Microsoft® Excel 2013:
Level 2 of 3

ERIC A. WEINSTEIN
Suffolk County Community College

D1298972

LABYRINTH
LEARNING™

Berkeley, CA

Microsoft Excel 2013: Level 2

Copyright © 2014 by Labyrinth Learning

LABYRINTH
LEARNING™

Labyrinth Learning
2560 9th Street, Suite 320
Berkeley, California 94710
800.522.9746
On the web at lablearning.com

President:
Brian Favro

Product Development Manager:
Jason Favro

Managing Editor:
Laura Popelka

Production Editor:
Margaret Young

Production Manager:
Rad Proctor

eLearning Production Manager:
Arl S. Nadel

eLearning Development:
Judy Mardar and Andrew Vaughnley

Developmental Editors:
Trisha Conlon and Sandra Rittman

Indexing:
Joanne Sprott

Cover Design:
Mick Koller, SuperLab Design

Interior Design:
Mark Ong, Side-by-Side Studio

All rights reserved. Printed in the United States of America. No part of this material protected by this copyright notice may be reproduced or utilized in any form or by any means, electronic or mechanical, including photocopying, recording, scanning, or by information storage and retrieval systems without written permission from the copyright owner.

Labyrinth Learning™ and the Labyrinth Learning logo are trademarks of Labyrinth Learning. Microsoft® is a registered trademark of Microsoft Corporation in the United States and/or other countries and is used by Labyrinth Learning under license from owner. This title is an independent publication not affiliated with Microsoft Corporation. Other product and company names mentioned herein may be the trademarks of their respective owners.

Labyrinth Learning is independent from Microsoft Corporation, and not affiliated with Microsoft in any manner. While this publication may be used in assisting end users to prepare for a Microsoft Office Specialist exam, Microsoft, its designated program administrator, and Labyrinth Learning do not warrant that the use of this publication will ensure passing a Microsoft Office Specialist exam.

The example companies, organizations, products, people, and events depicted herein are fictitious. No association with any real company, organization, product, person, or event is intended or inferred.

Screenshots reprinted with permission.

ITEM: 1-59136-492-2
ISBN-13: 978-1-59136-492-4

Manufactured in the United States of America.

QVS 10 9 8 7 6 5 4 3 2 1

Table of Contents

EXCEL 2013 LESSON 7: FORMATTING CELL CONTENTS, ADVANCED SKILLS

EXCEL 2013 LESSON 8: MANAGING MULTIPLE-SHEET WORKBOOKS

EXCEL 2013 LESSON 11: UTILIZING GRAPHICS AND TEMPLATES

Quick Reference Tables

Preface

In today's digital world, knowing how to use the most popular suite of desktop software applications is critical. Our goal is to teach new users how to take advantage of this technology and to help experienced users understand how the applications have changed from previous versions. We begin with fundamental concepts and take learners through a systematic progression of exercises, resulting in skill mastery.

An online student resource center accompanies this book. It contains Concepts Review quizzes, student exercise files, and other learning tools. The URL for the student resource center is printed on the inside front cover of this textbook.

Supplemental Options

Video Tutorials: Our easy-to-follow instructional design is complemented with hundreds of videos that demonstrate the concepts and skills covered in this textbook. All videos can be accessed online with a single license key. Videos are an option for all learners. Keys can be purchased at http://lablearning.com/Store/Shop-Videos.

eLab Course Management System: eLab is a web-based learning systems that integrates seamlessly with this textbook. eLab is an option for students enrolled in instructor-led courses that have adopted eLab as part of their course curriculum.

Visual Conventions

This book uses visual and typographic cues to guide students through the lessons. Some of these cues are described below.

`Type this text`	Text you type at the keyboard is printed in this typeface.
Action words	The important action words in exercise steps are presented in boldface.
Ribbon	Glossary terms are presented in black text with a blue background.
⚠️ TIP	Tips, notes, and warnings are called out with special icons.
Command→ Command→ Command→ Command	Commands to execute from the Ribbon are presented like this: Ribbon Tab→Command Group→Command→Subcommand.
FROM THE KEYBOARD Ctrl + S to save	These margin notes present shortcut keys for executing certain tasks.
FROM THE RIBBON File→Save	These margin notes show Ribbon paths for executing certain tasks.

Acknowledgements

This textbook has benefited greatly from the reviews and suggestions of the following instructors.

Kim Anderson, *Elgin Community College*

Ann Blackman, *Parkland College*

Robert Caruso, *Santa Rosa Junior College*

Lori Collins, *Pike-Lincoln Technical Center*

Rose Corgan, *University of Cincinnati Blue Ash*

Julie Davis, *Mt. Diablo Adult Education (Loma Vista Adult School)*

Teresita Galvizo, *South East High*

Evangelina Garner, *South Texas Vocational Technical institute*

Reuben Gradsky, *North Carolina State University and Wake County Tech*

Michael Heath, *River Parishes Community College - Technical Education Campus*

Leonard James, *Placer School for Adults*

Ray Janosko, *Community College of Allegheny County*

Joan Johnson, *Lake Sumter Community College*

Kathy Lavieri, *Great Oaks Institute of Technology and Career Development*

Teresa Loftis, *San Bernardino Adult School*

Linda Maatta, *Davis College*

John Mims, *Central New Mexico Community College Workforce Training Center*

Kay Nelson, *The Lifelong Learning Center, Missoula County Public Schools*

Monika Olsen, *Acalanes Adult Education*

Diane Perreault, *Sacramento City College*

Kari Phillips, *Davis Applied Technology College*

Sonya Sample, *Greenville Technical College*

Maryla Scarpa, *Vincennes University Jasper*

Jeff Stern, *Sheridan Technical Center*

Mary Jo Slater, *Community College of Beaver County*

Cynthia Wade, *CierraTEC*

Ali Ware, *Humboldt County Office of Education*

EXCEL 2013

Formatting Cell Contents, Advanced Skills

LEARNING OBJECTIVES

After studying this lesson, you will be able to:

- Format worksheets using preset themes
- Work with dynamic and static date functions
- Create custom number formats
- Apply conditional formatting to flag positive and negative trends
- Create cell names for navigation and formulas

In this lesson, you will build on the formatting techniques you have learned with techniques such as the Format Painter, which allows you to efficiently apply consistent formatting. Moreover, you will use Excel's Conditional Formatting tool, which can format values that fall within an acceptable range, thus drawing attention to those values. Lastly, you will name cells and ranges so they are easier to locate within the worksheet and can be more easily utilized within formulas.

Formatting with Excel

Having completed the third quarter income statement for Green Clean, a janitorial product supplier and cleaning service contractor, you want to determine how well the company has performed compared to the prior year. With your spreadsheet modified to include prior year data, you format the income statement to highlight important information. You also name cells and ranges within the spreadsheet so they may be more easily located.

Green Clean			
Income Statement Comparison			
3rd Quarter			
	Current Year	Prior Year	Dollar Change
REVENUES			
Sales	$ 704,785	$ 687,525	$ 17,260
Finance Charge Revenue	12,054	12,578	(524)
Total Revenues	$ 716,839	$ 700,103	$ 16,736
Vehicle Costs	63,226	67,498	(4,272)
Wages	373,937	362,495	11,442
Total Costs	$ 571,164	$ 559,957	$ 11,207
Net Income (Loss)	$ 145,675	$ 140,146	$ 5,529
Net Income to Total Revenues	20.3%	20.0%	33.0%
Date Created	11-Nov-2013		Check Figure
Date Reviewed	15-Nov-2013		$ 16,734
Elapsed Days	4		
Date Printed	11/15/2013 10:23 AM		

Formatting can make important spreadsheet data more easily understandable.

Working with the Format Painter and Quick Styles

Video Library   http://labyrinthelab.com/videos   Video Number: EX13-V0701

The Format Painter applies formatting from existing worksheet cells, while Quick Styles apply predefined formats to cells. Both of these tools can greatly simplify the formatting of a worksheet.

The Format Painter

The Format Painter lets you copy text and number formats from one cell to another. This can be extremely helpful if you have a cell to which many formatting options have been applied and you do not wish to go through the process of applying each option individually to another cell or range of cells.

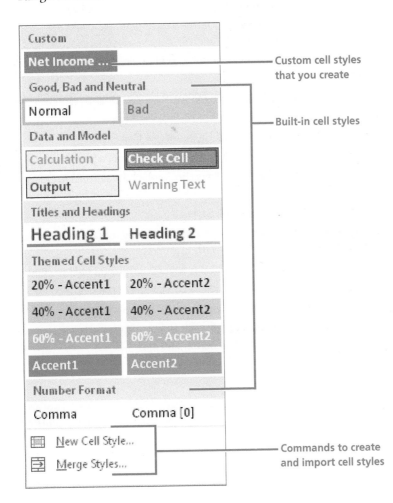

Custom cell styles that you create

Built-in cell styles

Commands to create and import cell styles

Applying Quick Styles to Cells

You can apply Excel's built-in cell styles, also called Quick Styles, or create your own styles for a uniform worksheet design. A cell style's formatting may include the font, number format, borders, or fill.

New cell styles that you create appear in the Custom section of the styles list. They are based on the workbook theme, so the colors change automatically to match any new theme applied. Among the built-in styles, only the Themed Cell Styles change colors. Any styles you create or edit apply only to the currently open workbook. The Merge Styles command in the Styles list allows you to import styles created in a different workbook into the current workbook.

QUICK REFERENCE	WORKING WITH THE FORMAT PAINTER AND CELL STYLES
Task	**Procedure**
Copy formats to one other cell or range	▪ Click the cell with the desired formatting and choose Home→Clipboard→Format Painter. ▪ Select the destination cell or range.
Copy formats to multiple locations	▪ Click the cell with the desired formatting and double-click Home→Clipboard→Format Painter. ▪ Select the destination cells or ranges; when finished, click Format Painter or tap Esc.
Apply a Quick Style to a cell or range	▪ Select the destination cells and choose Home→Styles→Cell Styles. ▪ Select the desired style from the list.
Create a cell style	▪ Choose Home→Styles→Cell Styles→New Cell Style. ▪ Click the Format button, select the desired formatting options, and click OK. ▪ Name the style in the Style dialog box, select the formatting categories to be included, and click OK.
Modify a cell style	▪ Choose Home→Styles→Cell Styles. ▪ Right-click the desired style and choose Modify (or Duplicate to create a new style based on the existing style). ▪ Click the Format button, select the desired formatting options, and click OK. ▪ Select the formatting categories to be included; click OK.
Import cell styles from a different workbook	▪ Open the workbook from which you wish to import styles. ▪ In the destination workbook, choose Home→Styles→Cell Styles→Merge Styles, choose the source workbook name, and click OK.

When you double-click the Format Painter, you can scroll through the worksheet to reach the desired location(s). You can also click a sheet tab to copy formatting to a different worksheet.

Change Formatting

In this exercise, you will copy the formatting from one cell to a range of cells. You also will apply cell styles and create a custom style.

1. Open **EX07-D01-ISComp** from the **EX2013 Lesson 07** folder and save it as **EX07-D01-ISComp-[FirstInitialLastName]**.

   Replace the bracketed text with your first initial and last name. For example, if your name is Bethany Smith, your filename would look like this: EX07-D01-ISComp-BSmith.

2. Follow these steps to apply consistent formats to the column headers using the Format Painter:

   Ⓐ Select **cell B4**.   Ⓑ Choose **Home→Clipboard→ Format Painter**.

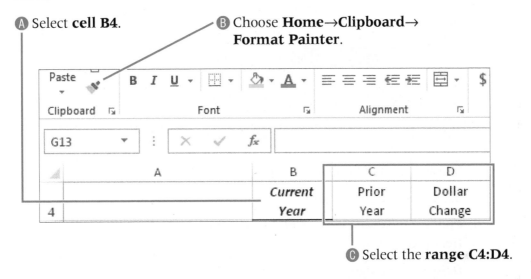

   Ⓒ Select the **range C4:D4**.

The formatting from cell B4 is applied to the range C4:D4. Because you only clicked it once, the Format Painter button is no longer active. If you had double-clicked it, it would still be active.

Apply Cell Styles

3. Select the **range A1:A3**.

4. Follow these steps to apply a built-in cell style:

Ⓐ Choose **Home→Styles→Cell Styles**.

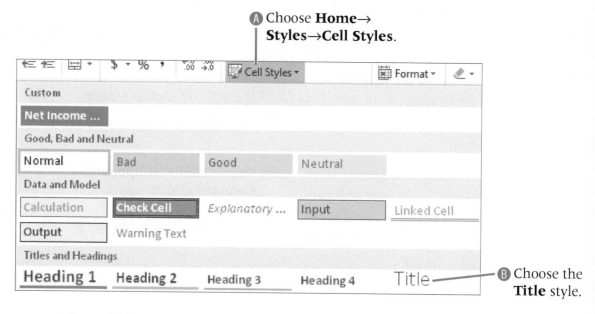

Ⓑ Choose the **Title** style.

Your styles may differ from those shown.

5. Select the **range B25:D25**.

6. Choose **Home→Styles→Cell Styles** 📝 and select **Total** from within the Titles and Headings group.

7. Deselect the range.

   Because of the cell style selected, the range displays bold formatting with a top and double bottom border.

Create a Custom Cell Style

8. Choose **Home→Styles→Cell Styles** 📝.

9. Choose **New Cell Style** at the bottom of the list.

10. Follow these steps to begin creating a cell style:

Ⓐ Type **Net Income Ratio** here.

Ⓑ Click the **Format** button.

Ⓒ Select the **Number** tab.

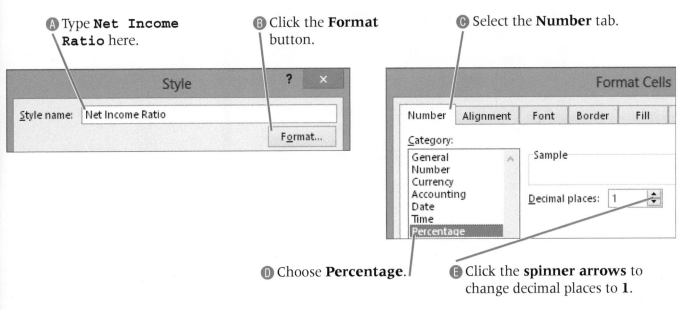

Ⓓ Choose **Percentage**.

Ⓔ Click the **spinner arrows** to change decimal places to **1**.

11. With the Format Cells dialog box still displayed, select the **Fill** tab.

12. Choose a dark fill color, such as the fourth color in the sixth column of the Theme Colors palette.

13. Follow these steps to set the text characteristics for the cell style:

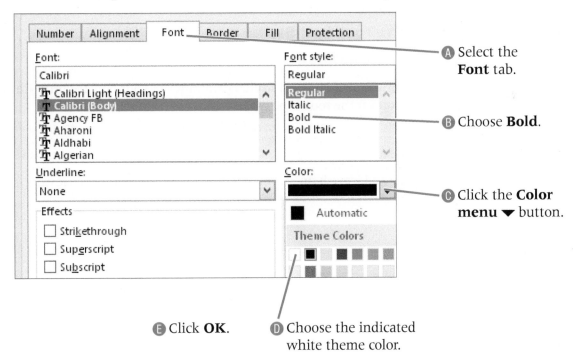

Ⓐ Select the **Font** tab.

Ⓑ Choose **Bold**.

Ⓒ Click the **Color menu ▼** button.

Ⓔ Click **OK**.

Ⓓ Choose the indicated white theme color.

Notice that your changes are shown in the Style dialog box.

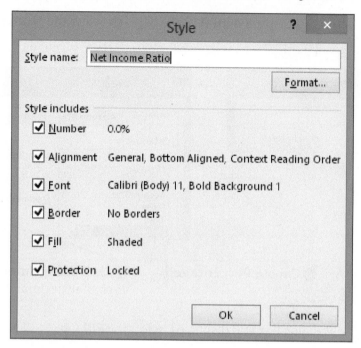

All the categories with a checkmark will be applied to the style. You can remove the checkmark from any formatting you don't want to use.

14. Click **OK** to close the Style dialog box.

Apply the Custom Cell Style

15. Select the **range A27:D27**.

16. Choose **Home→Styles→Cell Styles** and select your **Net Income Ratio** style from the **Custom** group at the top of the list.

    The range now displays your custom cell style, including bold, white font, and a dark fill color.

17. Deselect the range.

18. Save the file and leave it open; you will modify it throughout this lesson.

Formatting with Themes

Video Library http://labyrinthelab.com/videos Video Number: EX13-V0702

Themes allow you to easily apply formatting to entire workbooks. You can modify a theme by changing the font set, color palette, or graphic effect design. And, you can save the modifications as a custom theme that can be reused with other workbooks.

Themes allow you to choose a set of compatible fonts, one for headings and one for body text, which are identified at the top of the Font list. Likewise, the ten theme colors display at the top of the list when you are applying colors (such as fill color or font color).

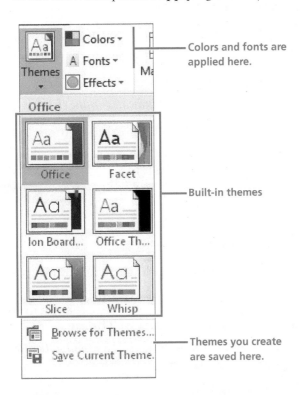

Colors and fonts are applied here.

Built-in themes

Themes you create are saved here.

Excel 2013

QUICK REFERENCE	APPLYING, MODIFYING, AND SAVING THEMES
Task	**Procedure**
Apply a theme to a workbook	■ Choose Page Layout →Themes→Themes 🖳 and choose the desired theme.
Modify and save a theme	■ Choose Page Layout→Themes→Themes 🖳 and choose the desired theme.
	■ Change the colors, fonts, and effects as desired.
	■ Choose Page Layout→Themes→Themes 🖳 →Save Current Theme, enter a theme name, and click Save.

Use Themes in a Workbook

In this exercise, you will apply a theme to the workbook. You also will modify a theme and explore how it would be saved.

1. Save your file as **EX07-D02-ISComp-[FirstInitialLastName]**.

2. Click the **Page Layout view** 🔲 button in the Status Bar.
   The view buttons are located to the left of the zoom slider.

3. Choose **Page Layout→Themes→Themes** 🔲.
   Office is the default theme applied to new workbooks.

4. Point at various themes and observe the different effects shown in Live Preview.
   Note that you may be able to scroll down to display additional themes.

5. Choose the **Integral** theme and click anywhere within the worksheet data.
   The colors and font in the workbook now correspond to those indicated in the theme.

6. Locate the **Status Bar** at the bottom-left corner of the Excel window to see that this theme displays the worksheet on one page.

   If this worksheet contained more data, and therefore extended beyond one page, you could quickly determine this by looking here.

◄ ►	**Sheet1**
READY	PAGE: 1 OF 1

Modify and Explore Saving a Theme

7. Choose **Page Layout→Themes→Theme Fonts** A Fonts ▾.

8. Point at various font families and observe the different effects in Live Preview.

9. Choose the **Arial** theme fonts.

10. Choose **Page Layout→Themes→Themes→Save Current Theme**.
    The Save Current Theme dialog box displays. Notice the default folder for saving themes on your system. You could enter a filename to save the modified theme.

11. Click **Cancel** so that you *do not* save the theme.

12. Save the file and leave it open.

Inserting Date Functions and Formatting

Video Library   http://labyrinthelab.com/videos   Video Number: EX13-V0703

The date functions, which utilize a similar syntax to that of statistical functions like SUM and AVERAGE, display either today's date or a date of your choice. Excel determines the current date according to your computer's clock feature.

Working with Dates

Dates are used in workbooks in two ways. First, you can simply type and display dates in cells using various formats such as 11/20/14; November 20, 2014; or 20-Nov-14. Second, you can use dates in formulas. For example, you may want to compute the number of days an invoice is past due. You calculate this as the difference between the current date and the due date of the invoice.

Date Serial Numbers

When you enter a date in a cell, Excel converts the date to a serial number between 1 and 2,958,525. These numbers correspond to the period from January 1, 1900, through December 31, 9999. The date January 1, 1900, is assigned the serial number 1; January 2, 1900, is assigned the serial number 2; etc. Serial numbers extend all the way to December 31, 9999. When dates are converted to numbers, you can use the numbers/dates in calculations.

Excel 2013

Excel recognizes an entry as a date as long as you enter it using a standard date format.

Function	Description
TODAY()	Displays the current system date and calculates the serial number. The date updates automatically when the worksheet is recalculated or reopened.
NOW()	Displays the current system date and time and calculates the serial number. The date and time update automatically when the worksheet is recalculated or reopened.
DATE(year, month, day)	Returns a specific date displayed in the default date format and calculates the serial number. The date does not update when the worksheet is recalculated or reopened.

Do not type anything within the parentheses of the TODAY and NOW functions.

QUICK REFERENCE	CREATING DATE AND TIME FUNCTIONS
Task	**Procedure**
Insert a date or time function	■ Click the cell in which you wish to place the function result. ■ Click Insert Function f_x and choose Date & Time. ■ Select the function you wish to create; click OK. ■ Enter the appropriate function arguments (if necessary); click OK.

Use the TODAY Function and Format a Date

In this exercise, you will create formulas to calculate the current date, and you will format dates.

1. Save your file as **EX07-D03-ISComp-[FirstInitialLastName]**.

2. Select **cell B30**.

3. Type **9/1/14** and then click **Enter** ✓.

4. Display the **Home** tab and locate the **Number** group.

   Notice the number format style displayed is Date, which Excel formatted for you when you typed the number in the date format.

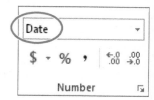

5. Choose **Home→Number→dialog box launcher** 🔲.

   The Format Cells dialog box opens with the Number tab displayed.

6. Follow these steps to change the date format:

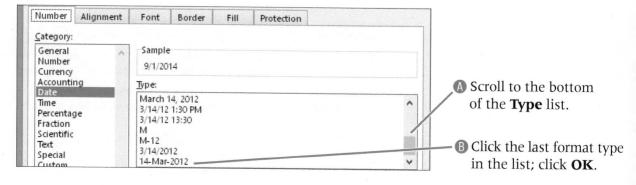

Ⓐ Scroll to the bottom of the **Type** list.

Ⓑ Click the last format type in the list; click **OK**.

7. Ensure that **cell B30** is still selected, and then tap Delete.

   Look at the Number group on the Home tab and notice that even when you remove the contents of the cell (the date), the number format for the cell will remain as Date.

Use the TODAY Function and Calculate Dates

8. Follow these steps to enter the TODAY function in cell B30:

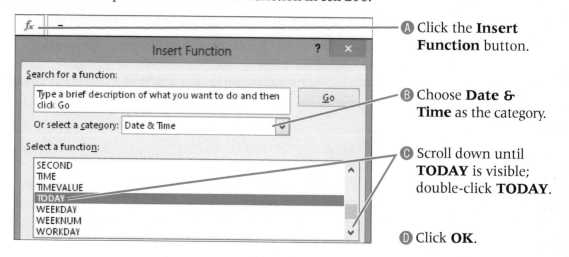

Ⓐ Click the **Insert Function** button.

Ⓑ Choose **Date & Time** as the category.

Ⓒ Scroll down until **TODAY** is visible; double-click **TODAY**.

Ⓓ Click **OK**.

The date will appear with the number formatting you set for the cell.

9. Select **cell B29** and enter the date that is four days prior to today.

10. Use the **Format Painter** to apply the date format from **cell B30** to **cell B29**.

11. Select **cell B31** and enter the formula **=B30-B29**.

   The result should equal 4. By subtracting dates in this manner, Excel can calculate the number of days between any two dates.

Use the NOW Function

12. Select **cell B32**, then type **=now (** and tap ⏎Enter.

   Excel automatically adds the closing parenthesis for the formula. Number signs (###) display across the cell width, which means that the date is too long to fit.

13. AutoFit **column B** by double-clicking the right edge of the header.

   The NOW function displays the current date and time, which will be updated the next time you open the worksheet.

14. Save the file and leave it open.

Excel 2013

Creating Custom Formats

Video Library   http://labyrinthelab.com/videos   Video Number: EX13-V0704

Excel's predefined number format options are usually sufficient, but you may also need a modified format. For example, you may want a date to display the year as two digits instead of four. Or, an identification or account number may need to be displayed with preceding zeros, such as 0004842. The Number tab of the Format Cells dialog box includes a Type box in which you can edit an existing number format or create a new one.

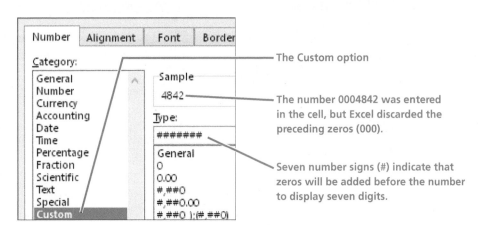

The Custom option

The number 0004842 was entered in the cell, but Excel discarded the preceding zeros (000).

Seven number signs (#) indicate that zeros will be added before the number to display seven digits.

Task	Procedure
Modify an existing number format to create a custom format	■ Select the cell/range to which you wish to apply a custom number format. ■ Choose Home→Number→dialog box launcher 🔲. ■ Select the Custom category and choose the format closest to the desired format. ■ Edit the formatting in the Type box and view the sample; click OK.

Modify a Date Format

In this exercise, you will edit the date format currently applied to the NOW function formula.

1. Save your file as **EX07-D04-ISComp-[FirstInitialLastName]**.

2. Select **cell B32**.

3. Follow these steps to modify the date format applied to the NOW function formula:

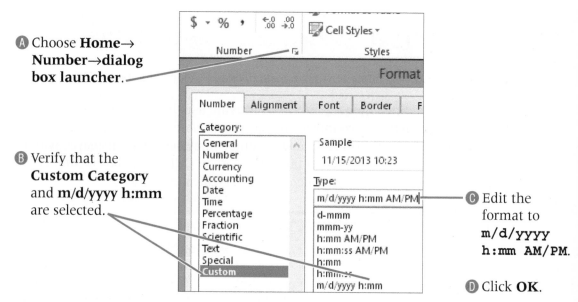

Ⓐ Choose **Home→ Number→dialog box launcher**.

Ⓑ Verify that the **Custom Category** and **m/d/yyyy h:mm** are selected.

Ⓒ Edit the format to **m/d/yyyy h:mm AM/PM**.

Ⓓ Click **OK**.

The time now displays either AM or PM.

4. Save the file and leave it open.

Working with Conditional Formatting

Video Library   http://labyrinthelab.com/videos   Video Number: EX13-V0705

The Conditional Formatting command applies formatting to cells that meet criteria that you set. Conditional formats are activated only when the criteria are met. For example, you may assign a yellow fill to a cell when its value is greater than 12. You may apply conditional formatting to cells containing values, text, dates, blanks, or errors. While conditional formatting can refer to a cell in a different sheet of the workbook, it cannot refer to cells in a different workbook.

Using Presets and Multiple Conditions

You can choose from conditional formatting presets on the Conditional Formatting menu for frequently used criteria, such as Greater Than, Equal To, Above Average, and Top 10 Items. You may set any number of conditional formats and create multiple rules to check for more than one condition in a cell. Conditional formatting rules are applied in the priority order you set. The Stop If True option, when selected in any rule, prevents further formatting by the remaining rules after a criterion is evaluated as True.

Creating a Conditional Formatting Rule

If no preset item on the Conditional Formatting menu has your desired criteria or formatting, you may create a new conditional formatting rule. The following illustration defines the parts of the New Formatting Rule dialog box. The options vary in the lower half of the dialog box depending on the rule type you select.

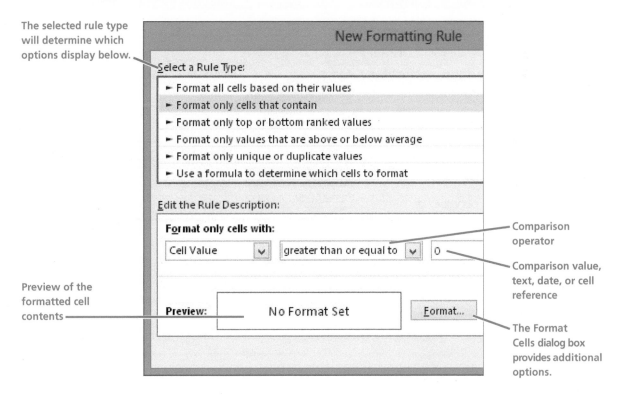

The selected rule type will determine which options display below.

Preview of the formatted cell contents

Comparison operator

Comparison value, text, date, or cell reference

The Format Cells dialog box provides additional options.

Excel 2013

Formatting with Graphics

You can choose to conditionally format cells with data bars, a color scale, or an icon set. These graphics identify values that are average, above average, and below average in the selected cell range. You may select a menu preset or create a custom rule using any of these visual aids.

Equipment Lease		7,844	8,200	✖	(356)
Insurance		18,230	17,500	✔	730
Rent		25,000	25,000	✖	-

Conditional formatting with data bars, a color scale, or icon sets helps to highlight data.

Use consistent formatting and limit the use of data bars, color scales, and icon sets on one worksheet. Using multiple styles could confuse the reader.

The Conditional Formatting Rules Manager

Conditional formatting rules can be created, edited, rearranged, and deleted within the Conditional Formatting Rules Manager dialog box. The following illustration displays the rules set within an entire worksheet.

A list of choices to display existing rules for a selected range or a worksheet

Buttons for creating a new rule and editing, deleting, or rearranging the order of a selected rule

Existing rules and their definitions

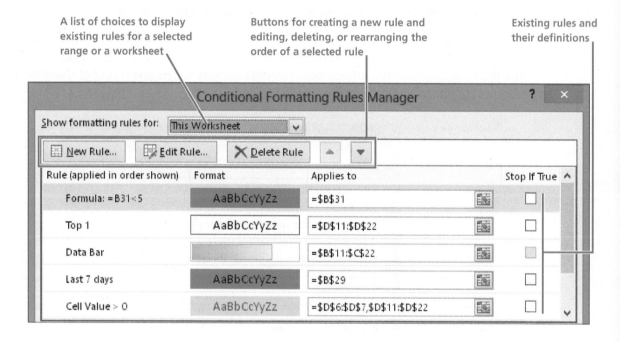

Task	Procedure
Apply preset conditional formatting	■ Select the cells to receive formatting. ■ Choose Home→Styles→Conditional Formatting 🔲, display a preset menu, and choose a command. ■ Edit options in the preset rule dialog box and click OK, if necessary.
Create a conditional formatting rule	■ Select the cells to receive formatting. ■ Choose Home→Styles→ Conditional Formatting 🔲→New Rule. ■ Choose a rule type and formatting options in the New Formatting Rule dialog box; click OK.
Apply conditional formatting with data bars, a color scale, or an icon set	■ Select the cells to receive formatting. ■ Choose Home→Styles→ Conditional Formatting 🔲→Data Bars, Color Scales, or Icon Sets. ■ Choose a preset item on the command's submenu or More Rules to create a custom rule.
Clear conditional formatting from specific cells	■ Select specific cells from which to remove formatting. ■ Choose Home→Styles→Conditional Formatting 🔲→Clear Rules→Clear Rules from Selected Cells.
Clear all conditional formatting from a worksheet	■ Display the desired worksheet. ■ Choose Home→Styles→Conditional Formatting 🔲→Clear Rules→Clear Rules from Entire Sheet.
Manage conditional formatting rules	■ Choose Home→Styles→Conditional Formatting 🔲→Manage Rules. ■ Choose Current Selection or a worksheet from the Show Formatting Rules For list. ■ Use buttons in the dialog box to create a new rule or select an existing rule and edit, delete, or change its order.

DEVELOP YOUR SKILLS EX07-D05
Apply Conditional Formatting

In this exercise, you will apply various types of conditional formatting to cell ranges. You will also create a conditional formatting rule and remove conditional formatting from a range.

1. Save your file as **EX07-D05-ISComp-[FirstInitialLastName]**.

2. Select the **ranges D6:D7** and the **range D11:D22**.

3. Choose **Home→Styles→Conditional Formatting→Highlight Cells Rules→Less Than**.

   Next you will create a highlighting rule to identify those line items that have decreased from the prior year.

Excel 2013

4. Follow these steps to apply conditional formatting:

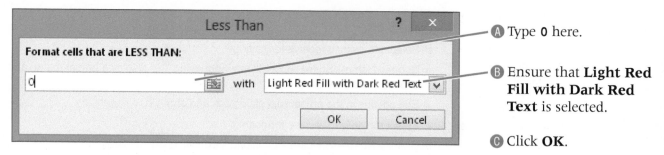

Ⓐ Type **0** here.

Ⓑ Ensure that **Light Red Fill with Dark Red Text** is selected.

Ⓒ Click **OK**.

5. With the prior ranges still selected, choose **Home→Styles→Conditional Formatting→Highlight Cells Rules→Greater Than**.

6. Repeat **step 4**, changing the format to **Green Fill with Dark Green Text**.

   All revenues and expenses that changed now show either a red or green background.

Create a Conditional Formatting Rule

7. Highlight **cell B29** and choose **Home→Styles→Conditional Formatting→Highlight Cells Rules→More Rules**.

   The New Formatting Rule dialog box appears.

8. Follow these steps to create a custom conditional formatting rule:

Ⓐ Select **Dates Occurring** here.

Ⓑ Select **In the Last 7 Days** here.

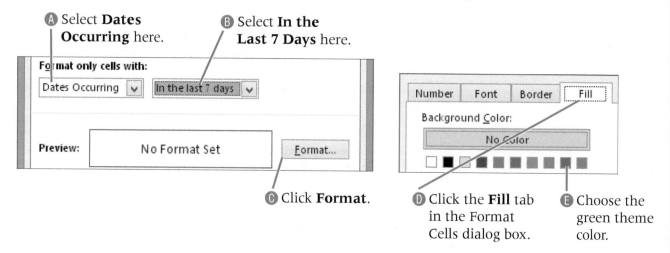

Ⓒ Click **Format**.

Ⓓ Click the **Fill** tab in the Format Cells dialog box.

Ⓔ Choose the green theme color.

9. Click **OK** to exit the Format Cells dialog box.

   Notice the green fill in the Preview box of the New Formatting Rule dialog box.

10. Click **OK** to exit the New Formatting Rule dialog box.

    The conditional formatting is applied to cell B29 to denote that the worksheet was created within the past week.

Format with Data Bars and a Top Rule

11. Select the **range B6:C7**.

12. Choose **Home→Styles→Conditional Formatting→Data Bars→Blue Data Bar**.

    The data bars display the relative size of each revenue item. You may choose either gradient or solid data bars.

13. Select the **range B11:C22** and choose **Home→Styles→Conditional Formatting→Data Bars→Orange Data Bar**.

    Data bars for revenues and expenses must be created separately, otherwise they will appear relative to one another (so the larger revenues would have big data bars and the smaller expenses would have small data bars).

14. Select the **range D11:D22** and choose **Home→Styles→Conditional Formatting→Top/ Bottom Rules→Top 10 Items**.

15. Change 10 to **1** in the Top 10 Items dialog box.

16. Choose **Red Border** from the **With** list and click **OK**.

    The highest expense item is now highlighted with a red border.

Format Using a Formula

In the next few steps, you will enter a formula that compares the date created to another date. If the result of this logical test is true, the cell's text will change to green.

17. Select **cell B30** and choose **Home→Styles→Conditional Formatting→New Rule**.

    The New Formatting Rule dialog box displays.

18. Follow these steps to create a conditional formatting rule using a formula:

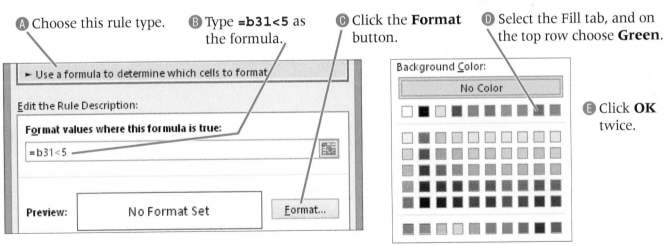

Ⓐ Choose this rule type.　Ⓑ Type **=b31<5** as the formula.　Ⓒ Click the **Format** button.　Ⓓ Select the Fill tab, and on the top row choose **Green**.

Ⓔ Click **OK** twice.

If Green Clean's goal of having schedules reviewed within fewer than five days has been met, cell B30 will display with green fill.

19. Select the **range B6:C7** and choose **Home→Styles→Conditional Formatting→Clear Rules→Clear Rules from Selected Cells**.

    The data bars disappear from the cells containing revenue figures.

20. Save the file and leave it open.

Naming Cells and Ranges

Video Library   http://labyrinthelab.com/videos   Video Number: EX13-V0706

You may use a descriptive name instead of cell references in formulas and for worksheet navigation. Range names are easier to type, recognize, and remember. Excel refers to these as defined names. You may create a name for one cell or a range of cells.

Naming Rules

Excel has a few rules for naming cells. Defined names:

- Must begin with a letter.
- Cannot resemble a cell reference, as in A3 or BC14.
- Cannot consist of the single letters C or R, which Excel interprets as column or row.
- Cannot contain spaces, hyphens, or symbols.
- May contain an underscore, period, or capital letter to connect words.

Creating Defined Names

Defined names are available throughout a workbook by default. You may define a name in one worksheet and use the name to navigate to its cell reference(s) from within any other worksheet.

You may create a name using a few different methods, the easiest of which is to type a name in the Name Box of the Formula Bar.

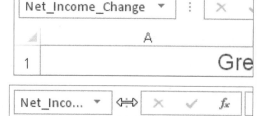

The Name Box may be widened by dragging the three dots between the Name Box and the Formula Bar.

QUICK REFERENCE	ASSIGNING DEFINED NAMES
Task	**Procedures**
Assign cell and range names	Use any of these three methods: ■ Select the desired cell(s), click in the Name Box, type the new name, and tap Enter. ■ Select the desired cell(s), choose Formulas→Defined Names→Define Name, type the new name, and click OK. ■ Select the desired cell(s) (including the column or row titles), choose Formulas→Defined Names→Create from Selection, select the location of the associated title, and click OK.

Using Defined Names

Defined names are mainly used to navigate workbooks and create linking formulas or calculation formulas.

Using Names to Navigate

Create defined names to move quickly to areas of the worksheet that you view or update frequently. To navigate to a named cell or range, you select its name from the Name list on the Formula Bar.

Using Names in Formulas

Formulas containing defined names help others to understand what the formulas are calculating. For example, the formula =AdvertisingTotal+MileageTotal is easier to understand than =AC10+AD10. Workbook users might prefer the linking formula =AdvertisingTotal, which uses a defined name, rather than =Advertising!B16. You may substitute a defined name for cell references in any formula. You may type the defined name or select it from the Use in Formula list on the Ribbon.

Excel 2013

TIP

If the error message #NAME? displays in a cell, ensure that the spelling of the name is the same in the formula and Name list and that the name was not deleted from the list.

Modifying and Deleting Defined Names

Use the Name Manager dialog box to view all defined names and edit their properties. You may add and delete names in Name Manager. Formula cells, however, display the error message #NAME?# after names have been deleted. You will need to edit the cell references in formulas that used any deleted name.

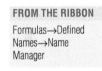

FROM THE RIBBON
Formulas→Defined Names→Name Manager

FROM THE KEYBOARD
Ctrl + F3

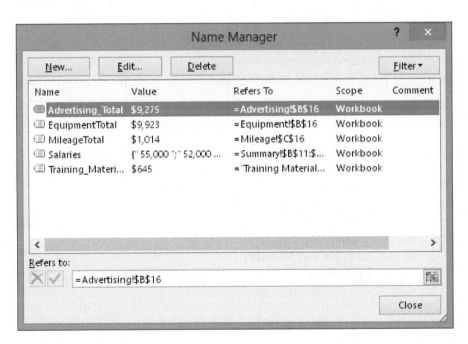

WARNING

To change the Refers To entry, use the Collapse button and point mode to select cells. Do not use arrow keys to edit the entry, as Excel would insert cell references rather than move the insertion point.

Task	Procedures
Name Cells	■ Select the range of cells, type a name in the Name Box, and tap ⌑Enter.
Create names from existing row or column titles	■ Select the labels and the cells to which they refer, and choose Formulas→Defined Names→Create from Selection.
	■ Place a checkmark to indicate the location of the labels, and click OK.
Change a defined name	■ Choose Formulas→Defined Names→Name Manager, choose an existing name, click Edit, edit the name, click OK, and click Close.
Change the range to which a name refers	■ Choose Formulas→Defined Names→Name Manager, and choose an existing name.
	■ Click the Collapse button next to Refers To, select the new range, and click the Expand button.
	■ Click Close, and click Yes to confirm the change.
Delete a defined name	■ Choose Formulas→Defined Names→Name Manager, choose an existing name, click Delete, click OK, and click Close.
Navigate to a defined range	■ Choose the name from the Name list in the Formula Bar.
Use a defined name in a linking formula	■ Select the cell to contain the summary formula, choose Formulas→Defined Names→Use in Formula, choose the defined name, and tap ⌑Enter.
Use one or more defined names in a calculation formula	■ Select the cell to contain the formula, and type the function beginning, such as =SUM(
	■ Choose Formulas→Defined Names→Use in Formula, choose the defined name, continue typing the formula and choose defined names as necessary, and tap ⌑Enter.

DEVELOP YOUR SKILLS EX07-D06

Create and Use Defined Names

In this exercise, you will create names for single cells and then navigate to important areas of the workbook. You also will use defined names to create linking formulas.

1. Save your file as **EX07-D06-ISComp-[FirstInitialLastName]**.

2. Select **cell D25**.

3. Follow these steps to name the cell:

Ⓐ Click in the **Name Box** at the left of the Formula Bar to select the D25 cell reference.

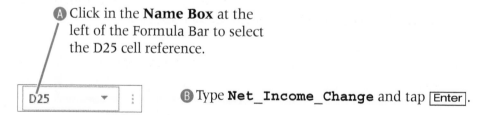

Ⓑ Type **Net_Income_Change** and tap ⌑Enter.

You must tap ⌑Enter after typing the name. If you simply click outside the Name Box, the name will not be created.

4. Select any cell other than D25, and then select **cell D25** again.

   The Name Box displays Net_Income_Change.

5. To view the entire name, drag the three dots between the Name Box and Formula Bar, if necessary.

6. Select **cell D27** and choose **Formulas→Defined Names→Define Name** 🔲.

7. In the New Name dialog box, type **Profit_Margin_Percentage** and click **OK**.

   Notice that the Scope option is set to Workbook. If you had multiple worksheets within this workbook, you could select the defined name from within any worksheet.

Use Names to Navigate and Create Formulas

You will now use defined names to create a "check" formula to confirm that the formulas in cells D25 and D27 are calculated properly.

8. Choose **Net_Income_Change** from the Name list in the Formula Bar to navigate to cell D25.

9. Navigate to **Profit_Margin_Percentage**.

10. Select **cell D30**, choose **Formulas→Defined Names→Use in Formula** 🔲, and choose the defined name **Net_Income_Change**.

11. Continue the formula by typing **/**.

12. Choose **Formulas→Defined Names→Use in Formula** 🔲.

13. Choose the defined name **Profit_Margin_Percentage** and confirm the formula.

    Since this "check" formula result is the same as the value in cell D8, you have confirmed that the formulas in cells D25 & D27 were calculated properly.

14. Save and then close the file. Exit **Excel**.

Concepts Review

To check your knowledge of the key concepts introduced in this lesson, complete the Concepts Review quiz by choosing the appropriate access option below.

If you are...	Then access the quiz by...
Using the Labyrinth Video Library	Going to http://labyrinthelab.com/videos
Using eLab	Logging in, choosing Content, and navigating to the Concepts Review quiz for this lesson
Not using the Labyrinth Video Library or eLab	Going to the student resource center for this book

Reinforce Your Skills

Work with Dates, Cell Styles, and Themes

In this exercise, you will enter a date function that will calculate the current date for you. You will apply cell styles to worksheet cells and change the fonts in the workbook theme.

Work with the Format Painter and Quick Styles

1. Start **Excel**. Open **EX07-R01-BudgetDate** from the **EX2013 Lesson 07** folder and save it as **EX07-R01-BudgetDate-[FirstInitialLastName]**.

2. Select **cell B24**.

3. Choose **Home→Clipboard→Format Painter** and highlight the **range B25:C25** to apply consistent formatting to it.

4. Select **cell C4** and choose **Home→Styles→Cell Styles**.

5. Choose an appropriate **Quick Style** from the list to draw attention to the balance.

6. Select **cells A7, A15, and A25** using the Ctrl key.

7. Choose **Home→Styles→Cell Styles** and choose an appropriate themed cell style.

Format with Themes

8. Choose **Page Layout→Themes→Theme Fonts** A Fonts ▾.

9. Point at various font themes to preview the workbook; choose a font theme.
   Remember that you can scroll to view all the font themes.

10. Evaluate how the data appear and change the font theme, if necessary, until you are satisfied.
    Your goal is to identify a font theme that is suitable for the worksheet data and easily comprehensible by the user.

11. Add any formatting that you think enhances the workbook design.

Insert Date Functions and Formatting

12. Select **cell B4**.

13. Click the **Insert Function** *fx* button.

14. Choose the **Date & Time** category if you do not see the TODAY function in the Most Recently Used category.

15. Scroll down, select the **TODAY** function, and click **OK**.

16. Click **OK** in the Function Arguments window.
    The date will be returned in the default format.

17. Choose **Home→Number→dialog box launcher** ▫.

18. Display the **Number** tab in the Format Cells dialog box. Scroll down if necessary, and choose the format that will display the date like 1-Jan-15.

    Excel uses March 14, 2012, as its example date; however, the date that appears within the worksheet will be the one you have created.

19. Save and then close the file. Exit **Excel**.

20. Submit your final file based on the guidelines provided by your instructor.

    To view examples of how your file or files should look at the end of this exercise, go to the student resource center.

REINFORCE YOUR SKILLS EX07-R02
Apply Conditional Formatting and Cell Names

In this exercise, you will apply conditional formatting to cell ranges to analyze trends. You will also create a custom number format and name cells.

Create Custom Formats

1. Start **Excel**. Open **EX07-R02-ShippingFee** from the **EX2013 Lesson 07** folder and save it as **EX07-R02-ShippingFee-[FirstInitialLastName]**.

2. Select **cell C21** and choose **Home→Number→dialog box launcher** 🔲.
   Notice that the contents of the range C21:D21 has been merged and centered.

3. Select the **Custom** category and choose **m/d/yyyy h:mm** as the format.

4. In the type box, edit the format to **m/d/yy h:mm AM/PM**; click **OK**.
   In addition to the date, cell C21 now shows the time and AM or PM as well.

Work with Conditional Formatting

5. Select the **range B4:B18**.

6. Choose **Home→Styles→ Conditional Formatting→ Highlight Cells Rules→A Date Occurring**.
   The A Date Occurring dialog box appears with the Yesterday option displayed.

7. Choose in **In the Last 7 Days** from the date list and choose **Green Fill with Dark Green Text** from the **With** list; click **OK**.

   The last four dates are highlighted in column B of the worksheet.

8. Select the **range E4:E18**.

9. Choose **Home→Styles→ Conditional Formatting→Color Scales→Green-White Color Scale**.

   The darkest green highlights the highest value, while the shades become lighter as the values decrease.

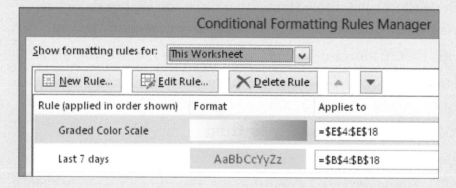

10. Select the **range C4:C18**.

11. Choose **Home→Styles→Conditional Formatting→Highlight Cells Rules→Text that Contains**.

12. Type **11** in the **Format Cells that Contain the Text** box and choose **Yellow Fill with Dark Yellow Text** from the **With** list; click **OK**.

    Next you will delete a conditional formatting rule.

13. Choose **Home→Styles→Conditional Formatting→Manage Rules**.

14. Choose to show formatting rules for **This Worksheet** and select the rule that displays yellow fill.

15. Click the **Delete Rule** button and click **OK**.

Conditional Formatting Rules Manager		
Show formatting rules for: This Worksheet ▼		
📋 New Rule... 📝 Edit Rule... ✖ Delete Rule ▲ ▼		
Rule (applied in order shown)	Format	Applies to
Graded Color Scale		=$E$4:$E$18
Last 7 days	AaBbCcYyZz	=$B$4:$B$18

Now only these two conditional formatting rules remain in effect for the worksheet.

Name Cells and Ranges

16. Select **cell D19**.

17. Highlight **cell D19** in the Name Box, type **EstimatedTotal**, and tap ⌷Enter⌷.

18. Follow the same steps to name **cell E19 ActualTotal**.

19. Select **cell F19**, type **=EstimatedTotal-ActualTotal**; confirm the formula.

    You have now calculated the total difference for all orders by using cell names within the formula.

20. Save and then close the file. Exit **Excel**.

21. Submit your final file based on the guidelines provided by your instructor.

    To view examples of how your file or files should look at the end of this exercise, go to the student resource center.

Apply Appropriate Formats

In this exercise, you will enter a date function that will calculate the current date. You will also apply cell styles to worksheet cells and change the fonts in the workbook theme.

Work with the Format Painter and Quick Styles

1. Start **Excel**. Open **EX07-R03-NonProfit** from the **EX2013 Lesson 07** folder and save it as **EX07-R03-NonProfit-[FirstInitialLastName]**.

2. Select **cell A4** and choose **Home→Clipboard→Format Painter** .

3. Select the **range B4:C4**, to which you will apply the formatting.

4. Select **cell A1**, choose **Home→Styles→Cell Styles**, and choose **Heading 1**.

Format with Themes

5. Choose **Page Layout→Themes→Theme Fonts** A Fonts▾.

6. Select the **Arial** theme.

Insert Date Functions and Formatting

7. Select **cell A12**, type **=NOW()**, and confirm your formula.

8. With **cell A12** selected, choose **Home→Number→Number Format ▼ menu→Long Date**.

   You decide that you do not like the appearance of the Long Date, so you will now create a custom date format.

Create Custom Formats

9. With **cell A12** highlighted, choose **Home→Number→dialog box launcher** .

10. Select the **Custom** category and choose **d-mmm** as the format.

11. In the Type box, edit the format to **d-mmm h:mm** and click **OK**.

Work with Conditional Formatting

12. Select the **range C5:C9**.

13. Choose **Home→Styles→Conditional Formatting→Color Scales→Red – White Color Scale**.

    This formatting applies the darkest shade of red to the highest rating, with progressively lighter shades applying to the ratings as they decrease.

14. With the **range C5:C9** selected, choose **Home→Styles→Conditional Formatting→Icon Sets > Three Traffic Lights (Unrimmed)**.

    Just like the color bars, the traffic light icons help to identify the magnitude of each rating.

15. With the **range C5:C9** selected, choose **Home→Styles→Conditional Formatting→Manage Rules**.

16. Select the **Icon Set** rule, choose **Delete Rule**, and click **OK**.

    Since the two rules accomplish the same goal, there is no need to display both.

Excel 2013

Name Cells and Ranges

17. Select **cell C5**.

18. Highlight **cell C5** in the Name Box, type **FamilySupporters**, and tap Enter.

19. Repeat **steps 17–18** to similarly name each cell in the **range C6:C9**.
    Remember that the apostrophe in Children's Assist *cannot be used within a defined name.*

20. Right-click the **row 10** heading and choose **Insert**.

21. Type **Average Rating** in **cell A10** and **=Average (** in **cell C10**.

22. Select **cell C5**.
    The defined name for cell C5 is entered into the formula.

23. Complete the formula by selecting each cell in the **range C6:C9**, using a comma to separate each cell reference.
    The defined names continue to display, making it easier to identify the components of the formula.

24. Save and then close the file. Exit **Excel**.

25. Submit your final file based on the guidelines provided by your instructor.

Apply Your Skills

Use the Format Painter, Themes, and Date Functions

In this exercise, you will use the Format Painter, apply themes to a worksheet, and insert the date using a date function.

Work with the Format Painter, Quick Styles, and Themes

1. Start **Excel**. Open **EX07-A01-RetailInventory** from the **EX2013 Lesson 07** folder and save it as **EX07-A01-RetailInventory-[FirstInitialLastName]**.

2. Select **cell B4** and apply the **Currency** cell style.

3. Use the **Format Painter** to apply the formatting from **cell A3** to the **range B3:C3**, and from **cell B4** to the **range B5:B8**.

4. Apply the **Mesh** theme to the workbook.
   Apply a theme of your choice if Mesh is not available.

5. Modify the workbook's theme font to **Corbel**.

Insert Date Functions and Formatting

6. Use a function to enter the current date in **cell A12**.

7. Format the entry in **cell A12** to display the current time in addition to the date.

8. Save and then close the file. Exit **Excel**.

9. Submit your final file based on the guidelines provided by your instructor.
   To view examples of how your file or files should look at the end of this exercise, go to the student resource center.

Add Conditional Formatting and Navigate with Cell Names

In this exercise, you will apply a conditional formatting rule to highlight low quantities of products in inventory. You will also navigate the worksheet using cell names.

Create Custom Formats and Work with Conditional Formatting

1. Start **Excel**. Open **EX07-A02-InternetInv** from the **EX2013 Lesson 07** folder and save it as **EX07-A02-InternetInv-[FirstInitialLastName]**.

2. Create a custom format for the date in **cell A12** so the time includes seconds.
   Within the type box, seconds are represented by ss.

3. Create a conditional formatting rule that highlights values below 200 in **column C**.
   Be sure not to apply the conditional formatting to the total row.

4. Create a conditional formatting rule that highlights values above 200 in **column C**.
   Be careful to apply a different highlight color. The second conditional format is not informative, so you decide to remove it.

5. Remove the conditional formatting rule you created in **step 4**.

Name Cells and Ranges

6. Ensure that the **range C4:C8** is still highlighted.
   Note in the name box that this range has already been named InternetQuantity.

7. Sum the product quantities in **cell C9** using this range name.

8. Create an appropriate defined name for **cell C9**.

9. Save and then close the file. Exit **Excel**.

10. Submit your final file based on the guidelines provided by your instructor.
    To view examples of how your file or files should look at the end of this exercise, go to the student resource center.

Format a Worksheet

In this exercise, you will use a variety of techniques to format a customer ratings worksheet.

Work with the Format Painter, Quick Styles, and Themes

1. Start **Excel**. Open **EX07-A03-CustomerRatings** from the **EX2013 Lesson 07** folder and save it as **EX07-A03-CustomerRatings-[FirstInitialLastName]**.

2. Use the **Format Painter** to apply formatting from **cell A4** to the **range B4:E4**.

3. Apply the **Title** cell style to **cell A1**.

4. Apply the **Facet** theme to the workbook.

5. Modify the theme color of the workbook to **Red Violet**.

Insert Date Functions and Formatting, and Create Custom Formats

6. Use the **Now** function to enter the date and time in **cell A12**.

7. Create a custom format for the dates in the **range B5:B9** to be consistent with Jan-01-2014.

Work with Conditional Formatting, and Name Cells and Ranges

8. Insert red data bars for all staff ratings.

9. Create a conditional formatting rule that highlights overall ratings greater than 3 with **Green Fill with Dark Green Text**.

10. Name the **range D5:D9** as **Staff_Ratings** and the **range E5:E9** as **Overall_Ratings**.

11. Write formulas in **cells D12 and E12**, using the range names you created, to show the average ratings.

12. Save and then close the file. Exit **Excel**.

13. Submit your final file based on the guidelines provided by your instructor.

Extend Your Skills

In the course of working through the Extend Your Skills exercises, you will think critically as you use the skills taught in the lesson to complete the assigned projects. To evaluate your mastery and completion of the exercises, your instructor may use a rubric, with which more points are allotted according to performance characteristics. (The more you do, the more you earn!) Ask your instructor how your work will be evaluated.

EX07-E01 That's the Way I See It

In this exercise, you will create a worksheet listing your ten favorite musical artists. For each artist, list their musical genre, your favorite song by the artist, the most recent album, and the number of songs of each that you own. You can use the Internet to search for information as necessary.

Save your file as **EX07-E01-MusicalArtists-[FirstInitialLastName]** in the **EX2013 Lesson 07** folder.

Create appropriate headers and column titles within the worksheet. Use the Format Painter to apply formats throughout, enter the necessary data, and use conditional formatting to identify the three artists whose songs appear most in your music library. Apply the theme of your choice. Use a function to display the current date at the top of the worksheet, and for each artist use a function to display the date on which their most recent album was released. Then, create formulas that calculate the number of days since the release of each artist's most recent album.

You will be evaluated based on the inclusion of all elements specified, your ability to follow directions, your ability to apply newly learned skills to a real-world situation, your creativity, and the relevance of your topic and/or data choice(s). Submit your final file based on the guidelines provided by your instructor.

EX07-E02 Be Your Own Boss

In this exercise, you will format a worksheet listing all landscape architects used by your company, Blue Jean Landscaping, and their associated customer ratings.

Open **EX07-E02-Landscape** from the **EX2013 Lesson 07** folder and it save as **EX07-E02-Landscape-[FirstInitialLastName]**.

Apply appropriate formatting within the worksheet and use the Format Painter to copy it throughout. Use conditional formatting to highlight the contractor with the highest customer ratings and apply cell names to each cell containing a rating. Lastly, use a function to insert a custom date below all worksheet data that displays the date and time of worksheet completion, along with either "AM" or "PM."

You will be evaluated based on the inclusion of all elements specified, your ability to follow directions, your ability to apply newly learned skills to a real-world situation, your creativity, and your demonstration of an entrepreneurial spirit. Submit your final file based on the guidelines provided by your instructor.

Transfer Your Skills

In the course of working through the Transfer Your Skills exercises, you will use critical-thinking and creativity skills to complete the assigned projects using skills taught in the lesson. To evaluate your mastery and completion of the exercises, your instructor may use a rubric, with which more points are allotted according to performance characteristics. (The more you do, the more you earn!) Ask your instructor how your work will be evaluated.

EX07-T01 Use the Web as a Learning Tool

Throughout this book, you will be provided with an opportunity to use the Internet as a learning tool by completing WebQuests. According to the original creators of WebQuests, as described on their website (WebQuest.org), a WebQuest is "an inquiry-oriented activity in which most or all of the information used by learners is drawn from the web." To complete the WebQuest projects in this book, navigate to the student resource center and choose the WebQuest for the lesson on which you are currently working. The subject of each WebQuest will be relevant to the material found in the lesson.

WebQuest Subject: Effective application of conditional formatting

Submit your file(s) based on the guidelines provided by your instructor.

EX07-T02 Demonstrate Proficiency

You have created an information card that will be given to all customers at Stormy BBQ. You will be collecting customer information so you can maintain a customer list and use it to contact customers with promotional offers.

Open **EX07-T02-CustInfo** from the **EX2013 Lesson 07** folder and save it as **EX07-T02-CustInfo-[FirstInitialLastName]**.

Use the Format Painter to apply the existing formats throughout the worksheet. Ensure that the headers in rows 1 and 2 are consistent, and that the titles in row 4 are consistent. Enter the information for five of your friends in rows 5–9 and apply the formatting from row 5 throughout. Apply a theme of your choice to the worksheet and create a defined name for the range of data in rows 5–9. Lastly, insert a "created on" date (with appropriate label) that displays both the date and time of completion below all worksheet data. Write a paragraph (minimum of three sentences) below the data that details a new promotional offer that you plan to initiate utilizing the customer data collected.

Submit your final file based on the guidelines provided by your instructor.

EXCEL 2013

Managing Multiple-Sheet Workbooks

LEARNING OBJECTIVES

After studying this lesson, you will be able to:

- Sort worksheet rows in alphabetic and numeric order
- View nonadjacent areas of large worksheets and view multiple worksheets simultaneously
- Create formulas that summarize data from multiple worksheets
- Copy worksheets and their formats
- Print multiple worksheets of a workbook

In this lesson, you will learn several techniques for working with multiple-sheet workbooks. You will sort worksheet rows, freeze headings, and adjust print options. You will split the worksheet window to compare data from separate areas of a worksheet. You will organize workbooks by copying worksheets, moving worksheets, and linking formulas. Lastly, you will print selected worksheets by issuing a single command.

Tracking Project Expenses

Green Clean, a janitorial product supplier and cleaning service contractor, has developed a project budget. Your job is to create a workbook that tracks the year-to-date expenditures and consolidates the information on a summary worksheet. The summary worksheet will give you an instant overview of the amounts spent compared to the budget allocations. Formulas in the summary worksheet will be linked to cells in the detail sheets, where all the necessary detail information is stored.

green clean

	A	B
1	Advertising Tracking Sheet	
2		
3		Amount Spent
4	September	-
5	October	2,000
6	November	6,075
7	December	1,200
8	January	
9	February	
10	March	
11	April	
12	May	
13	June	
14	July	
15	August	
16	Total	$9,275

	A	B
1	Equipment Tracking Sheet	
2		
3		Amount Spent
4	September	8,547
5	October	3,640
6	November	5,072
7	December	1,211
8	January	
9	February	
10	March	
11	April	
12	May	
13	June	
14	July	
15	August	
16	Total	$9,923

	A	B	C
1	Mileage Tracking Sheet		
2			
3			Amount
3		Mileage	Spent
4	September	720	317
5	October	885	389
6	November	280	123
7	December	420	185
8	January		-
9	February		-
10	March		-
11	April		-
12	May		-
13	June		-
14	July		-
15	August		-
16	Total	2,305	$1,014

	A	B	C
1	Training Materials Tracking Sheet		
2			
3		Amount Spent	
4	September	145	
5	October	1,620	
6	November	(1,705)	
7	December	730	
8	January		
9	February		
10	March		
11	April		
12	May		
13	June		
14	July		
15	August		
16	Total	$645	

	A	B	C
1	Green Clean		
2	Budget and Expenses		
3			
4	General and Capital Expenses	Budget Allocation	Year-to-Date Spent
5	Advertising	40,000	9,275
6	Equipment	25,000	9,923
7	Mileage	8,000	1,014
8	Training Materials	7,000	645

The summary worksheet tracks the totals from the detail sheets.

Sorting Worksheet Data

Video Library   http://labyrinthelab.com/videos   Video Number: EX13-V0801

Excel can easily sort lists organized in alphabetic or numeric order. For example, you may sort by name, date, item number, or dollar amount. A sort is performed on all adjacent rows. You may, however, decide to select only certain rows to sort.

If a sorting problem arises and Undo is unavailable, close the workbook without saving it. Reopen the workbook to restore its original appearance.

Sorting by a Single Column

The Sort A to Z and Sort Z to A buttons let you sort quickly by one column. Sort A to Z sorts records in ascending order from lowest to highest, and Sort Z to A sorts in descending order from highest to lowest. Excel sorts all rows in the adjacent list unless it determines that the list has a header row.

Sorting Selected Rows

If the list contains rows you do not want included in the sort, you must select the rows you *do* want sorted before clicking one of the sort buttons. Excel will use column A as the sort key by default.

To keep data together for each record, always select *one cell* or *entire rows* before sorting. Do not highlight several cells in one column and then sort, as this sorts the selected cells only. The other cells belonging to each record will not move.

Sorting by Multiple Columns

The Sort dialog box is used to specify multiple sort keys for multiple-column sorts. For example, a worksheet displays last names in column A and first names in column B. Using the Sort dialog box, you may instruct Excel to sort the rows by last name and then by first name. You may also sort by more than two columns.

Last Name	First Name
Duran	Timothy
Alejo	Carmen
Martin	Michael
Carter	Aaron
Wintz	Siobhan
Carter	Adam

An unsorted list

Last Name	First Name
Alejo	Carmen
Carter	Aaron
Carter	Adam
Duran	Timothy
Martin	Michael
Wintz	Siobhan

A list sorted by last name and then first name

Excel 2013

Task	Procedure
Sort by a single column	■ Select one cell in the desired column on or under the header row. ■ Choose Data→Sort & Filter→Sort A to Z ⒜ or Sort Z to A ⒵
Sort selected rows by a single column	■ Select a cell in the sort key column, and select the rows to be sorted. ■ Choose Data→Sort & Filter→Sort A to Z ⒜ or Sort Z to A ⒵
Sort by multiple columns	■ Select any cell within the data to be sorted and choose Data→Sort & Filter→Sort. ■ Choose the first column to be sorted from the Sort By list; change the Sort On and Order settings, if necessary. ■ Click Add Level to add additional sort categories and change their settings, if necessary. ■ If the list to be sorted has a header row, place a checkmark next to My Data Has Headers; click OK.

Sort Worksheet Columns

In this exercise, you will use the sort buttons and Sort dialog box to sort lists in a workbook.

1. Open **EX08-D01-ProjectBudget** from the **EX2013 Lesson 08** folder and save it as **EX08-D01-ProjectBudget-[FirstInitialLastName]**.

   Replace the bracketed text with your first initial and last name. For example, if your name is Bethany Smith, your filename would look like this: EX08-D01-ProjectBudget-BSmith.

2. Click the **Prior Year** sheet tab.

3. Follow these steps to sort the General and Capital Expenses by amount:

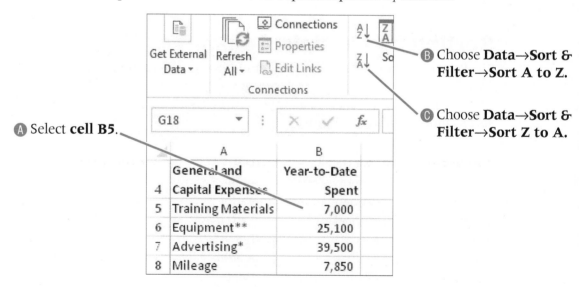

Ⓐ Select **cell B5**.

Ⓑ Choose **Data→Sort & Filter→Sort A to Z.**

Ⓒ Choose **Data→Sort & Filter→Sort Z to A.**

After sorting from A to Z you saw that the figures were presented from smallest to largest. Since this data will look better with the largest expenses on top, you decided to change the appearance and sort from Z to A.

4. Follow these steps to sort the Advertising Breakdown from largest to smallest:

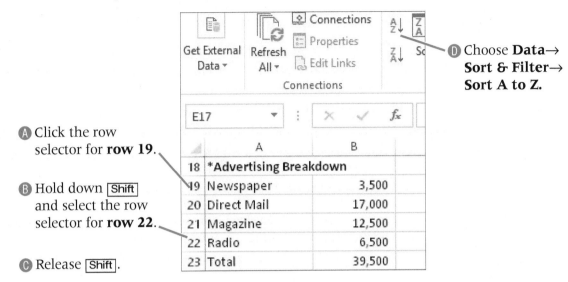

Ⓓ Choose **Data→ Sort & Filter→ Sort A to Z.**

Ⓐ Click the row selector for **row 19.**

Ⓑ Hold down Shift and select the row selector for **row 22.**

Ⓒ Release Shift.

Only the selected data rows are sorted. You did not include the total in your selection.

5. Select any cell in the **range A11:C16**.

6. Choose **Data→Sort & Filter→Sort** 🔤.

   The Sort dialog box appears.

7. Choose the options as shown to set the Sort By (first sort) settings.

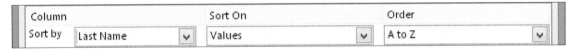

8. Follow these steps to finish setting the sort criteria:

Ⓐ Click **Add Level** to add a second sort category.

Ⓑ Choose **Labor Expenses** for the second sort and make sure **Values** and **Largest to Smallest** are set as shown.

Ⓒ Make certain the **My Data Has Headers** option box is checked.

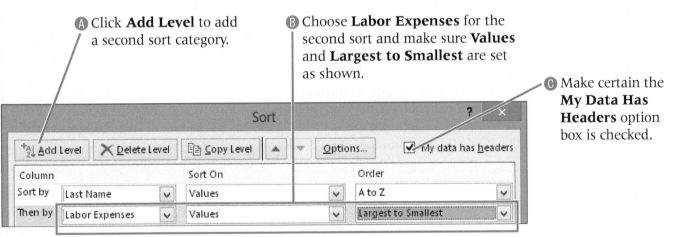

The sort will be performed on last names and then on labor expenses.

9. Click **OK**.

   Notice that Adam Carter has higher labor expenses, and therefore appears above Aaron Carter.

10. Choose **Data→Sort & Filter→Sort** 📊.

11. Change the second sort criteria to **First Name** (sorted A to Z) and then click **OK**.
    Now that First Name is the second sort category, Aaron Carter appears above Adam Carter.

12. Save the file and leave it open. You will modify it throughout this lesson.

Using Flexible Worksheet Views

Video Library   http://labyrinthelab.com/videos   Video Number: EX13-V0802

Excel allows you to view two areas of a large worksheet that normally could not be displayed together. When you are finished viewing this way, you can restore the worksheet to its original view. Two or more worksheets in the same workbook or different workbooks can also be viewed at once.

Freezing Rows or Columns

When you select the Freeze Panes command, Excel freezes all rows above the selected cell and all columns to the left of the selected cell. This "locks" the frozen rows and columns in place so they remain visible on the screen. This can be particularly useful for viewing headings while you scroll through a worksheet.

FROM THE RIBBON
View→Window→
Freeze Panes

Splitting the Worksheet Window

At times, you will want to split the window to scroll within two areas of a worksheet. For example, you may want to compare data in rows 3–15 with rows 203–215. You can use the Split command for this purpose. This type of command is called a toggle, as you click it once to switch it on and again to switch it off.

Splitting Compared to Freezing

Freezing is useful for keeping headings consistently visible. However, you may not easily view two nonadjacent groups of data by freezing rows and/or columns. Splitting the window allows you to view two or four nonadjacent groups. Each pane has its own set of scroll bars. You may drag the split bar to adjust the number of rows or columns displayed in each pane.

In this split window, each pane may be scrolled to view nonadjacent areas of the worksheet.

	A	B
10	**Last Name**	**First Name**
11	Alejo	Carmen
12	Carter	Aaron
15	Martin	Michael
16	Wintz	Siobhan

— Split bar

In this frozen window, headings remain visible regardless of where you scroll.

	A	B	C	D
1	Green Clean	Website Usage		
2		Year 1		
3				
4	Last Name	Jan	Feb	Mar
18	Company N	18.5	36.0	15.5
19	Company O	7.0	2.0	16.0
20	Company P	1.5	0.0	0.0

TIP

Use either Split or Freeze, but not both together. One does not operate correctly when the other is in effect.

QUICK REFERENCE	CONTROLLING WORKSHEET VIEWS
Task	**Procedure**
Freeze columns and rows	■ Select the cell below and to the right of the area to be frozen. ■ Choose View→Window→Freeze Panes ▦ menu ▼→Freeze Panes.
Freeze columns	■ Select the cell in row 1 of the column to the right of the column(s) to be frozen. ■ Choose View→Window→Freeze Panes ▦ menu ▼→Freeze Panes.
Freeze rows	■ Select the cell in column A of the row below the row(s) to be frozen. ■ Choose View→Window→Freeze Panes ▦ menu ▼→Freeze Panes.
Unfreeze all	■ Choose View→Window→Freeze Panes ▦ menu ▼→Unfreeze Panes.
Split a window between columns or rows	■ Select the first cell in the column to the right of (or row below) where the split is to occur. ■ Choose View→Window→Split ▭.
Adjust a split	■ Drag the split bar that divides the window panes.
Remove a split	■ Choose View→Window→Split ▭.

Freeze and Split Worksheets

In this exercise, you will freeze both rows and columns, and you will split a worksheet window into two panes to scroll and compare data in two areas.

1. Save your file as **EX08-D02-ProjectBudget-[FirstInitialLastName]**.

2. Choose the **Website Usage** worksheet and select **cell B5**.

3. Choose **View→Window→Freeze Panes** ▦ →**Freeze Panes**.

   The area above and to the left of cell B5 is frozen, indicated by a horizontal and a vertical separation line.

4. Scroll to the right until the company totals are visible, and then scroll down to view the monthly totals.

   The frozen column A and rows 1-4 remain visible, as you have frozen those areas of the worksheet.

5. Choose **File→Print** and view the preview in Backstage view.

   The frozen panes do not affect printing, therefore the entire worksheet would print.

6. Tap [Esc] to exit the view without printing.

7. Press [Ctrl]+[Home] to jump back to the home cell.

   Cell B5 is now the home cell because you froze the window panes at that location.

8. Choose **View→Window→Freeze Panes ▦→Unfreeze Panes**.

   Since you cannot both freeze and split a worksheet simultaneously, you unfreeze the worksheet here so you may next split it.

Display Split Bars

9. Follow these steps to split the window between columns:

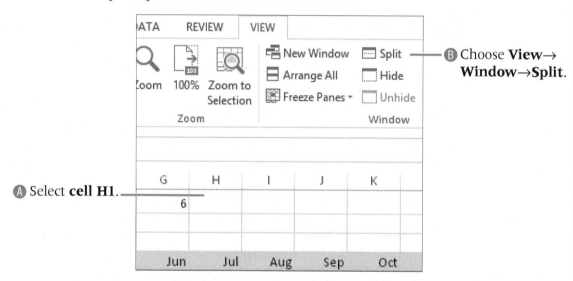

   The window displays two panes with a gray split bar between them.

10. Drag the scroll bars within each pane and note that the panes move independently of one another.

11. Follow these steps to move the split bar:

Ⓐ Point to the split bar until the mouse pointer changes to a two-headed arrow.

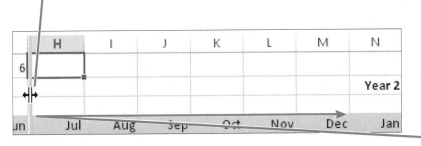

Ⓑ Drag to the right until the split bar is to the right of **column M**.

Ensure that the split bar is positioned to the right of Column M in the window on the left.

12. Choose **View→Window→Split** 🔲 to remove the split.

   Unlike Freeze Panes, the Split command toggles on and off when you click the same button.

13. Select **cell N5** and choose **View→Window→Split**.

   This time, the window splits into four panes because the pointer was not in the first cell of a row or column. The row 4 labels are in the upper panes because you selected a cell in row 5.

	L	M	N	O
1				
2			Year 2	
3				
4	Nov	Dec	Jan	Feb
5	13.0	7.0	2.0	7.5
6	18.0	17.5	10.0	8.5
7	0.0	0.0	0.0	4.0

14. Drag the scroll bars within each pane, and note that the panes move independently of one another.

15. Choose **View→Window→Split** 🔲 to remove the split.

16. Save the file and leave it open.

Viewing Worksheets in Multiple Windows

Video Library   http://labyrinthelab.com/videos   Video Number: EX13-V0803

As an alternative to splitting the worksheet window, you can display two areas of a large worksheet at once in separate windows. You can even display two or more worksheets in this way. The worksheets may be from the same workbook or different workbooks. This method allows you to compare, copy, or move data between worksheet areas more easily. Each window is numbered, and only one window can be active at one time.

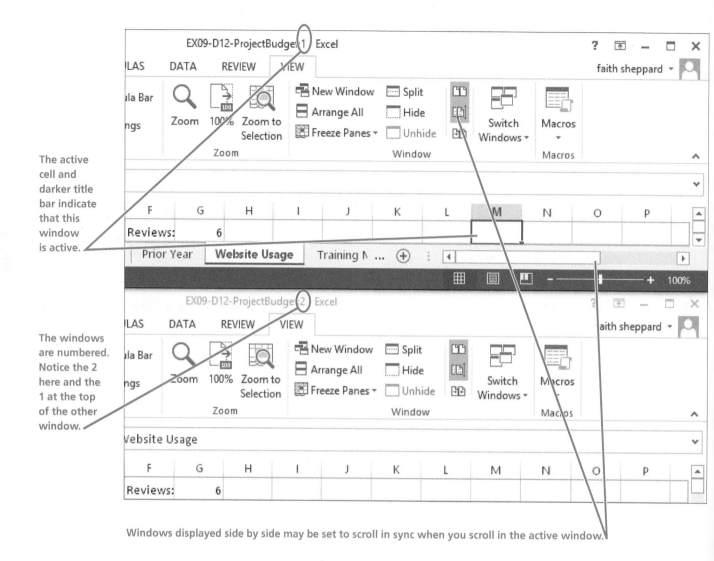

The active cell and darker title bar indicate that this window is active.

The windows are numbered. Notice the 2 here and the 1 at the top of the other window.

Windows displayed side by side may be set to scroll in sync when you scroll in the active window.

Synchronous Scrolling

Once windows are arranged, they may be scrolled independently with the scroll bars in each window. However, you may want to use synchronous scrolling so that the view in both windows moves simultaneously in the same direction as you scroll in the active window. This feature can keep the rows or columns aligned in the windows to help you compare data. To use synchronous scrolling, the windows must be set to be viewed side by side.

Creating Custom Worksheet Views

You can save certain display settings and print settings as custom views to redisplay later. You can create multiple custom views in a worksheet. A custom view, however, can be applied only to the worksheet for which you created the custom view.

To manage custom views, include the worksheet name when creating a custom view name.

Task	Procedure
View two areas of the same worksheet	■ Choose View→Window→New Window. ■ Choose View→Window→Switch Windows menu ▼ and select the desired active window. ■ Choose View→Window→View Side by Side. If necessary, select the second window and click OK. The active window will appear on top or to the left.
View two worksheets from the same workbook	■ Display the first worksheet, and choose View→Window→New Window. ■ Click the tab of the second worksheet in the new window and arrange the windows as desired.
View two worksheets from different workbooks	■ Display the first worksheet. ■ Choose File→Open, navigate to the desired workbook, display the second worksheet, and arrange the windows as desired.
Scroll windows synchronously	■ Use one of the previous procedures to set up two or more windows and choose View→Window→View Side by Side. ■ If Synchronous Scrolling does not turn on automatically, choose View→Window→Synchronous Scrolling.
Arrange windows	■ Choose View→Window→Arrange All and select a display option from the list.
Create a custom view	■ Change the worksheet display and print settings as desired. ■ Choose View→Workbook Views→Custom Views and click Add. ■ Enter a view name, and select the desired options.
Display a custom view	■ Choose View→Workbook Views→Custom Views. ■ Double-click the desired view in the Custom Views dialog box.

DEVELOP YOUR SKILLS EX08-D03

Arrange Multiple Worksheet Windows

In this exercise, you will view nonadjacent areas of a worksheet in separate windows and scroll them synchronously. You will also arrange two worksheets from a workbook to view them simultaneously.

1. Save your file as **EX08-D03-ProjectBudget-[FirstInitialLastName]**.

2. Display the **Website Usage** worksheet.

3. Choose **View→Window→New Window**.

   The Excel title bar displays EX08-D03-ProjectBudget-FirstInitialLastName:2 to indicate the window you just created.

4. Choose **View→Window→Switch Windows** and select **EX08-D03-ProjectBudget-FirstInitialLastName:1**.

   The EX08-D03-ProjectBudget-FirstInitialLastName:1 window is now the active window.

5. Choose **View→Window→View Side by Side**.

   The EX08-D03-ProjectBudget-FirstInitialLastName:1 window appears to the left of the other window because it was active when you chose the side-by-side view. If you have other workbooks open, a dialog box will appear from which you can choose the desired workbook. If the windows do not appear side-by-side, this will be remedied in the next step.

6. Choose **View→Window→Arrange All** ▤, choose **Horizontal**, and click **OK**.

The windows are arranged top to bottom.

7. Choose **View→Window→Synchronous Scrolling** ▣ from either window to toggle off synchronous scrolling.

The Synchronous Scrolling toggle button now should not appear highlighted when the window is active.

8. Follow these steps to compare data between the two worksheets:

Ⓐ Select **cell B5** in the EX08-D03-ProjectBudget-FirstInitialLastName:1 worksheet.

Ⓑ Choose **View→Window→Freeze Panes→Freeze Panes**.

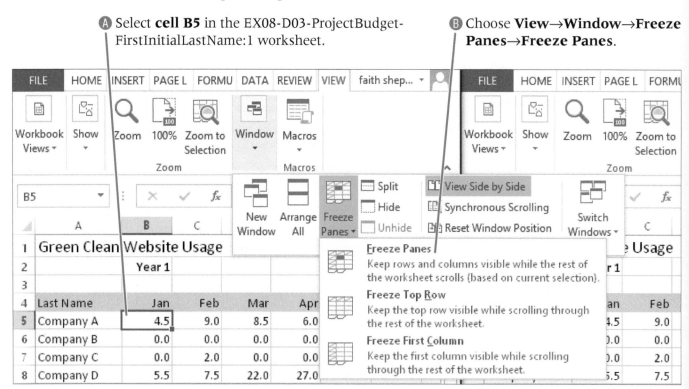

Ⓒ Repeat the prior two steps for the second worksheet.

Ⓓ Scroll to the right in the second worksheet until **column N** appears.

Since you turned off synchronous scrolling, only the active worksheet scrolled here.

9. Choose **View→Window→Synchronous Scrolling** ▣ to toggle on synchronous scrolling.

10. Click in the **EX08-D03-ProjectBudget-FirstInitialLastName:1** window, scroll to the right, and watch the other window scroll as well.

11. Click in the **EX08-D03-ProjectBudget-FirstInitialLastName:2** window and close it.

12. Choose **View→Window→New Window** .

13. Click the **Summary** sheet tab in the **EX08-D03-ProjectBudget-FirstInitialLastName:2** window.

14. Choose **View→Window→Arrange All**, select **Tiled**, and click **OK**.

    The Summary sheet and Website Usage sheet display side by side. Since synchronous scrolling is off, you could scroll one sheet without impacting the other.

15. Close the **Summary** sheet window, maximize the **Website Usage** sheet window, and **Unfreeze** the panes.

16. Save the file and leave it open.

Printing Multipage Worksheets

Video Library   http://labyrinthelab.com/videos   Video Number: EX13-V0804

Excel offers a variety of options that can improve the appearance of multipage worksheets when they are printed.

Sizing Options

The Page Setup and Scale to Fit command groups on the Page Layout tab contain options to help fit large worksheets on printed pages.

You can use the orientation, margin presets, paper size, and scaling presets available in the Print tab of Backstage view to correct the worksheet size just before printing.

Margins

Margins determine the space between the edge of the paper and the worksheet. You may choose from three preset margin layouts—Normal, Wide, and Narrow—as well as a Custom Margins option. Choose Narrow to fit more columns and rows on the printed page. Choose Custom Margins to launch the Page Setup dialog box with the Margins tab displayed. On this tab you may set specific worksheet margins and center the worksheet horizontally and/or vertically on the paper.

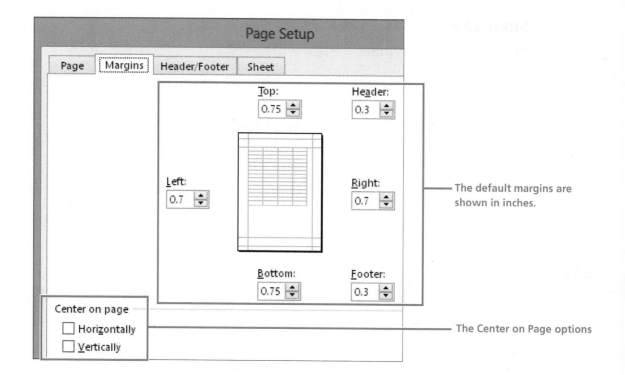

The default margins are shown in inches.

The Center on Page options

Orientation

Orientation indicates the direction of printing. Portrait is the default and prints across the narrow edge of the paper. Landscape orientation prints across the wide edge of the paper.

Portrait orientation   Landscape orientation

Size

The Size option refers to the paper size. The default is Letter 8.5" x 11" paper, while alternatives include Legal 8.5" x 14" paper.

Print Area

To print only a specific portion of your worksheet, you may set any range of cells as the print area. The Set Print Area command makes the range permanent until you set a different range or choose Clear Print Area to restore the entire worksheet for printing.

Scale to Fit

The Scale to Fit command group on the Page Layout tab provides automated scaling options to adjust the worksheet size for printing.

- **Width:** You may reduce the size of a worksheet containing many columns to fit its width on one, two, or more pages, as appropriate.
- **Height:** You may reduce the size of a worksheet containing many rows to fit its height on one, two, or more pages, as appropriate.
- **Scale:** To adjust the width and height in the same proportion, change the Scale, which is set to 100 percent by default. To use Scale, the Width and Height must be set to Automatic.

To reset the Height and Width to normal size, choose Automatic from each drop-down list. Make certain to change Scale to 100%, as the percentage does not reset automatically. The Undo command cannot reverse any Scale to Fit settings.

QUICK REFERENCE	SETTING PRINT OPTIONS
Task	**Procedure**
Display Page Layout View	■ Choose View→Workbook Views→Page Layout View 🔲 or click the Page Layout View button.
Change to preset margins	■ Choose Page Layout→Page Setup→Adjust Margins 🔲 menu ▼ and choose Normal, Wide, or Narrow.
Change specific margins	■ Choose Page Layout→Page Setup→Adjust Margins 🔲 menu ▼ and choose Custom Margins. ■ Change the Top, Bottom, Left, or Right margins.
Center the worksheet on printed page(s)	■ Choose Page Layout→Page Setup→dialog box launcher 🔲; click the Margins tab. ■ Under Center on Page, place a checkmark next to Horizontally and Vertically.
Change the orientation	■ Choose Page Layout→Page Setup→Change Page Orientation 🔲 menu ▼ and choose Portrait or Landscape.
Change paper size	■ Choose Page Layout→Page Setup→Choose Page Size 🔲 menu ▼ and choose a paper size.
Scale the worksheet to fit on fewer pages	■ Choose Page Layout→Scale to Fit, select 100% in the Scale box, type the desired percentage, and tap Enter.
Scale the worksheet width or height	■ Choose Page Layout→Scale to Fit→Width menu ▼ or Height menu ▼ and set the desired number of pages.
Set a print range	■ Select the desired cells, and choose Page Layout→Page Setup→Print Area ▼→ Set Print Area.
Remove the print range	■ Choose Page Layout→Page Setup→Print Area 🔲 menu ▼→Clear Print Area.

Use Orientation, Margin, and Sizing Options

In this exercise, you will change the orientation and margins. You also will scale a worksheet to print on fewer pages. You will use commands on the Ribbon as well as in the Page Setup dialog box.

1. Save your file as **EX08-D04-ProjectBudget-[FirstInitialLastName]**.

2. Display the **Website Usage** worksheet in **Page Layout View** at **40%** zoom.

   When you change sizing options you can see those changes within Page Layout view, but not within Normal view.

   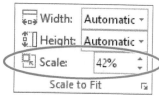

3. Choose **Page Layout→Page Setup→Change Page Orientation** →**Landscape**.

   Note that the entire worksheet will not fit on one page in Landscape orientation.

4. Choose **Page Layout→Page Setup→Adjust Margins** →**Narrow**.

   Decreasing the margins allows more columns and rows to fit on a page.

5. Go to **Page Layout→Scale to Fit→Scale**, change the scale to **42**, and tap Enter.

   The data now fits on one page, but would be too small to read if it were printed.

6. Change 42% in the Scale box to **100** and tap Enter.

   You manually changed the scale back to 100 because the Undo button wouldn't have worked in this instance.

7. Choose **Page Layout→Scale to Fit→Height menu ▼→1 page**.

   Now that the height is set to one page, the entire worksheet fits on two pages across.

Set the Print Area and Adjust Margins

8. Display the **Website Usage** worksheet in **Page Layout** view at **100%** zoom.

9. Follow these steps to set the print area for a portion of the year 1 data:

Ⓐ Choose **View→Workbook Views→Normal View**.

Ⓑ Select the range **A1:G14**.

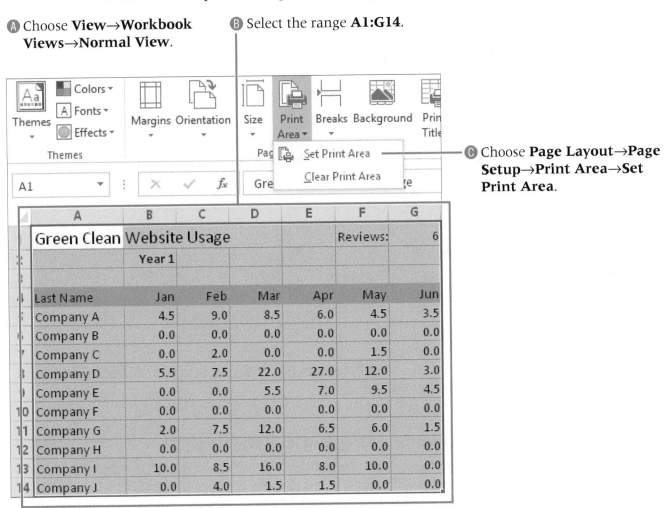

Ⓒ Choose **Page Layout→Page Setup→Print Area→Set Print Area**.

The print area appears surrounded by a border when you click any cell within the worksheet.

10. Choose **File→Print**.

    Notice that Excel would print only the cells that you set as the print area.

11. Exit Backstage view and choose **Page Layout→Page Setup→Print Area**▣**→Clear Print Area**.

    The border disappears because the print area has now been reset.

12. Display the **Summary** worksheet in Page Layout view.

13. Choose **Page Layout→Page Setup→Adjust Margins**▢**→Custom Margins**.

    If multiple custom margins options appear, select the last one within the menu.

14. In the Center on Page area, place a checkmark next to **Horizontally** and **Vertically**, and click **OK**.

   The worksheet would now be centered on the page if it were printed.

15. Save the file and leave it open.

Headers and Footers

Video Library   http://labyrinthelab.com/videos   Video Number: EX13-V0805

Headers print at the top of every page and footers print at the bottom of every page. Excel provides a variety of predesigned headers and footers. You may even create customized headers and footers to suit your needs and create a different header and footer on odd and even pages for double-sided printing.

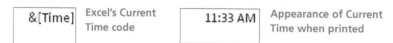

Summary			1 of 1				11/14/2012
Green Clean					Reviews:		
Budget and Expenses			11/13/2012				

A header displayed in Page Layout view

Use Page Layout view or the Print Preview in Backstage view to see headers and footers. They do not display in Normal view.

Creating and Formatting Headers and Footers

Headers and footers are created most conveniently in Page Layout view. Excel divides headers and footers into left, center, and right sections of the page. You need not fill in all three sections. To activate a section, just click in it to display the Design tab filled with header and footer options. When you choose an option from the Header & Footer Elements command group, Excel displays a code to represent the item. When you click outside the header section, Excel converts the code to properly display the selected option.

&[Time]	Excel's Current Time code

11:33 AM	Appearance of Current Time when printed

You may format headers and footers by changing elements such as the font, size, and color.

|

Task	Procedure
Display Page Layout view	■ Choose View→Workbook Views→Page Layout View 🖾 or click Page Layout on the Status Bar.
Select a predesigned page header or footer	■ Display Page Layout 🔲 view. ■ Select Click to Add Header above or Click to Add Footer below the worksheet. ■ Choose Header & Footer Tools→Design→Header & Footer→Header (or Footer) menu ▼ and choose a predesigned item.
Create a custom page header or footer	■ Display Page Layout 🔲 view. ■ Select the left, center, or right header section above, or footer section below, the worksheet. ■ Type text and set options from the Header & Footer Elements command group.
Set header and footer margins	■ Choose Page Layout→Page Setup→dialog box launcher 🖾. ■ Click the Margins tab and change the Header or Footer margin.
Create a different header and/or footer to print on page 1	■ Choose Page Layout→Page Setup→dialog box launcher. ■ Click the Header/Footer tab, place a checkmark next to Different First Page, and click OK. ■ Display the worksheet in Page Layout view, and create the desired header/footer on pages 1 and 2.
Create different headers and/or footers to print on odd and even pages	■ Choose Page Layout→Page Setup→dialog box launcher. ■ Click the Header/Footer tab, place a checkmark next to Different Odd and Even Pages, and click OK. ■ Display the worksheet in Page Layout view, create the desired header/footer on an odd page, and then create the desired header/footer on an even page.
Remove a header or footer	■ Select any section of the header or footer, choose Header & Footer Tools→Design→Header & Footer→Header (or Footer) menu ▼, and choose (None).

DEVELOP YOUR SKILLS EX08-D05

Set the Header and Footer

In this exercise, you will select predefined headers and footers, remove a footer, create custom headers and footers, and change the margins for these items.

1. Save your file as **EX08-D05-ProjectBudget-[FirstInitialLastName]**.

2. Select the **Website Usage** worksheet.

3. Choose **Page Layout view** and change the zoom level to **75%**.

4. Scroll up to the top of the page, if necessary, and choose **Click to Add Header**.

				Click to add header
Green Clean Website Usage			Reviews:	6
	Year 1			

The center header section is activated, and the Design tab displays.

5. Choose **Header & Footer Tools→Design→Header & Footer→Header** and select **Page 1 of ?**.

The "?" will update within the header to show the total number of pages.

6. Scroll to the bottom of the page.

7. Select **Click to Add Footer** in the center footer section.

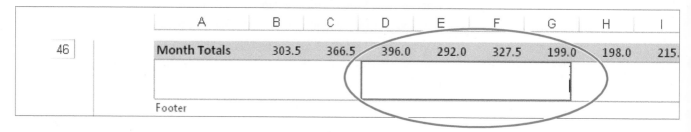

8. Choose **Header & Footer Tools→Design→Header & Footer→Footer→Website Usage**.

The sheet name now displays within the footer of each page.

9. Select the footer, choose **Header & Footer Tools→Design→Header & Footer→Footer**, and select **(None)** to remove the footer.

10. Select the left header section, choose **Header & Footer Tools→Design→Header & Footer Elements→Sheet Name**.

The Sheet Name code is displayed.

11. To complete the header, type a comma, tap Spacebar, and choose **Header & Footer Tools→Design→Header & Footer Elements→File Name**.

Although the header presently displays the codes for Sheet Name and File Name, the actual names will appear.

12. Select the right header section, type your name, and click outside the header.

13. Click any cell within the spreadsheet and select **Page Layout→Page Setup→dialog box launcher**.

14. Follow these steps to change the header and footer margins:

Ⓐ Display the **Margins** tab.

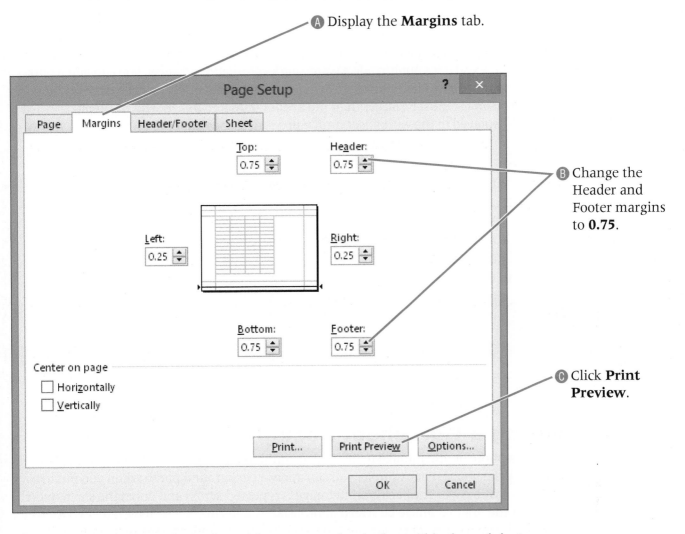

Ⓑ Change the Header and Footer margins to **0.75**.

Ⓒ Click **Print Preview**.

Excel 2013

Note that the header and footer now overlap the data within the worksheet.

15. Click the **Page Setup** link at the bottom of the list of print options.

16. Under the Margins tab, change the **Header and Footer** margins to **0.3**, click **OK** and exit backstage view.

17. Save the file and leave it open.

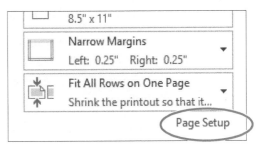

Adding a Watermark Image

Video Library   http://labyrinthelab.com/videos   Video Number: EX13-V0806

A watermark is a lightly shaded notation such as *Confidential* or *Draft* that appears behind document data. Excel does not include a watermark command; however, you can add a photo or transparent image to a header or footer to achieve a watermark effect on each page of the worksheet. The image must be larger than the header or footer area in which you place it. The image is not displayed in the worksheet until you deselect the header or footer.

.0.0	8.5	16.0	8.0	10.0	0.0	2.5	8.5	12.5	17.0	9.5	4.5	0
.8.5	36.0	15.5	25.5	16.0	10.0	2.5	1.5	17.0	24.5	16.0	13.5	2
7.0	2.0	16.0	4.5	13.0	8.0	4.0	2.0	14.0	3.5	9.0	3.0	16
4.5	9.0	8.5	6.0	4.5	3.5	0.0	2.0	4.5	11.5	13.0	7.0	0
0.0	0.0	0.0	0.0	14.0	17.5	17.5	12.5	0.0	24.0	35.0	19.5	18
5.5	25.5	16.0	10.0	2.5	1.5	17.0	24.5	16.0	13.5	5.5	7.5	2
.6.0	4.5	13.0	8.0	4.0	2.0	14.0	3.5	9.0	3.0	0.0	0.0	16
5.0	19.5	22.0	0.0	0.0	0.0	0.0	0.0	0.0	0.0	0.0	0.0	1
3.5	366.5	396.0	292.0	327.5	199.0	198.0	215.5	282.0	379.5	378.0	310.5	256

A logo watermark

Applying a Worksheet Background

You can use a photo or other image to fill the background and then turn off the gridlines to better display the image. For example, you can apply a background photo when you publish a workbook as a web page. The background image is repeated across and down the sheet, which requires that the original image be scaled appropriately and contrast well with the worksheet text colors. The image cannot be adjusted in Excel. The background image will not be included on a printed worksheet.

Green Clean Website Usage			
	Year 1		
Last Name	Jan	Feb	Mar
Company A	4.5	9.0	8.5
Company B	0.0	0.0	0.0
Company C	0.0	2.0	0.0
Company D	5.5	7.5	22.0

A photo background should contrast well with worksheet text.

QUICK REFERENCE	ADDING A WATERMARK AND BACKGROUND TO SHEETS

Task	Procedure
Add a watermark image to a worksheet	▪ Select the left, center, or right section of the header or footer.
	▪ Choose Header & Footer Tools→Design→Header & Footer Elements→Picture, navigate to the desired image, and double-click the image.
	▪ Choose Header & Footer Tools→Design→Header & Footer Elements→Format Picture and adjust the size, cropping, and image control as desired.
Remove a watermark image	▪ Click in the appropriate header or footer section, which selects &[Picture], and tap Delete.
Apply a repeating background to a worksheet	▪ Choose Page Layout→Page Setup→Background, navigate to the desired image file, and double-click the image.
Remove a background	▪ Choose Page Layout→Page Setup→Delete Background.

Excel 2013

DEVELOP YOUR SKILLS EX08-D06
Apply a Watermark and Background to Sheets

In this exercise, you will add both a watermark effect and a "Draft" background image to a worksheet.

1. Save your file as **EX08-D06-ProjectBudget-[FirstInitialLastName]**.

2. Display the **Website Usage** sheet in **Page Layout** view and select the center header section.

   The page numbering within the header should now be selected.

3. Choose **Header & Footer Tools→Design→Header & Footer Elements→Picture** .

4. Navigate to your **EX2013 Lesson 08** folder through the From a File section, select **EX08-D06-GreenWater**, and click **Insert**.

   The header section displays the code &[Picture] in place of the page numbering, but the image is not displayed while the header is selected.

Website Usage				Reviews:		6	
Year 1							
Jan	Feb	Mar	Apr	May	Jun	Jul
4.5	9.0	8.5	6.0	4.5	3.5	0.0
0.0	0.0	0.0	0.0	0.0	0.0	0.0
0.0	2.0	0.0	0.0	1.5	0.0	0.0
5.5	7.5	22.0	27.0	12.0	3.0	4.5
0.0	0.0	5.5	7.0	9.5	4.5	13.0
0.0	0.0	0.0	0.0	0.0	0.0	0.0
2.0	7.5	12.0	6.5	6.0	1.5	0.5

5. Click any cell in the worksheet to deselect the header.

   The image now displays on every page of the worksheet and would appear if it were printed.

6. Display the **Summary** sheet in Normal view.

7. Choose **Page Layout→Page Setup→Background** .

8. Navigate to your **EX2013 Lesson 08** folder through the From a File section, select **EX08-D06-DraftBack**, and click **Insert**.

Excel now repeats as many copies of the word "Draft" as will fit based on the image size.

9. Press Ctrl + P to display the Print tab of Backstage view

Notice in the preview that the background would not print.

10. Exit **Backstage view** without printing; save the file and leave it open.

Setting Title Rows and Columns

Video Library   http://labyrinthelab.com/videos   Video Number: EX13-V0807

You may specify one or more rows as title rows and one or more columns as title columns. Title rows and columns are printed on every page of a worksheet. This can be beneficial when worksheet data extends to multiple pages and requires headers to be fully understood.

The Title Rows and Title Columns options are not available if you display the Page Setup dialog box from within the Print tab of Backstage view. To use these options, you must launch the Page Setup dialog box from the Page Layout tab.

Sheet Options

The Sheet Options command group of the Page Layout tab contains options that affect the worksheet view and all printed pages of the worksheet. You may choose some options separately for viewing the worksheet and for printing.

Gridlines

By default, light gray gridlines surround every cell in the worksheet view. However, these gridlines do not print by default. In large worksheets, you may find it useful to print with gridlines to help track data across rows and down columns.

Company J	0.0	4.0	1.5
Company K	7.0	2.0	16.0
Company L	0.0	24.0	35.0

The printed worksheet without gridlines (the default setting)

Company J	0.0	4.0	1.5
Company K	7.0	2.0	16.0
Company L	0.0	24.0	35.0

The printed worksheet with gridlines

Headings

By default, column headings (letters A, B, C, etc.) and row headings (numbers 1, 2, 3, etc.) do not print. Similar to gridlines, these can also be included on the printed worksheet, if desired.

Task	Procedure
Print title rows on every page	■ Choose Page Layout→Page Setup→Print Titles ▦. ■ Click in the Rows to Repeat at Top box. ■ Drag to select the desired rows in the worksheet; click Print Preview or OK.
Print title columns on every page	■ Choose Page Layout→Page Setup→Print Titles ▦. ■ Click in the Columns to Repeat at Left box. ■ Drag to select the desired columns in the worksheet; click Print Preview or OK.
Print gridlines	■ Choose Page Layout→Sheet Options→Gridlines→Print Gridlines.
Print column and row headings	■ Choose Page Layout→Sheet Options→Headings→Print Headings.

Excel 2013

Set Sheet Options

In this exercise, you will set options to print repeating title rows and title columns, gridlines, and row and column headings on a multipage worksheet.

1. Save your file as **EX08-D07-ProjectBudget-[FirstInitialLastName]**.

2. Display the **Website Usage** worksheet in **Page Layout** view; click **cell A1**.

3. Choose **Page Layout→Page Setup→Print Titles** ▦.

4. Follow these steps to set title rows and title columns:

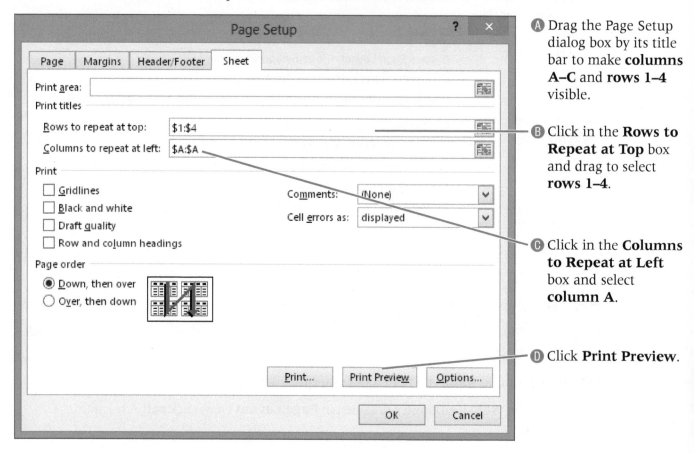

Ⓐ Drag the Page Setup dialog box by its title bar to make **columns A–C** and **rows 1–4** visible.

Ⓑ Click in the **Rows to Repeat at Top** box and drag to select **rows 1–4**.

Ⓒ Click in the **Columns to Repeat at Left** box and select **column A**.

Ⓓ Click **Print Preview**.

5. Click the **Next Page** button below the print preview in Backstage view.

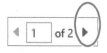

Note that the title rows and column repeat on the second page of the printed worksheet.

6. Exit Backstage view without printing; then display **Normal** view.

Turn Gridlines and Headings On and Off

7. Choose **Page Layout→Sheet Options→Gridlines→View Gridlines** to turn gridlines off.

8. Follow these steps to turn gridlines back on and to display gridlines and headings when you print:

Ⓐ Choose **Page Layout→Sheet Options→Gridlines→View Gridlines**.

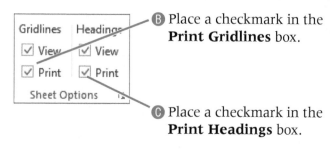

Ⓑ Place a checkmark in the **Print Gridlines** box.

Ⓒ Place a checkmark in the **Print Headings** box.

9. Choose **File→Print** and click the **Zoom to Page** 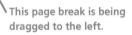 in the lower-right corner of Backstage view to zoom in.

Gridlines appear as dotted lines but will print as solid lines. The column headings and row headings display as well.

10. Exit **Backstage view** without printing; save the file and leave it open.

Working with Page Breaks

Video Library   http://labyrinthelab.com/videos   Video Number: EX13-V0808

You can use Page Break Preview to see where Excel's automatic page breaks occur in a worksheet and which part of the worksheet will be printed. This view also allows you to insert additional page breaks manually when they are needed. In Page Break Preview, the print area appears in white. Nonprinting areas appear in gray.

Adjusting Automatic Page Breaks

Excel formats most printed worksheets by inserting automatic page breaks when pages are full. An automatic page break appears as a dashed line. You may adjust the location of a page break by clicking and dragging it in Page Break Preview. The page break then displays as a solid line, indicating that it is a manual page break.

	M	N	O	P	Q	R	S	T	U
1									
2		Year 2							
3									
4	Dec	Jan	Feb	Mar	Apr	May	Jun	Jul	Aug
5	7.0	2.0	7.5	12.0	6.5	6.0	1.5	0.5	9.0
6	17.5	10.0	8.5	16.0	8.0	10.0	0.0	2.5	8.5
7	0.0	0.0	4.0	1.5	1.5	0.0	0.0	3.5	0.0
8	27.0	18.5	36.0	15.5	25.5	21.*	10.0	2.5	6.5
9	12.0	7.0	2.0	16.0	4.5	13.0	8.0	14.0	16.0

This page break is being dragged to the left.

When adjusting page breaks, you cannot *increase* columns or rows on a full page without adjusting other print options.

Inserting and Removing Page Breaks

You must select a cell in an appropriate column or row before inserting a manual page break. The page break appears as a solid line in the column to the left of or the row above the selected cell. You may remove any manual page break. If necessary, Excel inserts automatic page breaks after you remove manual page breaks.

QUICK REFERENCE	SETTING PAGE BREAKS
Task	**Procedure**
Adjust an automatic page break	■ Choose Page Break Preview 🔲 from the Status Bar. ■ Drag a vertical dashed automatic page break line to the left or a horizontal page break line up.
Add a manual page break	■ Choose Page Break Preview 🔲 from the Status Bar. ■ Select a cell below and/or to the right of the desired page break location. ■ Choose Page Layout→Page Setup→Breaks 🔛 menu ▼→Insert Page Break; or, right-click the cell and choose Insert Page Break.
Remove a manual page break	■ Choose Page Break Preview 🔲 from the Status Bar. ■ Select the cell to the right of the desired vertical page break line and/or below a horizontal page break line. ■ Choose Page Layout→Page Setup→Breaks 🔛 menu ▼→Remove Page Break; or, right-click the cell and choose Remove Page Break.

DEVELOP YOUR SKILLS EX08-D08
Work with Page Breaks

In this exercise, you will move, add, and remove a page break in Page Break Preview.

1. Save your file as **EX08-D08-ProjectBudget-[FirstInitialLastName]**.

2. On the **Website Usage** worksheet, press ⌨Ctrl + ⌨Home to display **cell A1**.

3. Click the **Page Break Preview** button from the Status Bar.

4. Click anywhere on the blue automatic page break line and drag to the left until it is to the left of **column N**.

5. Select a cell within **page 1** and choose **File→Print**.

6. Click the **Zoom to Page** 🗗 button at the lower-right corner of the print preview in Backstage view.

   Notice that page 1 ends with column M, which contains the December data for year 1.

7. Exit Backstage view without printing.

8. In **Page Break Preview**, select any cell in **column H**, which contains July data.

9. Choose **Page Layout→Page Setup→Breaks** 🔛**→Insert Page Break**.

   A solid blue, manual page break line now appears to the left of column H.

10. Point to any cell in **column T**, right-click, and choose **Insert Page Break**.

    Do not move the pointer off column T as you right-click.

11. Use either method you just learned to add a page break to the left of **column Z**.
    The worksheet would now print on five pages.

12. Select any cell in **column H**.

13. Choose **Page Layout→Page Setup→Breaks** ⊟→**Remove Page Break**.

14. Point to any cell in **column T**, **right-click**, and choose **Remove Page Break**.

15. Use either method you just learned to remove the page break to the left of **column Z**.
    The worksheet now contains only one page break to the left of column N.

16. Save the file and leave it open.

Using Multiple Worksheets

Video Library   http://labyrinthelab.com/videos   Video Number: EX13-V0809

Like pages in a word-processing document, multiple worksheets are a convenient way to organize data logically into more manageable sections. Any worksheet can contain formulas that perform calculations on data contained in other worksheets. For example, you may set up a summary worksheet that totals data from multiple detail worksheets. You may also change the default number of sheets for new workbooks using the Excel Options dialog box.

Selecting Multiple Sheets

Cell entries and formatting may be created in the same cell or range of multiple sheets simultaneously. This action is recommended when the sheets have an identical structure. You can also perform other simultaneous actions to the selected sheets, such as inserting a row.

The three highlighted tabs are selected.

QUICK REFERENCE	USING MULTIPLE SHEETS
Task	**Procedure**
Change the default number of sheets for new workbooks	▪ Choose File→Options, and select the General category. ▪ In the When Creating New Workbooks section, indicate the desired number of sheets and click OK.
Select multiple worksheets	▪ Display the first sheet to be included in the selection. ▪ Hold down ⌨Ctrl and click each additional sheet tab desired; or, hold down ⇧Shift and click a sheet tab to include a consecutive range of sheets.
Remove sheets from the selection	▪ Hold down ⌨Ctrl and click a sheet tab to deselect it, click a sheet tab outside the selection to cancel a multiple selection; or, hold down ⇧Shift and click the first selected sheet tab to cancel an adjacent selection.

Select Multiple Sheets

In this exercise, you will change the number of sheets in new workbooks and select multiple worksheets.

1. Save your file as **EX08-D09-ProjectBudget-[FirstInitialLastName]**.

2. Choose **File→Options** to display the General options in the Excel Options dialog box.

3. Follow these steps to change the default number of sheets in a workbook:

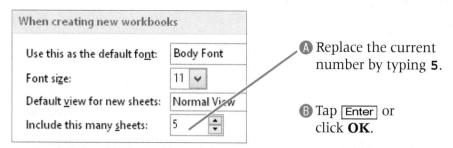

Ⓐ Replace the current number by typing **5**.

Ⓑ Tap [Enter] or click **OK**.

4. Press [Ctrl]+[N] to start a new workbook.
   Notice the five sheet tabs at the bottom of the worksheet window.

5. Close the new workbook without saving.

6. Display the **Excel Options** dialog box again, change the default number of sheets to **1**, and click **OK**.

7. With the **Summary** sheet active, hold down [Ctrl] and click the **Mileage** sheet tab.
   Both sheet tabs have a light background to indicate that they are selected.

8. Hold down [Ctrl] and click the **Mileage** sheet tab to remove it from the selection.

9. Follow these steps to select adjacent sheets:

Ⓐ Ensure that the **Summary** sheet is active.

Ⓑ Hold down [Shift] and click the **Mileage** sheet tab.

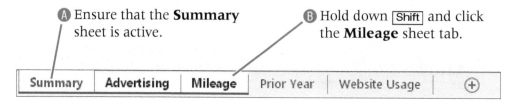

Ⓒ Notice that the three contiguous sheet tabs have a light background.

10. Select **cell A16**, choose **Home→Font→Bold** Ⓑ, type **Total**, and tap [Enter].

11. Hold down [Shift] and click the **Summary** sheet tab to cancel the multiple sheet selection.

12. Display the **Mileage** sheet and notice that the cell entry appears in **cell A16**.

13. Save the file and leave it open.

Linking Cells and Formulas

Video Library   http://labyrinthelab.com/videos   Video Number: EX13-V0810

Excel lets you link cells from different worksheets in the same workbook or in other workbooks. Linking places values from a source worksheet into a destination worksheet.

Why Link Cells?

Linking creates totals in summary worksheets from values in detail worksheets. This lets you keep detailed information in the detail sheets and see the totals in the summary worksheet. If the contents of the original cells are changed, the appropriate cell in the summary worksheet updates automatically.

Creating Linking Formulas

As with normal formulas, before you create a linking formula, you must select the cell in the summary worksheet where you want the result to appear. Also, as with all other formulas, a linking formula begins with the equals (=) sign.

You may type a linking formula, but using the mouse to select cells is more accurate and highly recommended.

Linking Cells from Other Worksheets in Formulas

The formulas shown will link the contents of one cell from a detail worksheet to a cell in the summary worksheet. The sheet name and cell reference are separated by an exclamation point (!). If the sheet name contains spaces or other non-alphabetic characters, the sheet name must be surrounded by single quotes ('), as in the second example.

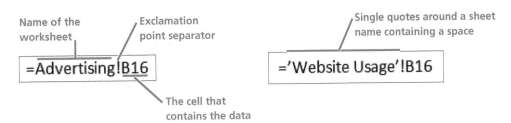

You may create calculation formulas on a summary worksheet using data from multiple detail worksheets. The following example sums the sales from four quarterly sheets to result in the yearly total. Notice that commas are used to separate the four cell references.

=SUM(Quarter1!D18, Quarter2!D18, Quarter3!D18, Quarter4!D18)

Excel 2013

Linking Cells from Other Workbooks in Formulas

If the source cell is in a different workbook, you must include the full workbook name in square brackets. Because the example workbook name contains a space, single quotes (') are included before the workbook name and after the worksheet name. Selecting the cell with the mouse will add all of this syntax for you.

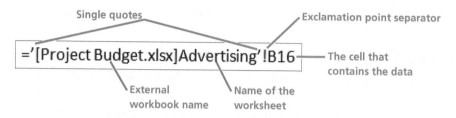

Single quotes

Exclamation point separator

='[Project Budget.xlsx]Advertising'!B16 — The cell that contains the data

External workbook name

Name of the worksheet

Create a Linking Formula

In this exercise, you will create a formula to link a cell in the Advertising worksheet to the Summary worksheet.

1. Save your file as **EX08-D10-ProjectBudget-[FirstInitialLastName]**.

2. Display the **Advertising** worksheet.

3. Select **cell B16**, choose **Home→Editing→AutoSum Σ**, and tap ⎡Enter⎤.
   The total should equal 8,075. Notice that AutoSum summed the entire range B4:B15. This is desirable because AutoSum will keep a running total as you enter data throughout the year.

4. Display the **Summary** worksheet, select **cell C5**, and type an equals (**=**) sign.

5. Display the **Advertising** worksheet.
   Excel displays the Advertising worksheet. The sheet name Advertising appears in the Formula Bar followed by an exclamation point.

6. Select **cell B16**.
   The linking formula =Advertising!B16 displays in the Formula Bar.

7. Complete the formula by tapping ⎡Enter⎤.
   Excel displays the Summary worksheet with the completed link in cell C5. The number 8,075 appears in cell C5.

8. Display the **Advertising** worksheet.

9. Select **cell B7**, type **1200**, and tap ⎡Enter⎤.
   The total in cell B16 displays 9,275.

10. Repeat the **above steps** to link the total amount spent in the **Mileage** worksheet to the **Summary** Worksheet.

11. Copy the formula in **cell D5** of the **Summary** worksheet to the **range D6:D8** on that worksheet.

    Cells C5 and C7 now display dynamic values, always reflecting the current value in the source cell. You will similarly fill in cells C6 and C8 later in this lesson.

12. Save the file and leave it open.

Using 3-D Cell References in Formulas

Video Library   http://labyrinthelab.com/videos   Video Number: EX13-V0811

Excel also allows you to perform calculations using the contents of the same cell address in multiple worksheets. This is called a 3-D cell reference. Contrast the following linking formula and normal summing formula with a formula containing a 3-D cell reference.

Type of Formula	Example	What It Does
Linking	=Supplies!C6	Displays the contents from cell C6 in the Supplies worksheet
Normal	=Supplies!C6 + Utilities!C6	Sums cell C6 from the Supplies and Utilities worksheets only
3-D	=SUM(Supplies:Equipment!C6)	Sums cell C6 in all worksheets from Supplies through Equipment in the workbook

Why Use a 3-D Reference?

Using a 3-D reference provides two advantages over normal cell references in a multi-sheet formula. First, you do not have to click the cell in each worksheet to build the formula. Also, the formula automatically includes the specified cell from additional worksheets that you insert within the worksheet range.

Deleting a worksheet or moving a worksheet tab to outside the range in the 3-D reference removes that worksheet's values from the formula result.

Creating a 3-D Reference

Functions that you may use to create 3-D references include SUM, AVERAGE, COUNT, MAX, MIN, and some statistical functions. A formula may contain a single cell or a cell range as a 3D reference. The cell or range must also contain the same type of data, such as values.

QUICK REFERENCE	CREATING 3-D CELL REFERENCES IN FORMULAS
Task	**Procedure**
Create a 3-D reference	▪ Design all worksheets so that the cell contents to be calculated are in identical cell addresses.
	▪ Select the cell to contain the formula in the summary worksheet, and type the function beginning, such as =SUM(.
	▪ Click the first sheet tab and hold down Shift while clicking the last sheet tab to be referenced.
	▪ In the sheet currently displayed, select the cell or range to be referenced, and complete the formula.

DEVELOP YOUR SKILLS EX08-D11

Create a 3-D Cell Reference

In this exercise, you will create 3-D cell references to one cell in several worksheets. You will also create a 3-D reference to a cell range.

1. Save your file as **EX08-D11-ProjectBudget-[FirstInitialLastName]**.

2. Display the **Summary** worksheet.

3. Follow these steps to create a formula that determines the total number of employee reviews of the data by adding the values in cell G1 in each worksheet:

Ⓐ Select **cell G1** in the **Summary** worksheet.

Ⓑ Type **=sum(** .

Ⓒ Click the **Advertising** sheet tab, hold down Shift, click the **Website Usage** sheet tab, and release Shift.

Ⓓ Select **cell G1** and click **Enter** ✓.

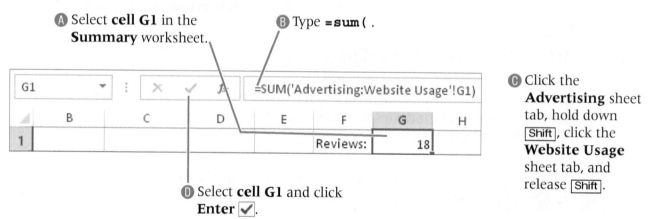

The formula result should be 18.

4. Save the file and leave it open.

Copying Worksheets

Video Library   http://labyrinthelab.com/videos   Video Number: EX13-V0812

Rather than inserting new blank sheets, you can use the Move or Copy Sheet command to copy an existing worksheet and then edit the duplicate.

The Move or Copy Dialog Box

A *copied* worksheet created with the Move or Copy Sheet command is an exact duplicate of the original. To move or copy a worksheet to another workbook, both workbooks must be open. Placing a checkmark in the Create a Copy box creates a *copy.* Leaving the box blank *moves* the selected worksheet. A worksheet moved to another workbook no longer exists in the original workbook.

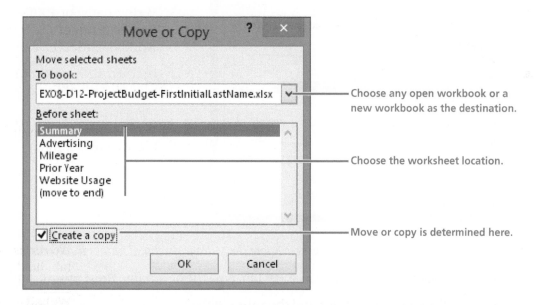

QUICK REFERENCE	COPYING AND MOVING WORKSHEETS
Task	**Procedure**
Copy or move a worksheet using a command	▪ Select the desired sheet tab to be copied or moved.
	▪ Choose Home→Cells→Format ⊞→Move or Copy Sheet; or, right-click the sheet tab and choose Move or Copy.
	▪ Choose the destination workbook or a new blank worksheet from the To Book list, and select the worksheet position.
	▪ To copy, place a checkmark in the Create a Copy box. To move, leave the box empty.
Copy or move a worksheet in the same workbook by dragging	▪ To move, drag the sheet tab to the desired location within the tabs.
	▪ To copy, hold down Ctrl and drag the sheet tab.

Create a Copy of a Worksheet

In this exercise, you will make two copies of the Advertising worksheet to create new sheets named Equipment and Training Materials.

1. Save your file as **EX08-D12-ProjectBudget-[FirstInitialLastName]**.

2. Display the **Advertising** worksheet.

3. Choose **Home→Cells→Format ⊞→Move or Copy Sheet**.

4. Follow these steps to create a copy of the Advertising worksheet:

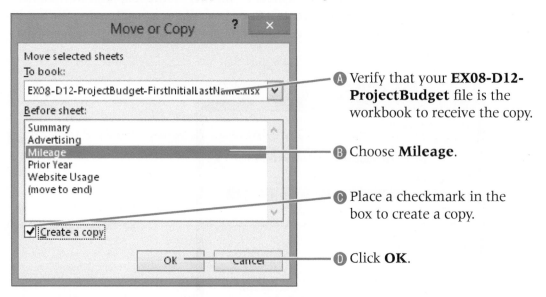

Ⓐ Verify that your **EX08-D12-ProjectBudget** file is the workbook to receive the copy.

Ⓑ Choose **Mileage**.

Ⓒ Place a checkmark in the box to create a copy.

Ⓓ Click **OK**.

Excel positions the duplicate worksheet before the Mileage sheet and names it Advertising (2).

5. Double-click the Advertising (2) sheet tab, type the new name **Equipment**, and tap ⌨Enter⌨.

6. Change the entries in **cell A1** and the **range B4:B7**.

◢	A	B
1	Equipment Tracking Sheet	
2		
3		Amount Spent
4	September	8,547
5	October	3,640
6	November	5,072
7	December	1,211

7. Right-click the **Advertising** sheet tab and choose **Move or Copy**.

8. In the dialog box, choose **(Move to End)** from the Before Sheet list, place a checkmark in the **Create a Copy** box, and click **OK**.

9. Change the name of the new sheet to **Training Materials**.

Your sheet tabs should look like these. If necessary, drag a sheet tab to the correct position.

Summary	Advertising	Equipment	Mileage	Prior Year	Website Usage	**Training Materials**

10. Edit the title in **cell A1** of the **Training Materials** worksheet and change the numbers in the **range B4:B7**.

	A	B	C
1	Training Materials Tracking Sheet		
2			
3		Amount Spent	
4	September	145	
5	October	1,620	
6	November	(1,705)	
7	December	730	

11. Link the totals within the **Training Materials** worksheet and the **Equipment** worksheet to the **Summary worksheet**.

Copy the Salaries Worksheet from a Different Workbook

12. Open **EX08-D12-Salaries** from the **EX2013 Lesson 08** folder, right-click the **Salaries** sheet tab, and choose **Move or Copy**.

13. Follow these steps to copy the Salaries worksheet:

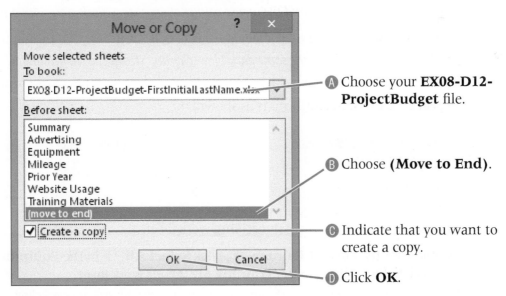

Ⓐ Choose your **EX08-D12-ProjectBudget** file.

Ⓑ Choose **(Move to End)**.

Ⓒ Indicate that you want to create a copy.

Ⓓ Click **OK**.

14. Close the **Salaries** workbook. Save the **Project Budget** workbook and leave it open.

Copying Formats between Worksheets

Video Library   http://labyrinthelab.com/videos   Video Number: EX13-V0813

Excel provides multiple ways to copy cell formatting from one worksheet to another without copying the text or numbers within the cells. The most basic of these methods is to use the Format Painter.

Use the Format Painter to copy formatting to cells in the target worksheet. You may select one or more cells, columns, or rows, or the entire worksheet before using the Format Painter button. The column width or row height is not applied unless you select an entire column or row before using the Format Painter.

Use the Select All ◢ button above the top-left corner of the worksheet to select the entire worksheet.

DEVELOP YOUR SKILLS EX08-D13
Use the Format Painter to Copy Formats

In this exercise, you will copy formatting from one worksheet to another. You will also apply formatting from one worksheet to two other worksheets.

1. Save your file as **EX08-D13-ProjectBudget-[FirstInitialLastName]**.

2. Display the **Summary** worksheet.

3. Select **cell A2** and choose **Home→Clipboard→Format Painter** ✔.
   Cell A2 displays a marquee, and the mouse pointer changes to a block cross with a paintbrush.

4. Display the **Advertising** worksheet and select **cell A1** to copy the format to that cell.
   The font in cell A1 now has the same dark blue color and size as the subheading in the Summary worksheet.

5. Repeat **steps 3–4** to copy formats as shown.

From the Summary Worksheet	To the Advertising Worksheet
Cell D4	Cell B3
Range A16:B16	Range A16:B16

6. Click **Select All** ◢ on the **Advertising** worksheet.

7. Double-click the **Format Painter** ✔, click **Select All** ◢ in the **Equipment** worksheet, and click **Select All** ◢ in the **Training Materials** worksheet.
   These two worksheets now have the same formatting as the Advertising worksheet.

8. Click the **Format Painter** ✔ to deactivate it. Click anywhere in the worksheet to deselect the cells.
   Deactivating the Format Painter ensures that you will not accidentally include formatting elsewhere, but does not undo the current formatting.

9. Display the **Mileage** worksheet and use the **Format Painter**  to copy the number and font formatting from **cell B4** to **cell C4**.

10. Use the **fill handle** to copy the formula and cell formatting in cell C4 down the column to **row 15**.

    Some of the cells will display zeros or dashes (depending on the default settings on your computer) because some values have not yet been entered into column B.

11. Deselect the highlighted cells.

12. Save the file and leave it open.

Excel 2013

Paste Options

Video Library   http://labyrinthelab.com/videos   Video Number: EX13-V0814

You may use options on the Paste menu to control the type of formatting and content applied to the target cells. Options on the Paste menu vary depending on the attributes of the copied selection. Clicking the Paste drop-down menu button on the Ribbon displays the menu.

The Paste Options button appears at the lower-right corner of the destination cell(s) so you can customize after a copy-and-paste action is performed. When the button is clicked, the same options display as on the Paste menu on the Ribbon. The button disappears upon the next action you take.

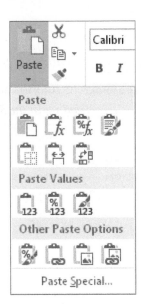

The Paste menu on the Ribbon

The Paste Options button

Pointing to an option in the Paste menu displays a preview of the result in the worksheet. The buttons and their actions are listed here.

PASTE MENU BUTTONS

Button	Name	Paste Action in the Destination Cell
	Paste	Pastes the source cell's contents and applies all its formatting
	Formulas	Pastes the source cell's contents and applies the destination cell's formatting
	Formulas & Number Formatting	Pastes the source cell's contents, applies the source cell's number format, and applies all other destination cell formatting
	Keep Source Formatting	Pastes the source cell's contents and applies all its formatting (used when pasting from an outside source)
	No Borders	Pastes the source contents and applies all its formatting except borders
	Keep Source Column Widths	Pastes the source cell's contents and applies the source cell's column width to the destination column
	Transpose	Pastes the source range's contents and formatting but reverses the row and column data
	Values	Pastes the value resulting from a formula (but not the formula) and applies the destination cell's formatting
	Values & Number Formatting	Pastes the value resulting from a formula (but not the formula), applies the source cell's number format, and applies all other destination cell formatting
	Values & Source Formatting	Pastes the value resulting from a formula (but not the formula) and applies the source cell's formatting
	Formatting	Applies the source cell's formatting but does not paste its contents
	Paste Link	Creates a linking formula to the source cell and applies the source cell's formatting
	Picture	Pastes a picture of the selected range as an object on top of the spreadsheet (or into other document, such as a Word document)
	Linked Picture	Pastes a picture of the selected range and creates a link to update the picture if any source cell is changed

Paste Special

The Paste Special command contains a dialog box with many of the same options that are on the Paste menu. The Operation options allow you to add a copied value to (or subtract it from) the existing value in the destination cell, multiply the values, or divide the destination values by their corresponding copied values. Certain other options are only available here as well.

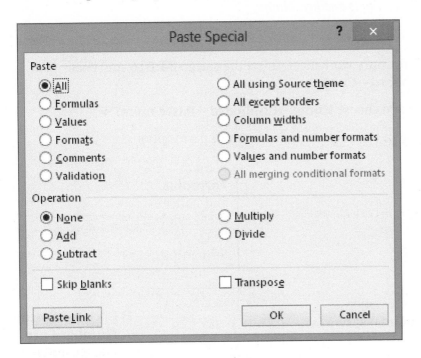

QUICK REFERENCE	USING THE FORMAT PAINTER, PASTE OPTIONS, AND PASTE SPECIAL
Task	**Procedure**
Copy formats to one other cell or range	▪ Click the cell that has the format(s) you wish to copy. ▪ Choose Home→Clipboard→Format Painter [icon], and select the cell/range to which you wish to copy the format(s).
Copy formats to multiple locations	▪ Click the cell that has the format(s) you wish to copy. ▪ Double-click Home→Clipboard→Format Painter [icon], and select the cell/range to which you wish to copy the format(s).
Apply an option while pasting using the Ribbon	▪ Select a cell or range of cells and choose Home→Clipboard→Copy. ▪ Choose Home→Clipboard→Paste menu ▼ and choose the desired option.
Apply an option after pasting	▪ Copy and paste the desired cell or range of cells. ▪ Click the Paste Options button at the lower-right corner of the destination cell(s) and choose an option.
Apply an option using Paste Special	▪ Select and copy a cell or range of cells. ▪ Select the destination cell or range of cells. ▪ Choose Clipboard→Paste menu ▼→Paste Special, choose the desired option in the Paste Special dialog box, and click OK.

Use Paste Options and Paste Special

In this exercise, you will copy data from a column and paste it across a row, and you will add the values of copied cells to values in the corresponding destination cells. You will also copy only the column width formatting from one column to another column.

1. Save your file as **EX08-D14-ProjectBudget-[FirstInitialLastName]**.

2. Display the **Summary** worksheet, select the **range B4:B16**, and choose **Home→Clipboard→Copy**.

3. Select **cell H4** and choose **Home→Clipboard→Paste menu** ▼.

4. Follow these steps to view the result of various paste options:

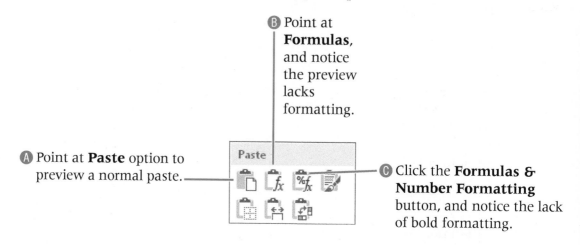

Ⓑ Point at **Formulas**, and notice the preview lacks formatting.

Ⓐ Point at **Paste** option to preview a normal paste.

Ⓒ Click the **Formulas & Number Formatting** button, and notice the lack of bold formatting.

5. **Undo** ↶ the paste.

6. Follow these steps to copy cell values without formatting:

Ⓐ Copy the **range B4:B16**.   Ⓑ Select **cell H4**.

Ⓓ Choose **Values**.

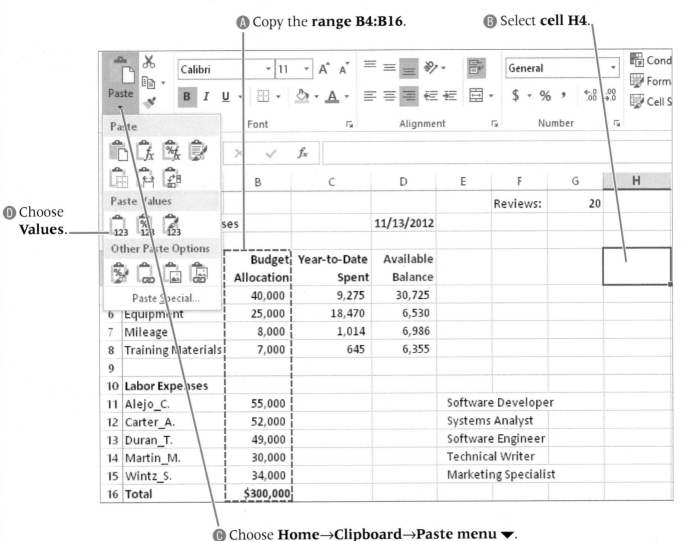

Ⓒ Choose **Home→Clipboard→Paste menu ▼**.

7. Select the range **B4:B16** and choose **Home→Clipboard→Copy**.

8. Select **cell H4**, choose **Home→Clipboard→Paste Menu ▼→Formatting**, and widen **column H** to fit all entries.

   The formatting of column H is now consistent with the rest of the worksheet.

9. Select the **range A11:A15** and choose **Home→Clipboard→Copy**.

10. Display the **Salaries** worksheet, select **cell B3**, and choose **Home→Clipboard→Paste**.

    The employee names have replaced some values on the Salaries worksheet. You will now transpose these names in order to correct this issue.

11. Click the **Paste Options** button and choose **Transpose**.

▲	A	B	C
1	Salaries Tracking Sheet		
2			
3		Alejo_C.	
4	September	Carter_A.	4,333
5	October	Duran_T.	4,333
6	November	Martin_M.	4,333
7	December	Wintz_S.	4,333
8	January		📋 (Ctrl) ▾

▲	B	C	D	E	F
3	Alejo_C.	Carter_A.	Duran_T.	Martin_M.	Wintz_S.
4	4,583	4,333	4,083	2,500	–

The employee names are transposed across row 3 and the original values in the range B4:B7 are displayed.

12. Right-align the **range B3:F3** to align with the numbers below these employee names.

13. Display the **Advertising** worksheet, select **cell B3**, and choose **Copy**.

14. Display the **Salaries** worksheet.

15. Select **cell G16** and choose **Home→Clipboard→Paste menu ▾→Paste Special**.

16. Choose **Column Widths** and click **OK** in the Paste Special dialog box.
    Only the column width is applied from the source cell to all cells in column G.

17. Autofit the height of **row 3**, if necessary.

18. Calculate the monthly totals in the **range G4:G15** and link the totals in row 16 to the **range C11:C15** on the **Summary** worksheet. Format the range as necessary.

19. On the **Summary** worksheet, calculate the **Available Balances** in the range **D11:D15**. Copy the formula in **cell B16** to the range **C16:D16**.

Add Copied Values to Destination Cells
Next, you will use Paste Special to add the values from one range to another.

20. Display the **Summary** worksheet, select the **range B5:B8**, and press ⌈Ctrl⌉ + ⌈C⌉.

21. Select **cell H5** and choose **Home→Clipboard→Paste menu ▾→Paste Special**.

22. In the Paste Special dialog box, choose **Add**, and click **OK.**
    The value in cell B5 was added to the value in cell H5. The result in cell H5 should be 80,000. Each of the other values in the range B6:B8 was added to its corresponding cell in column H.

23. Delete the contents of **column H**.

24. Save the file and leave it open.

Printing Multiple-Sheet Workbooks

Video Library   http://labyrinthelab.com/videos   Video Number: EX13-V0815

Excel prints the active worksheet when you choose the Quick Print command on the Quick Access toolbar. If you are working with a multiple-sheet workbook, you may use various techniques to set options and print multiple sheets simultaneously.

Applying Page Setup Options to Multiple Sheets

You may adjust the margins, page orientation, headers and footers, and a variety of other settings that affect the printed worksheet. Apply these settings to multiple worksheets by first using Ctrl to select nonadjacent sheet tabs or Shift to select adjacent sheet tabs.

Printing Multiple Sheets

You may print all sheets without selecting their tabs by choosing the Print Entire Workbook option in the Print tab of Backstage view. You may print only certain sheets by using Ctrl to select the desired sheet tabs and choosing Print or Quick Print.

DEVELOP YOUR SKILLS EX08-D15
Preview and Print Selected Sheets

In this exercise, you will select multiple sheets, change their orientation, and preview them all at once.

1. Save your file as **EX08-D15-ProjectBudget-[FirstInitialLastName]**.

2. With the **Summary** worksheet active, hold down Shift, and click the **Mileage** sheet tab.

3. Choose **Page Layout→Page Setup→Change Page Orientation→Landscape**.

4. Choose **File→Print**.

    Notice that the Print Active Sheets setting is selected. The bottom of the preview area displays "1 of 4," which indicates that four sheets are active and would print if you were to click Print.

5. Use the **Next Page** ▶ command to browse through the worksheets.

    Notice that the orientation of the four sheets is landscape.

6. Tap Esc to exit **Backstage view**; click any unselected sheet tab to deselect multiple sheet tabs.

Excel 2013

Select Multiple Nonadjacent Sheets

7. Display the **Advertising** worksheet.

8. Hold down Ctrl, click the **Mileage** sheet tab, click the **Salaries** sheet tab, and release Ctrl.
   Three sheets are selected.

9. Right-click any selected sheet tab and choose **Ungroup Sheets**.
   Now only one worksheet is active.

10. Choose **File→Print**.

11. In the Settings area of the Print tab, click **Print Active Sheets** and choose **Print Entire Workbook**.
    You may use this option to print the entire workbook without first selecting the sheets.

12. Press Esc to exit Backstage view without printing.

13. Save and close the file. Exit **Excel**.

Concepts Review

To check your knowledge of the key concepts introduced in this lesson, complete the Concepts Review quiz by choosing the appropriate access option below.

If you are...	Then access the quiz by...
Using the Labyrinth Video Library	Going to http://labyrinthelab.com/videos
Using eLab	Logging in, choosing Content, and navigating to the Concepts Review quiz for this lesson
Not using the Labyrinth Video Library or eLab	Going to the student resource center for this book

Reinforce Your Skills

Sort and Print Multiple Worksheets

In this exercise, you will use the Sort dialog box to sort worksheet rows. You will also arrange worksheets so you can view both open account balances and whether customers have defaulted in the past. Finally, you will print multiple worksheets.

Sort Worksheet Data

1. Start **Excel**. Open **EX08-R01-BalanceDue** from the **EX2013 Lesson 08** folder and save it as **EX08-R01-BalanceDue-[FirstInitialLastName]**.

2. On the **Balance Due** worksheet, select any account number below the **row 3 heading**.

3. Choose **Data→Sort & Filter→Sort A to Z** ![A to Z icon].
   The list is sorted by the Account Number column. Now you will sort on two sort keys.

4. Select any data cell below the **row 3** headings, choose **Data→Sort & Filter→Sort**, change the **Sort By** level to **Outstanding Balance**, and then set the **Order** to **Z to A**.

5. Click **Add Level**, change the **Then by** field to **Account Number**, and ensure **Order** is set to **Smallest to Largest**.

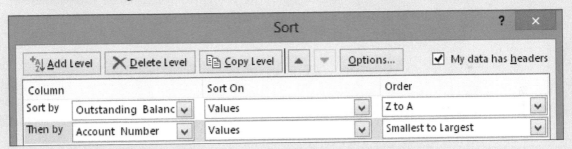

6. Click **OK** to perform the sort on two sort keys.

Use Flexible Worksheet Views

7. Choose **View→Window→New Window** ![New Window icon] and select the tab of the **Previous Default** worksheet.
   Notice that the two Balance Due worksheets that are now open display :1 and :2 after the workbook name in the title bar.

8. Choose **View→Window→Arrange All** ![Arrange All icon], select **Vertical**, and click **OK**.
   Note how easily you can now compare the data within the two worksheets.

9. **Close** ![X icon] the second Balance Due worksheet, and **maximize** ![maximize icon] the remaining window.

Print Multipage Worksheets

10. Choose **Page Layout→Scale to Fit→Scale** and change the scale to **200%**.

    In some instances, you will want to increase the size of your printed worksheet so it is easier to read.

11. Choose **File→Print** to view the print preview.

    Because of the scale increase, the worksheet does not fit on one page.

12. Exit **Backstage view** and choose **Page Layout→Page Setup→Adjust Margins→Narrow**.

    Reducing the margins allows for more of the worksheet to fit on the page.

13. Choose **File→Print** to view the print preview.

    The worksheet now fits on one page.

Use Multiple Worksheets

14. Choose **Options** to display the General options within the Excel Options dialog box.

    You intend to create more comparison workbooks with two worksheet tabs in the future, so you will change the default for new workbooks to include two worksheets.

15. Under **When Creating New Workbooks**, change the **Include This Many Sheets** option to **2**. Click **OK**.

16. Save and then close the file. Exit **Excel**.

17. Submit your final file based on the guidelines provided by your instructor.

    To view examples of how your file or files should look at the end of this exercise, go to the student resource center.

REINFORCE YOUR SKILLS EX08-R02

Copy and Link Worksheets

In this exercise, you will create formulas that link cells between worksheets, arrange worksheet tabs, and adjust print options.

Link Cells and Formulas

1. Start **Excel**. Open **EX08-R02-Marketing** from the **EX2013 Lesson 08** folder and save it as **EX08-R02-Marketing-[FirstInitialLastName]**.

2. On the **Summary** worksheet, select **cell B4** and type an equals sign.

3. On the **Eastern** worksheet, select **cell B4**, and type a plus sign.

    The formula now reads =Eastern!B4+. You will next add to this the figures within cell B4 on the other two worksheets.

4. Repeat the prior step for the **Western** and **Central** worksheets, remembering to type a plus sign between these two cell references. Press Enter.

    Excel displays the Summary worksheet, and shows a total of $32,000 in cell B4.

5. Drag the fill handle to copy this formula to the **range C4:E4**.

Use 3-D Cell References in Formulas

6. On the **Summary** worksheet, select **cell B5** and type =Sum(.

7. Select the **Eastern** sheet tab, press Shift, and select the **Central** sheet tab.

   All four sheet tabs are now highlighted, while the Eastern sheet remains active.

8. Select **cell B5** on the **Eastern** sheet (which is currently displayed), type a close parenthesis, and confirm the formula.

   This formula provides the same result as the formula in cell B4, but it was easier to construct. When data on multiple sheets line up in the same cells, as they do in this worksheet, 3-D cell references should always be used.

9. AutoFill with this formula the remaining quarters for **Area 2**, as well as all quarters for **Areas 3 and 4**.

Copying Worksheets

10. Click the **Eastern** sheet tab and click **Select All** .

11. Choose **Home→Clipboard** then double-click the **Format Painter** button.

    Because you double-clicked, the Format Painter will remain active after you apply it in the next step.

12. Display the **Western** sheet tab and click **Select All** .

    You were able to copy the formats in this manner because the sheets have an identical structure.

13. Repeat **step 12** to copy the formats to the **Central** and **Summary** worksheets.

14. Choose **Home→Clipboard→Format Painter** to deactivate the feature.

Print Multiple-Sheet Workbooks

15. Click the **Summary** sheet tab and choose **File→Print**.

16. In the **Settings** area, choose **Print Active Sheets→Print Entire Workbook**.

    If you were to now select print, all four worksheets would be printed.

17. Save and then close the file. Exit **Excel**.

18. Submit your final file based on the guidelines provided by your instructor.

    To view examples of how your file or files should look at the end of this exercise, go to the student resource center.

Sort, Link, and Organize Multiple Worksheets

In this exercise, you will sort expense data related to two monthly events hosted by Kids for Change. You will create linking formulas within a summary worksheet, and will organize the worksheets prior to printing.

Sort Worksheet Data

1. Start **Excel**. Open **EX08-R03-Events** from the **EX2013 Lesson 08** folder and save it as **EX08-R03-Events-[FirstInitialLastName]**.

2. On the **Fundraising** worksheet, select **cell N4** and highlight the **range N4:A7**.

3. Choose **Data→Sort & Filter→Sort Z to A** $\begin{smallmatrix}Z\\A\end{smallmatrix}$↓.

   The expense data is now sorted from highest to lowest based on the total column.

4. Repeat the prior two steps on the **Awards** worksheet.

Use Flexible Worksheet Views

5. Choose **View→Window→New Window** .

   Notice that the two Events worksheets that are now open display :1 and :2 after the workbook name in the title bar.

6. Choose **View→Window→Arrange All** , select **Horizontal**, and click **OK**.

   Note how easily you can now compare the data within the two worksheets.

7. **Close** ✕ the second Events worksheet and **maximize** ▢ the remaining window.

Print Multipage Worksheets

8. On the **Fundraising** worksheet select **cell H1**.

9. Choose **Page Layout→Page Setup→Breaks** →**Insert Page Break**.

   Because the active cell was within row 1 when you inserted this page break, only a vertical break is applied to the worksheet.

10. Choose **Page Layout→Page Setup→Print Titles** ; then click within the **Columns to Repeat at Left** box, select **column A,** and click **OK**.

    You will not see any change within the worksheet, however when you print you will see column A repeat on each printed page.

11. Repeat the prior two steps within the **Awards** worksheet.

Use Multiple Worksheets

12. Choose **File→Options** to display the General options within the Excel Options dialog box.

13. In the **When Creating New Workbooks** section, change the **Include This Many Sheets** option to **3**; click **OK**.

Link Cells and Formulas

14. Double-click the **Sheet3** worksheet tab and rename it **Summary**.

15. On the **Fundraising** worksheet, choose **Select All** 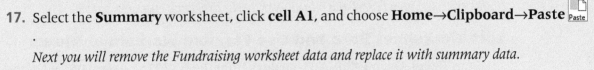.

16. Choose **Home→Clipboard→Copy** 📋.

    You can now paste all data and formatting into another worksheet.

17. Select the **Summary** worksheet, click **cell A1**, and choose **Home→Clipboard→Paste** 📋.
    .

    Next you will remove the Fundraising worksheet data and replace it with summary data.

18. Modify the title in **cell A1** to **Kids for Change - Summary**.

19. Select the **range B4:N7** and tap Delete.

20. Select **cell B4**, type **=**, choose the **Fundraising** worksheet tab, select **cell B4**, type **+**, choose the **Awards** worksheet tab, select **cell B4**, and tap Enter.

21. AutoFill the formula in **cell B4** to the **range B4:M7**.

    The Summary worksheet now displays the total expenses for all events.

Use 3-D Cell References in Formulas

22. On the **Summary** sheet, select **cell N4** and type **=Sum(**.

23. Select the **Fundraising** sheet tab, hold Shift, and select the **Awards** sheet tab.

24. Select **cell N4** on the Fundraising sheet, type a close parenthesis, and confirm the formula.

25. Select **cell N4** and choose **Home→Clipboard→Copy** 📋.

26. Highlight the **range N5:N8** and choose **Home→Clipboard→Paste menu ▼→Formulas**.

Copy Worksheets

27. Drag the **Summary** worksheet tab prior to the **Fundraising** worksheet to rearrange the order of the worksheets.

Print Multiple-Sheet Workbooks

28. Choose **File→Print**.

29. In the **Settings** area, choose **Print Active Sheets→Print Entire Workbook**.

    If you were to now select print, all three worksheets would be printed.

30. Save and then close the file. Exit **Excel**.

31. Submit your final file based on the guidelines provided by your instructor.

Apply Your Skills

Sort on Multiple Sort Keys

In this exercise, you will sort and adjust worksheets displaying customer orders.

Sort Worksheet Data and Use Flexible Worksheet Views

1. Start **Excel**. Open **EX08-A01-Orders** from the **EX2013 Lesson 08** folder and save it as **EX08-A01-Orders-[FirstInitialLastName]**.

2. Format the numbers in **column D** as **Comma style** with no decimal places.

3. AutoFit the width of **columns B–D**.

   Notice that the rows are currently sorted by Sales in column D.

4. Use the **Sort** dialog box to sort the rows using three sort keys:
   - Key 1: Area in smallest to largest order
   - Key 2: Customer in A to Z order
   - Key 3: Sales in largest to smallest order

   The rows for each area will be sorted within groups by customer according to their sales prices.

5. Freeze **rows 1–3** so the headers remain visible when you scroll down.

   Columns and rows cannot remain frozen when headers and footers are created, because Page Layout view must be used to do so. Therefore, you will unfreeze these rows so that you can create a header and footer in the upcoming steps.

6. Unfreeze **rows 1–3**.

Use Multiple Worksheets and Print Multipage Worksheets

7. Create a header that displays the filename at the top-right.

8. Create a footer that displays the current date at the bottom-right.

9. Use Ctrl to select **Sheet2** and **Sheet3**. Delete these sheets.

10. Save and then close the file. Exit **Excel**.

11. Submit your final file based on the guidelines provided by your instructor.

    To view examples of how your file or files should look at the end of this exercise, go to the student resource center.

Create a Linked Workbook

In this exercise, you will create a new workbook that contains three worksheets. You will also create linking formulas.

Link Cells and Formulas and Use 3-D Cell References

1. Start **Excel**. Open **EX08-A02-RegionSales** from the **EX2013 Lesson 08** folder and save it as **EX08-A02-RegionSales-[FirstInitialLastName]**.

2. Create defined names for each total in **row 7** of the region sheets. Name the totals in the **Eastern** worksheet **Eastern_January, Eastern_February**, and **Eastern_March**. Use similar names for the totals in the **Central** worksheet.

3. Use the defined names created in the prior step to include linking formulas in **rows 4–5** of the **Totals** worksheet to the totals in the detail sheets.

4. On the **Totals** worksheet, format the **range B4:D5** with **Accounting** number format displaying a $ sign and zero decimal places.

5. Create a **3-D cell reference** on the **Totals** worksheet in **cell B8** to add the number of accounts listed on the region worksheets.

   Notice that you are able to enter this formula in cell B8, even though the 3-D reference adds the contents of cell B9 on the other worksheets.

Copy Worksheets and Print Multiple-Sheet Workbooks

6. Move the **Totals** worksheet prior to the **Central** worksheet.

7. Copy the format of **cell A1** of the **Totals** worksheet to **cell A1** of the **Central** and **Eastern** worksheets.

8. Change the orientation to **Landscape** for all three worksheets by issuing one command.

9. Set the **Print Range** of the **Totals** worksheet to the **range A1:B6**.

10. Save and then close the file. Exit **Excel**.

11. Submit your final file based on the guidelines provided by your instructor.

    To view examples of how your file or files should look at the end of this exercise, go to the student resource center.

Sort, Link, and Organize Multiple Worksheets

In this exercise, you will sort expense data for two employees. You will create linking formulas within a summary worksheet, and will organize the worksheets prior to printing.

Sort Worksheet Data and Use Flexible Worksheet Views

1. Start **Excel**. Open **EX08-A03-Expenses** from the **EX2013 Lesson 08** folder and save it as **EX08-A03-Expenses-[FirstInitialLastName]**.

2. Sort the data within each worksheet, based on the total expenses, from smallest to largest.

3. View the worksheets in separate windows, and tile them horizontally.

Use Multiple Worksheets and Print Multipage Worksheets

4. Insert a page break within the worksheet so the last six months of the year display on a second page.

5. Set **column A** as a title column that will print on every page for each worksheet.

6. Adjust print options so **gridlines** display.

7. Increase the default number of worksheets to **3**, if necessary.

8. Close the second workbook; maximize the first workbook.

Link Cells and Formulas and Use 3-D Cell References in Formulas

9. Change the name of **Sheet3** to **Summary**. Create headers and a title for a summary worksheet that follows the format of the other two. Use the **Format Painter** to copy all formatting.

   Ensure that all components of the worksheet appear in the same cell as their counterparts in the other two worksheets.

10. Use **linking formulas** to create formulas throughout the monthly columns of the summary worksheet.

11. Create a **3-D cell reference** on the **Summary** worksheet to populate those **Total** cells for which this approach is appropriate. Use linking formulas for all other totals.

Copy Worksheets and Print Multiple-Sheet Workbooks

12. Move the **Summary** worksheet prior to the **David Sutton** worksheet.

13. Change the orientation to **Landscape** for all three worksheets by issuing one command.

14. Adjust the print options to print the **Entire Workbook**.

15. Save and then close the file. Exit **Excel**.

16. Submit your final file based on the guidelines provided by your instructor.

Extend Your Skills

In the course of working through the Extend Your Skills exercises, you will think critically as you use the skills taught in the lesson to complete the assigned projects. To evaluate your mastery and completion of the exercises, your instructor may use a rubric, with which more points are allotted according to performance characteristics. (The more you do, the more you earn!) Ask your instructor how your work will be evaluated.

EX08-E01 That's the Way I See It

You want to analyze your personal spending over the last three months. (If you do not wish to share your personal financial information, simply make up the figures.) Each monthly worksheet will list your personal expenses related to food, entertainment, and transportation. You will then create a summary worksheet that averages your expenses across the three months.

Open Excel and create a new, blank workbook named **EX08-E01-MyExpenses-[FirstInitialLastName]** in your **EX2013 Lesson 08** folder.

Create the first worksheet using appropriate headers and column titles. Fill in the necessary expense data, and use a formula to calculate the total expenses for the month. Use the Format Painter, where possible, to apply consistent formats to the second and third worksheets. Create a summary worksheet and use linking formulas to calculate your average expenses. Include a footer on the summary worksheet that displays the current date and your name. Change the page orientation to Landscape for all worksheets simultaneously, and ensure that each worksheet will print with gridlines displayed.

You will be evaluated based on the inclusion of all elements specified, your ability to follow directions, your ability to apply newly learned skills to a real-world situation, your creativity, and the relevance of your topic and/or data choice(s). Submit your final file based on the guidelines provided by your instructor.

EX08-E02 Be Your Own Boss

Blue Jean Landscaping has expanded to Draper, a small college town. In this exercise, you will sort and format a worksheet listing the hours worked for each client in the new location.

Open **EX08-E02-Draper** from your **EX2013 Lesson 08** folder and save it as **EX08-E02-Draper-[FirstInitialLastName]**.

Freeze the first three rows so you can view the headers as you scroll to the bottom of the worksheet. Find the last data row and create a new blank row to separate the data from the total row. Custom sort the users by category alphabetically and then by largest to smallest for the Totals column. Insert a page break that will display students on the second page, with all other client categories appearing on the first page. Lastly, increase the default number of worksheets within the workbook to five, as you will be creating extensive client listings in the future.

You will be evaluated based on the inclusion of all elements specified, your ability to follow directions, your ability to apply newly learned skills to a real-world situation, your creativity, and your demonstration of an entrepreneurial spirit. Submit your final file based on the guidelines provided by your instructor.

Transfer Your Skills

In the course of working through the Transfer Your Skills exercises, you will use critical-thinking and creativity skills to complete the assigned projects using skills taught in the lesson. To evaluate your mastery and completion of the exercises, your instructor may use a rubric, with which more points are allotted according to performance characteristics. (The more you do, the more you earn!) Ask your instructor how your work will be evaluated.

EX08-T01 WebQuest: Use the Web as a Learning Tool

Throughout this book, you will be provided with an opportunity to use the Internet as a learning tool by completing WebQuests. According to the original creators of WebQuests, as described on their website (WebQuest.org), a WebQuest is "an inquiry-oriented activity in which most or all of the information used by learners is drawn from the web." To complete the WebQuest projects in this book, navigate to the student resource center and choose the WebQuest for the lesson on which you are currently working. The subject of each WebQuest will be relevant to the material found in the lesson.

WebQuest Subject: Linking worksheets effectively

Submit your final file based on the guidelines provided by your instructor.

EX08-T02 Demonstrate Proficiency

You have built a budget workbook for Stormy BBQ with two worksheets, one for salaries and one for other expenses. You would like to ensure consistency throughout the workbook.

Open **EX08-T02-BudgetSummary** from your **EX2013 Lesson 08** folder and save it as **EX08-T02-BudgetSummary-[FirstInitialLastName]**. Use the Format Painter to copy the formatting from the Salaries worksheet to the Expenses sheet. Create a Summary worksheet containing identical formatting. Use 3-D cell references within this worksheet to summarize the total expenses for each month. Freeze columns A and B within each worksheet, name each of the sheet tabs (use your best judgment to create relevant names), and include a header within each worksheet that will display these names. Move the summary worksheet to the front of the workbook. When finished, use a single command to print only the salaries worksheet and the expenses worksheet.

Submit your final file based on the guidelines provided by your instructor.

Applying Advanced Functions and Data Analysis

LESSON OUTLINE

LEARNING OBJECTIVES

After studying this lesson, you will be able to:

- Build formulas with criteria IF functions and logical functions
- Use text functions to reformat data
- Use the PMT and FV functions to analyze loans and investments
- Adjust variables using Goal Seek and Solver
- Create what-if models in the Scenario Manager

I n this lesson, you will use advanced functions and what-if analyses to facilitate decision making. Complex worksheets for decision making often require advanced functions based on the values in other cells. With the criteria IF and SUBTOTAL functions, you can sum, average, or count values when specific criteria are satisfied. You can use logical functions to specify various criteria in formulas. Excel's text functions help you reformat data imported into Excel. The PMT function can determine the monthly payment for a business loan, while the FV function can determine the future value of investments. Several Excel tools, such as Goal Seek and Solver, allow you to perform a what-if analysis on worksheet data.

Analyzing a Fundraising Campaign

Green Clean, which sells janitorial products and contracts for cleaning services, works in conjunction with an environmental charity to raise funds to support environmental responsibility. You have been asked to track the fundraising efforts of the charity. Additionally, this charity plans to expand its operations to a new facility and has asked Green Clean to help secure the necessary funding. You will set up an Excel worksheet that calculates the loan repayment schedule for this facility using the PMT function and input variables. You will also use the Goal Seek and Solver tools to explore various financing scenarios.

	A	B
1	Loan Analysis	
2		
3	Phase 1 Site Plan Cost	$580,473.95
4		
5	**Loan**	
6	Loan Amount	$480,473.95
7	Interest Rate	5.45%
8	Number of Months	60
9	Monthly Payment	$ 9,166.67
10	Total Interest	$ 69,525.96
11		
12	**Total Cost**	
13	Down Payment	$100,000.00
14	Total Loan Payments	$549,999.92
15	Total Financed Cost	**$649,999.92**

Goal Seek and Solver can determine optimal financing level.

Creating Formulas Using Criteria IF Functions

Video Library http://labyrinthelab.com/videos Video Number: EX13-V0901

Excel provides functions that average, count, or sum cells that meet one or more criteria. Because Excel performs the necessary calculations instantaneously, the possibility of making an error when using these functions is small. Only cells meeting all criteria are averaged, counted, or summed.

Function Syntax

Criteria IF functions all utilize a combination of the same arguments.

FUNCTION ARGUMENTS	
Argument	**Description**
Range	The cells to be compared with the criteria
Criteria	Enclosed in quotation (") marks, the comparison value, text, or expression using a comparison operator, such as =, >, <, >=, <=, or <> (not equal to)
Sum range	(Optional) The potential cells to be summed. If this is omitted, the range will be summed.
Average range	(Optional) The potential cells to be averaged. If this is omitted, the range will be averaged.

The IF functions have the following structure, or syntax.

FUNCTION SYNTAX	
Function	**Description**
SUMIF	SUMIF(range,criteria,[sum range])
AVERAGEIF	AVERAGEIF(range,criteria,[average range])
COUNTIF	COUNTIF(range,criteria)
SUMIFS	SUMIFS(sum range,range1,criteria1,range2,criteria2)
AVERAGEIFS	AVERAGEIFS(average range,range1,criteria1,range2,criteria2)
COUNTIFS	COUNTIFS(range1,criteria1,range2,criteria2)

How the SUMIF Function Works

In the formula $=SUMIF(C5:C12,">=30000",C5:C12)$, the range to be evaluated is C5:C12. The criterion used to determine if a cell in the range should be summed is the second argument, greater than or equal to 30,000. The third argument, sum range, represents the cells that Excel will add together. In this formula, it's the same C5:C12 range.

Note that if the sum range is not specified in a SUMIF formula, the range will be used to evaluate criteria and to calculate the result. Therefore, the sum range could have been excluded from the above formula with the same result.

How the AVERAGEIF Function Works

In the formula =AVERAGEIF(C5:C12,">=30000",C5:C12), the range to be evaluated is C5:C12. The criterion used to determine if a cell in the range should be averaged is the second argument, greater than or equal to 30,000. The third argument, average range, represents the cells that Excel will average. In this formula, it is again the same C5:C12 range.

How the COUNTIF Function Works

In the formula =COUNTIF(C5:C12,">=30000"), the range to be evaluated is C5:C12. The criterion used to determine if a cell in the range should be counted is the second argument, greater than or equal to 30,000. The COUNTIF function does not include a third argument.

How the COUNTIFS Function Works

The formula =COUNTIFS(F5:F12,"Yes",G5:G12,"Yes") examines the ranges F5:F12 and G5:G12 for the word "Yes." Cells are counted only when the word "Yes" appears in both columns within the same row.

	A	B	C	D	E	F	G
		Nov.	Nov.	Dec.	Dec.	Achieved	Achieved
4	Team Leader	Goal	Raised	Goal	Raised	Nov. Goal?	Dec. Goal?
5	Abbott	$25,000	$24,500	$25,000	$31,810		Yes
6	Debowski	$90,000	$92,200	$100,000	$95,350	Yes	
7	Faber	$40,000	$44,475	$60,000	$52,500	Yes	
8	Lemus	$80,000	$79,620	$100,000	$110,350		Yes
9	Martinez	$70,000	$52,170	$70,000	$66,000		
10	Nguyen	$25,000	$25,250	$45,000	$48,000	Yes	Yes
11	Park	$25,000	$27,570	$30,000	$31,680	Yes	Yes
12	Weinstein	$50,000	$45,650	$70,000	$67,000		
13						Count:	2

Cells that satisfy the formula's COUNTIFS criteria

Create a SUMIF Function

In this exercise, you will use the SUMIF function to add cells containing $30,000 or greater in monthly fundraising.

1. Open **EX09-D01-Awards** from the **EX2013 Lesson 09** folder and save it as **EX09-D01-Awards-[FirstInitialLastName]**.

   Replace the bracketed text with your first initial and last name. For example, if your name is Bethany Smith, your filename would look like this: EX09-D01-Awards-BSmith.

2. Display the **November** worksheet and enter **Raised at Least $30,000** in **cell A13**.

3. Use **Format Painter** to copy the number format from cell C12 to **cell C13** and to format the **range A13:C13** as bold.

4. Widen **column A** to fit the text in **cell A13**.

   Next you will create a formula that adds the values in cells where the amount raised is at least $30,000.

5. Select **cell C13**.

6. Follow these steps to find the SUMIF function:

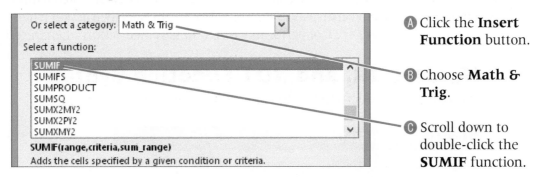

Ⓐ Click the **Insert Function** button.

Ⓑ Choose **Math & Trig**.

Ⓒ Scroll down to double-click the **SUMIF** function.

The Function Arguments dialog box appears for the SUMIF function.

7. If necessary, move the **Function Arguments** dialog box out of the way of **column C** by dragging its title bar.

8. Follow these steps to specify the SUMIF function arguments:

Ⓐ Select the **range C5:C12** in the worksheet.

Ⓑ Click in the **Criteria** box and type **>=30000**. Excel will add the quotation marks.

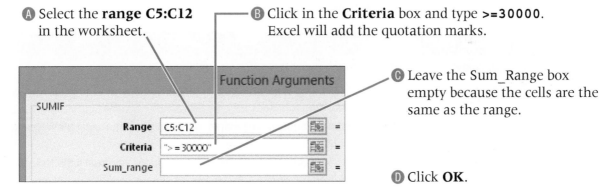

Ⓒ Leave the Sum_Range box empty because the cells are the same as the range.

Ⓓ Click **OK**.

9. Review the completed formula.

   The formula is =SUMIF(C5:C12,">=30000"). The result is $314,115.

10. Save the file and leave it open; you will modify it throughout this lesson.

Using Logical Functions in Formulas

Video Library   http://labyrinthelab.com/videos   Video Number: EX13-V0902

Excel provides several logical functions that allow you to customize criteria when comparing data. The IF function provides the basis for many of the formulas used for decision-making. You can use the AND, OR, and NOT functions in IF formulas to specify one or more criteria to be checked. AND requires that all conditions be met, while OR is satisfied if any one of the conditions is met. Excel displays *TRUE* or performs the specified action when the criteria are met. Excel displays *FALSE* or performs a different specified action when the criteria are not met.

IF, AND, OR, and NOT Function Syntax

The logical functions (IF, AND, OR, and NOT) have the following structure.

LOGICAL FUNCTION SYNTAX	
Function	**Syntax**
IF	IF(logical test,value if true,value if false)
AND	AND(condition1,condition2,…)
OR	OR(condition1,condition2,…)
NOT	NOT(condition)

The following table outlines the arguments of logical functions.

LOGICAL FUNCTION ARGUMENTS	
Argument	**Description**
Logical test	The condition being checked using a comparison operator, such as =, >, <, >=, <=, or <> (not equal to)
Value if true	The value, text in quotation (") marks, or calculation returned if the logical test result is found to be true
Value if false	The value, text in quotation (") marks, or calculation returned if the logical test result is found to be false
Condition	A logical expression to be evaluated as true or false; one of multiple expressions evaluated by an AND function or an OR function

How Logical Functions Work Together

The formula $=IF(AND(B5>=25000,B5<=50000),D5,"")$ is used to explain the function results shown in the following illustration.

Logical test | Result if true

F5 | f_x | =IF(AND(B5>=25000, B5<=50000), D5, "")

Result if false

	A	B	C	D	E	F
4	Team Leader	Goal	Amount Raised	Over (Under) Goal		Over (Under) $25K-$50K
5	Abbott	$25,000	$24,500	($500)		($500)
6	Debowski	$90,000	$92,200	$2,200		

Formula results

In this formula Excel looks to cell B5 to determine the result to display. If cell B5 is greater than or equal to $25,000, and is also less than or equal to $50,000, then the contents of cell D5 will display. If the conditions for cell B5 are not met, then a blank space (expressed as quotation, quotation) will appear in the destination cell. This is seen when copying the formula to cell F6, as shown above.

Alternatively, the logical test *NOT(L5=M5)* could be used in an IF formula to ensure that two values are not identical. If the value in L5 is not equal to the value in M5, the value-if-true action is performed; if the values are equal, the value-if-false action is performed.

IFERROR Function Syntax

The IFERROR function checks a formula for an error. The structure of the formula is *IFERROR(value,value if error)*.

The value represents the formula being checked for an error, while the value if error represents either the value, text in quotation marks, or calculation returned if the formula result is found to be an error. Excel checks formulas and returns the following error types.

ERROR TYPES

Error Type	Description	Common Cause
#DIV/0!	Value is divided by 0	Divisor cell referenced in the formula contains 0 or is empty
#N/A	Value not available	Cell referenced in the formula is empty
#NAME?	Text in a formula is not recognized	Misspelled or nonexistent range name in formula
#NULL!	Nonadjacent areas referenced in a formula	The existence of a space character instead of punctuation, such as a comma (,)
#NUM!	Invalid numeric value in a formula or function	Nonnumeric text in a function that requires a numeric argument
#REF!	Invalid cell reference	The deletion of cell(s) referenced in the formula
#VALUE!	Incorrect data type used in a formula	Cell referenced in the formula contains text rather than a value

How the IFERROR Function Works

Adding the IFERROR function to a formula allows you to display a descriptive message rather than the error type.

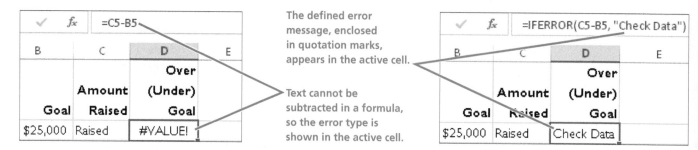

The defined error message, enclosed in quotation marks, appears in the active cell.

Text cannot be subtracted in a formula, so the error type is shown in the active cell.

Use Logical Functions

In this exercise, you will use the IF and AND functions to create a formula.

1. Save your file as **EX09-D02-Awards-[FirstInitialLastName]**.

2. On the **November** worksheet, select **cell F5** and choose **Formulas→Function Library→Logical→IF**.

   You may use the Function Library as an alternative to the Insert Function button on the Formula Bar.

3. If necessary, move the **Function Arguments** dialog box out of the way so you can see **columns B–D**.

4. Follow these steps to enter the IF function arguments:

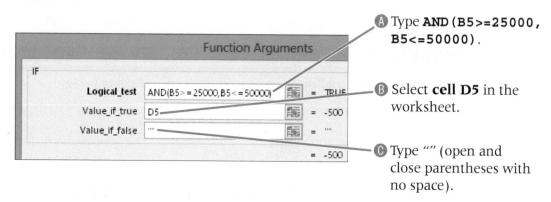

Ⓐ Type **AND(B5>=25000, B5<=50000)**.

Ⓑ Select **cell D5** in the worksheet.

Ⓒ Type "" (open and close parentheses with no space).

   In the Function Arguments dialog box, notice that the logical test evaluates as TRUE because both arguments are true.

5. Click **OK**.

   The result in cell F5 should appear as ($500).

6. Use **AutoFill** to copy the formula in cell F5 to the **range F6:F12**.

   Values appear in column F for five records that meet both conditions you specified with the AND function. The other formula cells in column F appear blank, which you specified as the Value-if-false argument.

7. Save and then close the file.

Using Functions to Format Text

Video Library   http://labyrinthelab.com/videos   Video Number: EX13-V0903

When workbook data is imported from sources other than Excel, the data may not be formatted as you wish. For example, employee last name, first name, and middle name may all be contained in one column instead of in three columns. Excel's text functions can help you clean up data.

If you are familiar with Excel macros and VBA (Visual Basic for Applications), you can create a macro to convert text in a range of cells for an entire worksheet rather than use functions.

Excel 2013

Changing the Case of Text with PROPER, LOWER, and UPPER

The PROPER function changes the first letter of each word in text to uppercase and the other letters to lowercase. The LOWER function changes all text to lowercase, and UPPER converts all text to uppercase. The syntax of these functions is *PROPER(text)*, *LOWER(text)*, and *UPPER(text)*. In the following illustration, the PROPER, LOWER, and UPPER formulas display results in column B.

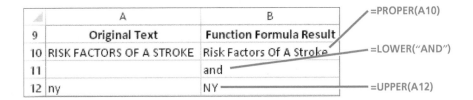

Eliminating Spaces with the TRIM Function

The TRIM function can be used to eliminate extra spaces within data. This can be particularly useful when data is imported from other programs. If you were to write the formula *=TRIM(" Operating Expenses ")*, the result would display as *Operating Expenses*. The spaces in front of *Operating* and after *Expenses* would be eliminated. The TRIM function retains spaces between words, which is why the space between *Operating* and *Expenses* would still display.

Using SUBSTITUTE to Replace Text

The SUBSTITUTE function changes specified text characters to a different set of characters. The function, which is case sensitive, looks for an exact match. If one is not found, the original text displays in the formula result cell. The syntax of the function is *SUBSTITUTE (text,old text,new text,[instance number])*.

SUBSTITUTE FUNCTION ARGUMENTS	
Argument	**Description**
Text	The text to be searched
Old text	The text to be replaced
New text	The text to be substituted for the old text
Instance number	(Optional) The occurrence of old text to be replaced within the full text. All instances are replaced if the instance number is omitted (e.g., "2" indicates that only the second occurrence of the old text should be replaced).

The formula =*SUBSTITUTE(J5,"Nurse Aid","Nurse Aide")* is entered in cell B5 and copied down column B. In this example, the optional instance number argument is not included because the text appears only once in the cell contents, and the formula displayed below in cell B7 refers to the text in cell J7.

=SUBSTITUTE(J7, "Nurse Aid", "Nurse Aide")			

Location of original text

B	**C**	**D**	**E**
Position	**Last Name**	**First Name**	**Area Code**
Physician	Howard	Alana	(619)
Physician	Ottome	John	(619)
Nurse Aide	Hardy	Brenda	(619)
Nurse Aide	Ford	Dedra	(619)

Unchanged entries —
Substituted entries —

The SUBSTITUTE function only replaces text for which it finds an exact match.

Calculating the Text Length with LEN

The LEN function counts characters, including spaces, in the specified text string. The syntax of the function is *LEN(text)*.

One popular use of the LEN function is to locate input errors. In the following example, the formula =*LEN(F5)* in cell H5 counts the characters in a phone number. The formula was copied down column H. Any result other than 8 indicates an input error.

=LEN(F5)		

F	**G**	**H**
Phone	**Employee Number**	**Input Error**
555-2435	Physician14	8
555-6869	Physician4	8
555-8189	Nurse AidNA1	8
555-00027	Nurse AidNA3	9

Using FIND to Locate Text

The FIND function locates specific text within a longer text string. The result returns the starting character position of the found text. You may specify an optional character number at which Excel is to start the search. Excel counts characters from the left of the text to arrive at this character. The syntax of the FIND function is *FIND(find text,within text,[character start number],[not found value])*. The following table describes the arguments of the FIND function.

FIND FUNCTION ARGUMENTS	
Argument	**Description**
Find text	The text to be found
Within text	The text in which the search will take place
Character start number	(Optional) The starting character for the search, counted from the left in the searched text; the first character, if the start number is omitted
Not found value	(Optional) The value returned when no match is found

The function =*FIND (" ",L5)* performs a search on the contents of cell L5. A space is found at the sixth character of the text, therefore the function result is 6.

Counting from the left of the text, the space is the sixth character.

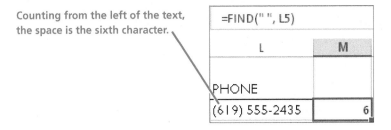

 The FIND function is similar to the Find command on the Home tab, except that it returns a result in the specified worksheet cell (the Find command only locates the text).

Using LEFT, MID, and RIGHT to Extract Text

Data copied in Excel from another application may contain extra characters that you do not want. You can use the LEFT, MID, and RIGHT functions to extract a certain number of characters, depending on their location in the text string. For example, you can use the RIGHT function to extract the last four digits of a social security number. The MID function counts the characters from the left until it arrives at the starting character number you specified. The extracted characters display in the formula result cell; the original text is not affected.

LEFT, MID, AND RIGHT FUNCTION SYNTAX	
Function	**Syntax**
LEFT	LEFT(text,[number of characters])
MID	MID(text,character start number,number of characters)
RIGHT	RIGHT(text,[number of characters])

LEFT, MID, AND RIGHT FUNCTION ARGUMENTS	
Argument	**Description**
Text	The text characters to be counted or extracted
Number of characters	(Optional for LEFT and RIGHT functions) The total characters to be extracted; the first character, if this argument is omitted
Character start number	The starting character to be extracted, counted from the left in the text; the first character, if the start number is omitted

	A	B
1	Text	Extracted Text
2	NA2 (temp)	NA2

The LEFT function: =LEFT(A2,3)

	A	B
1	Text	Extracted Text
2	44-258-777	258

The MID function: =MID(A2,4,3)

	A	B
1	Text	Extracted Text
2	999-99-2145	2145

The RIGHT function: =RIGHT(A2,4)

DEVELOP YOUR SKILLS EX09-D03

Use Functions to Format Text

In this exercise, you will use various text functions to clean up data.

1. Open **EX09-D03-DataCleanUp** from the **EX2013 Lesson 09** folder and save it as **EX09-D03-DataCleanUp-[FirstInitialLastName]**.

2. Select **cell B7** and then choose **Formulas→Function Library→Text Function** ⬛→ **SUBSTITUTE**.

3. If necessary, move the **Function Arguments** dialog box out of the way so you can see **row 7**.

4. Follow these steps to complete the Function Arguments dialog box:

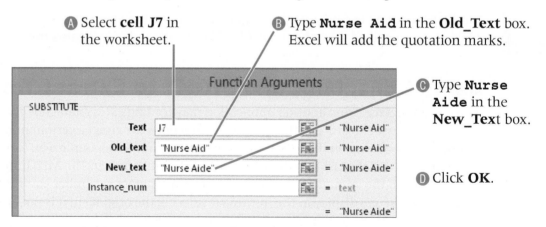

Ⓐ Select **cell J7** in the worksheet.

Ⓑ Type **Nurse Aid** in the **Old_Text** box. Excel will add the quotation marks.

Ⓒ Type **Nurse Aide** in the **New_Tex**t box.

Ⓓ Click **OK**.

Cell B7 displays Nurse Aide. *The Formula Bar displays* =SUBSTITUTE(J7,"Nurse Aid","Nurse Aide"). *The SUBSTITUTE function replaced the original text.*

5. Copy **cell B7** and paste in the **range B5:B8**.

The original text Physician *from cells J5 and J6 displays in cells B5 and B6. The original cells did not contain* Nurse Aid, *so no replacement was necessary.*

Split the Phone Numbers

Now you will split the phone numbers so the area code appears in column E and the remainder in column F.

6. Select **cell E5** and choose **Formulas→Function Library→Text Function** 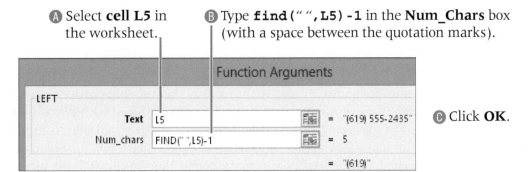**→LEFT**.

7. Follow these steps to complete the Function Arguments dialog box:

Ⓐ Select **cell L5** in the worksheet.　　Ⓑ Type **find(" ",L5)-1** in the **Num_Chars** box (with a space between the quotation marks).

Ⓒ Click **OK**.

The Formula Bar displays =LEFT(L5,FIND(" ",L5)-1). Cell L5 contains the text (619) 555-2435. The FIND function locates the space after the area code in cell L5. Including the space, the number of characters in (619) is six. You entered –1 to subtract the space character. The Num_Chars argument then evaluates as 5. The result in cell E5 is (619).

8. Use the **AutoFill** handle to copy **cell E5** down to the **range E6:E8**.

9. Select **cell F5** and choose **Formulas→Function Library→Text Function** **→RIGHT**.

10. Follow these steps to complete the Function Arguments dialog box:

Ⓐ Select **cell L5** in the worksheet.　　Ⓑ Type **len(L5)-find(" ",L5)** in the **Num_Chars** box (with a space between the quotation marks).

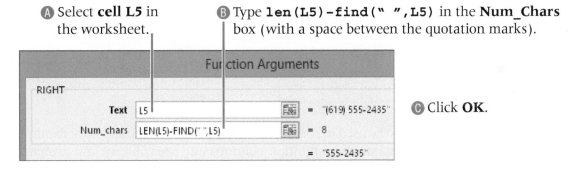

Ⓒ Click **OK**.

The Formula Bar displays =RIGHT(L5,LEN(L5)-FIND(" ",L5)). The result in cell F5 is 555-2435. The formula extracted eight characters of the phone number from the right of the entry.

The LEN function calculates 14 characters as the text length in cell L5. Again, the FIND function locates the space after the area code. The 6 characters up through the space are subtracted from 14. The Num_Char argument evaluates as 8 characters counted from the right.

11. Use the **AutoFill** handle to copy **cell F5** down to the **range F6:F8**.
    Notice that the phone number in cell F8 contains one extra digit.

12. Select **cell H5** and enter the formula **=len(f5)**.

13. Use the **AutoFill** handle to copy **cell H5** down to the **range H6:H8**.
    Cell H8 displays 9 as the character length, indicating an input error.

14. Save the file and leave it open.

Excel 2013

Using Flash Fill and the CONCATENATE Function

Video Library   http://labyrinthelab.com/videos   Video Number: EX13-V0904

A new feature in Excel 2013 is Flash Fill, which allows you to quickly create modified versions of text entries with similar characteristics. CONCATENATE is a function that can be used to combine multiple text entries within a single cell.

FROM THE RIBBON
Data→Data Tools→
Flash Fill

Flash Fill

You may find it useful to modify text within a worksheet so that portions of the text are copied to a new column. For example, when email addresses are listed within a column, you can use Flash Fill to insert the account name (text before the @) in an adjacent column. You need only type the account name for the first row (when using the Flash Fill button on the Ribbon) or the first two rows (when using Excel's automatic suggestions for filled data), after which Excel completes all remaining cells.

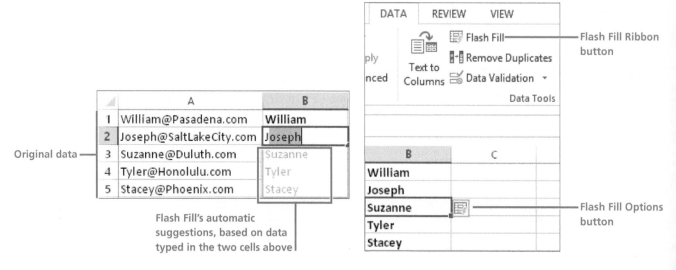

Flash Fill can also be used to combine text from multiple columns (for example, combining first, middle, and last names from multiple columns into one column) and to modify text (for example, adding dashes to a list of phone numbers to modify them from ########## to ###-###-####).

CONCATENATE Function

Similar to Flash Fill, the CONCATENATE function can combine existing text within a single cell. While it is appropriate to use Flash Fill when you are combining multiple columns of data, the CONCATENATE function is a better option when combining text entries from non-adjacent locations within a worksheet. The syntax of the CONCATENATE function is *CONCATENATE(text1,[text2],...)*.

	A	B	C
1	Text 1	Text 2	Formula Result
2	New	York	New York

The CONCATENATE function: =CONCATENATE(A2," ",B2)

Modify Text Using Flash Fill and CONCATENATE

In this exercise, you will use Flash Fill and CONCATENATE to further modify worksheet data.

1. Save your file as **EX09-D04-DataCleanUp-[FirstInitialLastName]**.

2. Type **Howard** in **cell C5**.

3. Select **cell C6** and then choose **Data→Data Tools→Flash Fill**.

   Excel locates the typed text (Howard) within the worksheet and fills column C with comparable text from each row.

4. Repeat the above steps to display **First Names** within **column D**.

5. Follow these steps to use the CONCATENATE function:

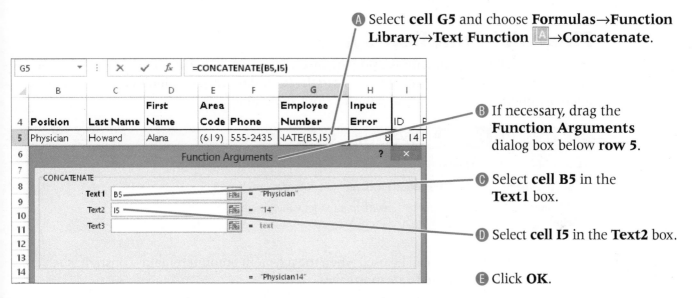

Ⓐ Select **cell G5** and choose **Formulas→Function Library→Text Function** [A] **→Concatenate**.

Ⓑ If necessary, drag the **Function Arguments** dialog box below **row 5**.

Ⓒ Select **cell B5** in the **Text1** box.

Ⓓ Select **cell I5** in the **Text2** box.

Ⓔ Click **OK**.

Cell G5 displays Physician14, *a combination of the text within cells B5 and I5.*

6. Copy the formula from **cell G5** to the **range G6:G8**.

7. Widen **column G** to display all the data.

8. Save and close the file.

Creating Financial Functions

Video Library   http://labyrinthelab.com/videos   Video Number: EX13-V0905

Excel provides a wide variety of financial functions that calculate important financial numbers. For example, Excel has basic financial functions for determining monthly payments on loans and the future value of investments.

PMT and FV Functions

The PMT function calculates the required payment for a loan when you specify the loan amount, interest rate, and number of payments you will make. The FV function calculates the future value of an investment when you specify the payment amount, interest rate, and number of payment periods.

Financial Function Syntax

You may enter financial functions using the Insert Function dialog box or by typing them. You may use the actual values or cell references in the formulas. Keep in mind that using the cell reference offers more flexibility and is, therefore, preferable.

GENERIC FORMAT FOR PMT AND FV FUNCTIONS	
Function	**Syntax**
PMT (Payment)	PMT(rate,periods,loan amount,[future value],[type])
FV (Future Value)	FV(rate,periods,payment,[present value],[type])

The PMT and FV functions can be used when the payment amount remains constant, such as with most car loans and fixed-rate mortgages.

PMT AND FV FUNCTION ARGUMENTS	
Argument	**Description**
Periods	The number of payments (typically made monthly) for a loan or number of deposits for an investment
Rate	The interest rate for each period of the loan/investment. Although loans are quoted as annual rates, payments are usually made monthly. Therefore, divide the interest rate by 12 in the formula. For example, a 7 percent annual rate would be expressed as 7%/12.
Payment	The amount invested in each period. It's always the same for each period.
Loan amount	The amount borrowed
Present value (optional)	The starting balance of an investment; not required if the starting balance is zero
Future value (optional)	The balance you wish to have at the end of an investment; not required if the balance will be zero
Type (optional)	Indicates when payments are due. You are not required to enter the default argument 0 (zero) if payments are made at the end of the period. Enter 1 if payments are due at the beginning of the period.

Converting Negative Numbers to Positive

Excel treats payments as money you owe, so the PMT and FV functions display the result as a negative number. Placing a minus (–) sign before the cell reference or function name (=–PMT) in the formula changes the result to a positive number, which may be more easily understood by the user.

Use the PMT and FV Functions

In this exercise, you will set up a worksheet to calculate the monthly payment on a construction loan using the PMT function. You also will use the FV function to calculate the future value of different pledge amounts.

1. Open **EX09-D05-Fundraising** from the **EX2013 Lesson 09** folder and save it as **EX09-D05-Fundraising-[FirstInitialLastName]**.

2. In the **Loan** worksheet, type **=B3-B13** in **cell B6**, **6%** in **cell B7**, and **60** in **cell B8**.
   The result in cell B6 is $600,000.00.

3. In **cell B9**, type **=-PMT(B7/12,B8,B6)**.
   The payment equals $11,599.68. Placing a minus sign before the PMT function converted the result to a positive amount. You divided the interest rate in cell B7 by 12 to convert the annual rate to a monthly rate because loan payments will be made on a monthly basis.

4. Format **cell B9** in **Accounting** format with **two decimal places**.

5. Enter the formula **=B9*B8** in **cell B14**; enter the formula **=B14-B6** in **cell B10**.
   Total loan payments in cell B14 equal $695,980.86, and total loan interest equals $95,980.86.

6. In **cell B15**, enter the formula **=B13+B14**.
   The total cost equals $795,980.86 to finance the phase 1 site plan.

Create the FV Function

7. In the **Investment** worksheet, enter **0** in **cell B5**, **2.5%** in **cell B7**, and **36** in **cell B8**.

8. In **cell B6**, enter the formula **=B3/B8**.
   The monthly contribution is $8,333.

9. Select **cell B9**.

10. Follow these steps to choose the FV function:

Ⓐ Click the **Insert Function** button beside the Formula Bar.

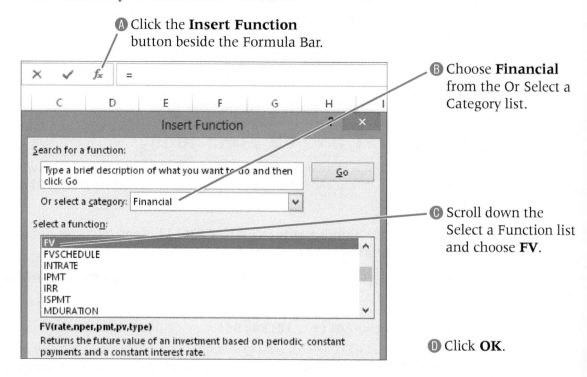

Ⓑ Choose **Financial** from the Or Select a Category list.

Ⓒ Scroll down the Select a Function list and choose **FV**.

Ⓓ Click **OK**.

11. Follow these steps to specify the function arguments:

Ⓐ If necessary, drag the **Function Arguments** dialog box off the range **A1:B9**.

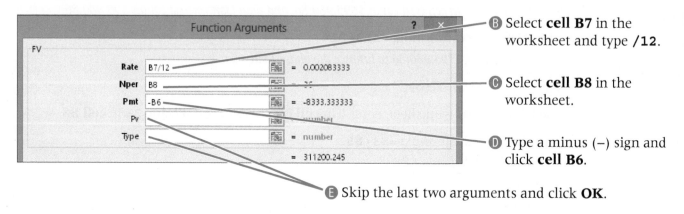

Ⓑ Select **cell B7** in the worksheet and type **/12**.

Ⓒ Select **cell B8** in the worksheet.

Ⓓ Type a minus (–) sign and click **cell B6**.

Ⓔ Skip the last two arguments and click **OK**.

The completed formula is =FV(B7/12,B8,-B6); the result of $311,200.24 appears in cell B9.

Include Optional Arguments

Now you will modify the FV formula for sponsors who are required to contribute an initial payment of 25 percent of the total pledge amount and make payments on the first of each month.

12. In **cell E5**, enter the formula **=E3*25%**.

    The result is $75,000.

13. Copy the **range B6:B9** to the **range E6:E9**.

14. Select **cell E6**, click in the **Formula Bar**, and edit the formula to **=(E3-E5)/E8**.

 The monthly contribution now is $6,250.

15. Select **cell E9** and click **Insert Function** ƒₓ.

16. Follow these steps to enter optional arguments:

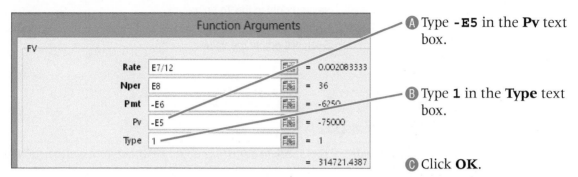

Ⓐ Type **-E5** in the **Pv** text box.

Ⓑ Type **1** in the **Type** text box.

Ⓒ Click **OK**.

The revised formula is =FV(E7/12,E8,-E6,-E5,1). The new total investment is $314.721.44. The -E5 argument is entered as a negative number. It indicates the starting balance, or the present value of the investment before the monthly payments begin. The Type argument of 1 indicates that payments will be made at the beginning of each month.

17. Change the number of months in **cells B8** and **E8** to **24**.

 By experimenting with the values for rate, number of periods, and payment, you create various plans.

18. Save the file and leave it open.

Using Data Analysis Tools

Video Library   http://labyrinthelab.com/videos   Video Number: EX13-V0906

Excel provides several tools to perform advanced what-if analyses: Goal Seek, Solver, and Scenario Manager. Each tool is best used in different situations. Goal Seek, for example, is useful when you know the formula answer you want but not the specific value in one cell that would achieve the answer.

Goal Seek

With Goal Seek, you set a goal for a specific formula result. For example, you will set a monthly payment goal of $10,000 in the Loan worksheet. The goal cell must contain a formula, which is a PMT function in this example. You will instruct Goal Seek to adjust the down payment to achieve the desired monthly payment.

QUICK REFERENCE	USING GOAL SEEK
Task	**Procedure**
Set up a Goal Seek solution	▪ Select the cell for which you want to set a goal. The cell must contain a formula.
	▪ Choose Data→Data Tools→What-If Analysis 📇→Goal Seek and type the desired goal in the To Value box.
	▪ Click in the By Changing Cell box and choose the worksheet cell for which Goal Seek will adjust the value.

DEVELOP YOUR SKILLS EX09-D06

Use Goal Seek

In this exercise, you will use Goal Seek to adjust the down payment for a construction loan based on a $10,000 monthly payment.

1. Save your file as **EX09-D06-Fundraising-[FirstInitialLastName]**.

2. Display the **Loan** worksheet and select **cell B9**.

3. Choose **Data→Data Tools→What-If Analysis 📇→Goal Seek**.

   Choosing the cell for which you wish to set a goal prior to starting Goal Seek will ensure that you set the goal for the correct cell.

4. Follow these steps to set the Goal Seek parameters:

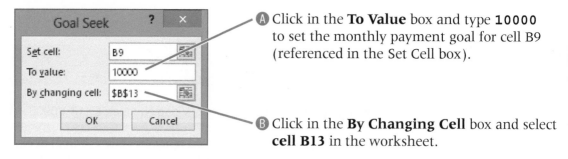

ⓐ Click in the **To Value** box and type **10000** to set the monthly payment goal for cell B9 (referenced in the Set Cell box).

ⓑ Click in the **By Changing Cell** box and select **cell B13** in the worksheet.

ⓒ Click **OK**.

   The Goal Seek Status dialog box indicates that Goal Seek found a solution for the goal. The down payment in the worksheet has been adjusted to $182,744.39.

5. Click **Cancel** in the Goal Seek Status dialog box to undo the change.

Use Goal Seek to Adjust the Interest Rate

You wish to know what the loan interest rate would be if the monthly payment were $12,000.

6. Select **cell B9**, choose **Data→Data Tools→What-If Analysis 📇→Goal Seek**, and type **12000** in the **To Value** box.

7. Click in the **By Changing Cell** box, select **cell B7**, and click **OK**.

   The interest rate is changed to 7.42%.

8. Click **OK** again in the Goal Seek Status dialog box to confirm the change.

9. Save the file and leave it open.

Solver

Video Library   http://labyrinthelab.com/videos   Video Number: EX13-V0907

Goal Seek adjusts only one variable at a time, but the Solver tool can solve problems when more than one variable requires adjustment. You may specify a precise objective cell value, as with Goal Seek, or you may specify that Solver determine the Max (maximum) or Min (minimum) value. In addition, Solver lets you specify one or more constraints. Constraints give you extra control by limiting a cell's possible range of values in the suggested solution.

See Excel Help for more information about the Solver's three solving methods: GRG Nonlinear, LP Simplex for linear problems, and Evolutionary for other problems.

Excel 2013

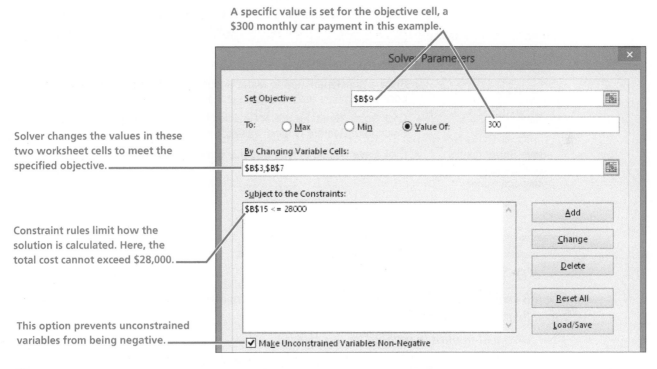

A specific value is set for the objective cell, a $300 monthly car payment in this example.

Solver changes the values in these two worksheet cells to meet the specified objective.

Constraint rules limit how the solution is calculated. Here, the total cost cannot exceed $28,000.

This option prevents unconstrained variables from being negative.

Solver is not part of the typical Office 2013 installation but is an add-in program. Your network administrator may not grant permission to install add-in programs.

Task	Procedure
Install or remove an add-in tool	■ Choose File→Options→Add-Ins. ■ Choose Excel Add-Ins in the Manage box and click Go. ■ In the Add-Ins dialog box, place a checkmark in the box for each desired add-in (removing checkmarks uninstalls add-ins currently installed), and click OK.
Set up a Solver solution	■ Choose Data→Analysis→Solver [?]; if desired, click Reset All. ■ Click in the Set Objective box and choose the worksheet cell for which you want to set a goal. ■ Choose Max or Min; or, choose Value Of and type a desired goal value. ■ Click in the By Changing Variable Cells box and choose one or more worksheet cells whose values you want Solver to adjust, using commas between cell references. ■ If desired, click Add and set constraint rules. ■ Place a checkmark next to Make Unconstrained Variables Non-Negative if only positive numbers are acceptable in the solution. ■ Click Solve. Read the Solver Results dialog box message, choose Keep Solver Solution or Restore Original Values, and click OK.
Save Solver results as a scenario to view again later	■ Click Save Scenario, type a scenario name, and click OK.

DEVELOP YOUR SKILLS EX09-D07

Use Solver

In this exercise, you will use Solver to determine the site plan cost and interest rate required to achieve the total financed cost that you specify.

The Solver add-in must be installed for this exercise.

1. Save your file as **EX09-D07-Fundraising-[FirstInitialLastName]**.

2. In the **Loan** worksheet, reenter the original value of **6%** in **cell B7**. Make certain that **cell B3** contains $700,000.00, **cell B8** contains 60, and **cell B13** contains $100,000.00.

3. Choose **Data→Analysis→Solver** [?].

4. If necessary, click the **Reset All** button and click **OK**.

5. Follow these steps to set the objective cell value and specify the variable cells:

Ⓐ Click in the **Set Objective** box and select **cell B15**.

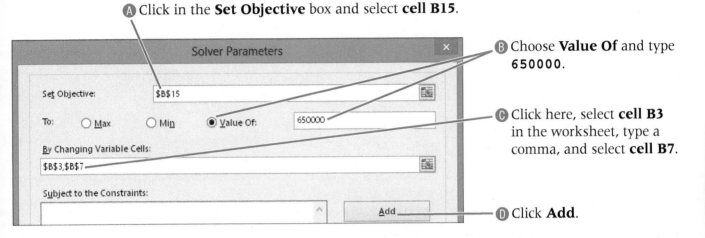

Ⓑ Choose **Value Of** and type **650000**.

Ⓒ Click here, select **cell B3** in the worksheet, type a comma, and select **cell B7**.

Ⓓ Click **Add**.

Ⓔ Select **cell B10**.

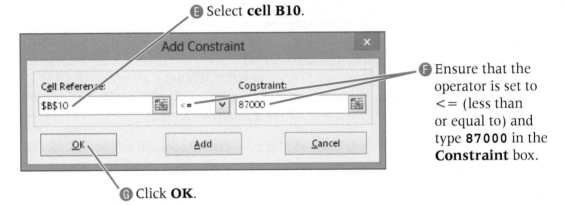

Ⓕ Ensure that the operator is set to <= (less than or equal to) and type **87000** in the **Constraint** box.

Ⓖ Click **OK**.

The constraint rule appears in the Subject to the Constraints list of the Solver Parameters dialog box.

6. Click **Solve**.

When Solver has completed its calculations, the Solver Results dialog box should report that a solution has been found that meets all conditions.

7. Follow these steps to accept the proposed solution:

Ⓐ Ensure that **Keep Solver Solution** is selected.

Ⓑ Ensure that there is no checkmark here.

Ⓒ Click **OK**.

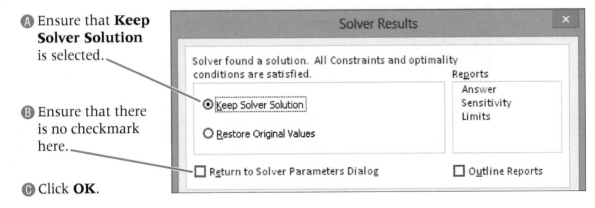

Compare your solution to the following example. Solver suggested a $580,473.95 site plan cost and 5.45 percent interest rate. The monthly payment recalculates as $9,166.67. The total financed cost and total interest are below the limits that you set ($650,000 and $87,000).

	A	B
1	Loan Analysis	
2		
3	Phase 1 Site Plan Cost	$580,473.95
4		
5	**Loan**	
6	Loan Amount	$480,473.95
7	Interest Rate	5.45%
8	Number of Months	60
9	Monthly Payment	$ 9,166.67
10	Total Interest	$ 69,525.96
11		
12	**Total Cost**	
13	Down Payment	$100,000.00
14	Total Loan Payments	$549,999.92
15	Total Financed Cost	**$649,999.92**

Use Solver to Adjust the Cost

You determine that a maximum $11,000 monthly payment is acceptable, and a local bank offers a 6 percent business loan. You wish to know the maximum site plan cost you can negotiate, but your research shows that $650,000 is the lowest bid you are likely to receive.

8. Choose **Data→Analysis→Solver** 📑, click **Reset All** and then click **OK**.

9. Follow these steps to set options in the Solver Parameters dialog box:

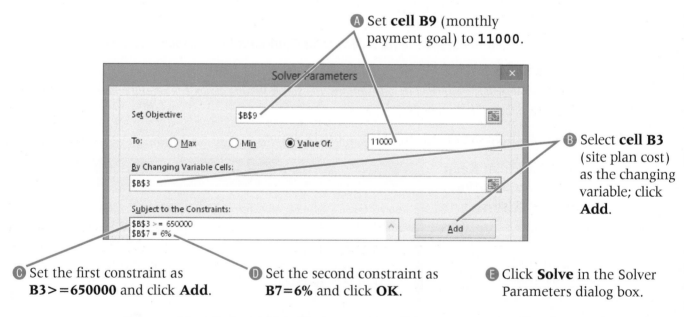

Ⓐ Set **cell B9** (monthly payment goal) to **11000**.

Ⓑ Select **cell B3** (site plan cost) as the changing variable; click **Add**.

Ⓒ Set the first constraint as **B3>=650000** and click **Add**.

Ⓓ Set the second constraint as **B7=6%** and click **OK**.

Ⓔ Click **Solve** in the Solver Parameters dialog box.

Solver could not find a solution. The interest rate still is 5.45 percent in cell B7 because the constraint for interest rate was ignored. You may not set a constraint for any cell used in the objective cell's formula. You must enter the desired interest rate in the worksheet.

10. Choose **Restore Original Values**, make sure there is no checkmark next to Return to Solver Parameters Dialog, and click **OK**.

11. In **cell B7**, change the interest rate to **6%**.

12. Choose **Data→Analysis→Solver** 📊, select the constraint rule **$B$7=6%**, click **Delete**, and click **Solve**.

    This time a solution was found. The site plan cost equals $668,981.65. This is the maximum price that you may negotiate to meet the $11,000 monthly payment goal.

13. Click **OK** to accept the proposed solution.

14. Save and close the file.

Scenario Manager

Video Library   http://labyrinthelab.com/videos   Video Number: EX13-V0908

Excel provides the Scenario Manager to create and save what-if models with up to 32 variables. This allows you to model virtually any what-if scenario. Scenario Manager does not solve for a specific variable value to achieve a formula result, as Goal Seek and Solver do. You may, however, save a Solver solution as a scenario.

What Is a Scenario?

A scenario is a group of values assigned to cells in a what-if model. The model calculates formula results based on the values you enter in the scenario. Scenarios are given names to identify them, and they are saved and organized using the Scenario Manager.

Managing Scenarios

You may create and manage a large number of scenarios in the Scenario Manager. This way, you may compare various scenarios and the results they achieve. The Scenario Manager also lets you display and print a summary of all scenarios. The scenario summary does not automatically update when you change any scenario values. You must create a new summary after scenario values are changed.

Adding Scenarios

It is recommended that you select the variable cells in the worksheet before issuing the Scenario Manager command. The Scenario Manager has an Add button that allows you to create new scenarios. Each scenario may contain different values. If you enter a formula for a variable, Excel will convert the result to a value.

Task	Procedure
Create a scenario	▪ Create defined names for all cells containing variables or result formulas affected by the variables.
	▪ Select the cells containing the desired variables but not cells with result formulas.
	▪ Choose Data→Data Tools→What-If Analysis→Scenario Manager and click Add.
	▪ In the Add Scenario dialog box, type a scenario name and click OK.
	▪ In the Scenario Values dialog box, edit values as desired and click OK.
Display a scenario in a worksheet	▪ Choose the desired scenario name in the Scenario Manager dialog box and click Show.
Edit a scenario	▪ Choose the desired scenario name in the Scenario Manager dialog box and click Edit.
	▪ In the Edit Scenario and Scenario Values dialog boxes, edit values as desired and click OK within each.
Display a summary of all scenarios	▪ Click the Summary button in the Scenario Manager dialog box.
	▪ Choose Scenario Summary or Scenario PivotTable Report.
	▪ Click in the Result Cells box and choose the cell(s) with result formulas based on the scenario values, using commas between cell references. Click OK.
Remove a scenario summary worksheet	▪ Right-click the Scenario Summary tab and choose Delete two times.

DEVELOP YOUR SKILLS EX09-D08

Use the Scenario Manager

In this exercise, you will use a model to analyze fundraising goals with certain budgeted expenses. You know that a lower expense-to-income percentage means resources are being used more effectively, so you will look at each component of the projected income to set achievable goals.

1. Open **EX09-D08-Scenarios** from the **EX2013 Lesson 09** folder and save it as **EX09-D08-Scenarios-[FirstInitialLastName]**.

2. Enter the model values in the **range B4:B7** as shown.

▲	A	B
4	Cash Contributions	1,000,000
5	In-Kind Contributions	50,000
6	Grants	30,000
7	Interest Income	20,000
8	Total Income	$ 1,100,000

3. In **cell B18**, enter the formula =B15/B8.

   The result equals 0.1. Notice that this formula divides the total expenses by the total income to compare the two amounts.

4. Format **cell B18** as **bold** and **Percent Style** with **two decimal places**.

   Expenses are 10 percent of net income. This model is the starting point from which you will create scenarios to see the effect on the targeted expenses versus income percentage.

5. Select the **range A4:B8**, then hold down Ctrl and select the **range A17:B18**.

6. Choose **Formulas→Defined Names→Create From Selection** , place a checkmark in the **Left Column** box (if necessary), and click **OK**.

7. Choose **Formulas→Defined Names→Name Manager** , view all defined names and their Refers To entries, and widen columns as necessary. Close the **Name Manager** dialog box.

8. Select the **range B4:B7**, choose **Data→Data Tools→What-If Analysis** →**Scenario Manager**, and click **Add**.

9. Follow these steps to set scenario options in the Add Scenario dialog box:

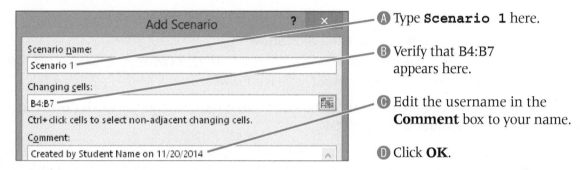

Ⓐ Type **Scenario 1** here.

Ⓑ Verify that B4:B7 appears here.

Ⓒ Edit the username in the **Comment** box to your name.

Ⓓ Click **OK**.

The Scenario Values dialog box appears as shown. Notice that Excel filled in the variable boxes with the current values from the range B4:B7 that you selected in the worksheet.

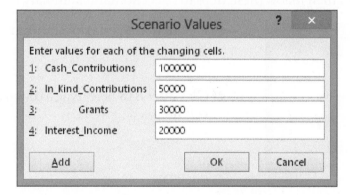

10. Click **OK** and review the new scenario name you just created.

11. Click **Add**, type **Scenario 2** as the scenario name, make sure the changing cells are **B4:B7**, and edit the comment to include your name. Click **OK**.

12. Change the variable for **Cash_Contributions** to **1500000** and the variable for **Grants** to **50000**. Click **OK**.

Scenario 1 and Scenario 2 now appear in the Scenario Manager dialog box.

Show the Results

13. With **Scenario 2** chosen, click the **Show** button and move the dialog box to view the worksheet values (if necessary).

Excel substitutes the scenario values into the model. The formula in cell B18 calculates the targeted expenses versus income result, which equals 6.79 percent.

14. Choose **Scenario 1** and click **Show**.

The Scenario Manager rapidly lets you see the results of various scenarios.

15. Add two new scenarios using this data:

Variable	Scenario 3 Values	Scenario 4 Values
Cash Contributions	500,000	3,250,000
In-Kind Contributions	25,000	53,000
Grants	25,000	200,000
Interest Income	25,000	80,000

16. Use the **Show** button to display the results of each scenario.

17. Choose **Scenario 3** and click **Show**.

    The expenses versus net sales are 19.13 percent. That's too high, so you will use Scenario Manager to adjust values until a desired result is achieved.

18. Click **Edit**, click **OK** in the Edit Scenario box, change the **Cash Contributions** value to **2000000**, and click **OK**.

19. Click **Show**.

    The result equals 5.30 percent. You can use these scenarios to determine which income items need to be adjusted to achieve an acceptable percentage.

20. Click **Summary** and then follow these steps to select Scenario Summary report options:

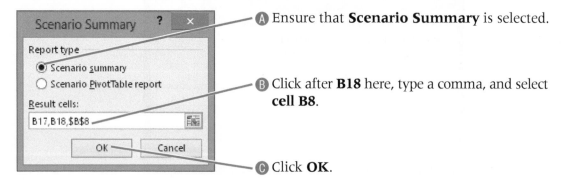

Ⓐ Ensure that **Scenario Summary** is selected.

Ⓑ Click after **B18** here, type a comma, and select **cell B8**.

Ⓒ Click **OK**.

Excel inserts the summary on a new worksheet named Scenario Summary. Review the summary, which displays the results data in the order you chose in the previous step.

21. Save and then close the file. Exit **Excel**.

Concepts Review

To check your knowledge of the key concepts introduced in this lesson, complete the Concepts Review quiz by choosing the appropriate access option below.

If you are...	Then access the quiz by...
Using the Labyrinth Video Library	Going to http://labyrinthelab.com/videos
Using eLab	Logging in, choosing Content, and navigating to the Concepts Review quiz for this lesson
Not using the Labyrinth Video Library or eLab	Going to the student resource center for this book

Reinforce Your Skills

Use Advanced Functions

In this exercise, you will use the COUNTIF function to count students who achieved a minimum test score on one test and COUNTIFS for multiple tests. You will also use the AND function and Flash Fill to complete the worksheet.

Create Formulas Using Criteria IF Functions

1. Start **Excel**. Open **EX09-R01-Grades** from the **EX2013 Lesson 09** folder and save it as **EX09-R01-Grades-[FirstInitialLastName]**.

   Now you will create a formula to count students who earned at least 70 points on Test 1. Kids for Change tracks the grades of certain students within its program.

2. Select **cell C13** and click **Insert Function** f_x.

3. Choose the **Statistical** category and double-click **COUNTIF** in the list.

   The Function Arguments dialog box displays.

4. Select **cells C4:C11** in the worksheet for **Range**.

5. Type **>=70** in the **Criteria** box and click **OK**.

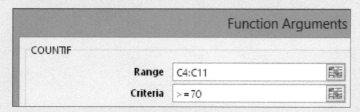

   The result is 6. Excel added quotation (") marks around the criteria in the formula
   =COUNTIF(C4:C11,">=70").

6. Copy the formula in **cell C13** to the **range D13:E13**.

   Now you will create a formula to count students who earned at least 70 points on every test. Only records meeting all the criteria in the COUNTIFS formula are counted.

7. Select **cell E14** and click **Insert Function** f_x.

8. With the **Statistical** category still selected, double-click **COUNTIFS** (not COUNTIF).

   The Function Arguments dialog box displays.

9. Select the **range C4:C11** in the worksheet for **Criteria Range1**.

10. Type **>=70** in the **Criteria1** box.

    Excel will add quotation (") marks around the criteria when you click the next text box.

11. Click in the **Criteria Range2** box and select the **range D4:D11** in the worksheet.

12. Copy "**>=70**" from the **Criteria1** box and paste it in the **Criteria2** box.

13. Click in the **Criteria Range3** box and select the **range E4:E11** in the worksheet.

14. Tap ⎡Tab⎤ to display the **Criteria3** box.

    Only five text boxes display in the dialog box at one time.

15. Paste ">=70" in the **Criteria3** box.

COUNTIFS			
Criteria1	">=70"	▦	= ">=70"
Criteria_range2	D4:D11	▦	= {82;90;98;70;54;82;94;73}
Criteria2	">=70"	▦	= ">=70"
Criteria_range3	E4:E11	▦	= {75;92;98;65;60;82;94;75}
Criteria3	">=70"	▦	= ">=70"
			= 5

16. Click **OK**.

▲	A	B	C	D	E
1	Kids for Change - Grade Calculations				
2					
3	Last	First	Test 1	Test 2	Test 3
4	Brown	Bernice	68	82	75
5	Espinoza	Marlo	87	90	92
6	Kim	Alicia	95	98	98
7	Lee	Jimmy	82	70	65
8	Savant	Susan	68	54	60
9	Soth	Ashley	91	82	82
10	Sulai	Raj	94	94	94
11	Warren	Reed	75	73	75
12					
13	Count >= 70		6	7	6
14	All tests				5

Five students earned a minimum score of 70 points on each of the three tests.

Use Logical Functions in Formulas

Students who achieve an exam average of 70 or higher are permitted to work with Kids for Change, while students whose average is between 60 and 70 have probationary status. You will use the AND function to determine which students are on probation.

17. Select **cell F4** and type `=Average(C4:E4)`.

18. Copy the formula to the **range F5:F11**.

    Review the average scores and note that Susan Savant's average falls between 60 and 70.

19. Select **cell G4** and type `=IF(AND(F4>60,F4<70),"Probation","")`.

    Because Bernice Brown's score does not fall between 60 and 70, a blank space is displayed.

20. Copy the formula to the **range G5:G11**.

    Since the formula dictates that the word Probation should appear for students whose scores fall above 60 and below 70, this result is displayed beside Susan Savant's scores.

Use Functions to Format Text

For students to use the Kids for Change computer facilities, they must have usernames, which consist of the student's last name, followed by the first two letters of their first name. You will use Flash Fill to populate the worksheet with usernames.

21. Select **cell H4**, type the username **BrownBe**, and tap Enter.

22. Select **cell H5** and begin typing **E**.

    Excel's Flash Fill feature suggests entries for the range H5:H11, each containing the student's last name, followed by the first two letters of his or her first name.

23. Tap Enter to confirm all suggested entries.

24. Save and close the workbook; exit **Excel**.

25. Submit your final file based on the guidelines provided by your instructor.

    To view samples of how your file or files should look at the end of this exercise, go to the student resource center.

REINFORCE YOUR SKILLS EX09-R02

Use the FV Function and Goal Seek

In this exercise, you will use the FV function to determine the future value of a savings account. You will then use Goal Seek to determine the interest rate required to save $200,000 by contributing $300 monthly for 18 years.

Create Financial Functions

1. Start **Excel**. Start a new workbook named **EX09-R02-Savings-[FirstInitialLastName]** and saved to your **EX2013 Lesson 09** folder.

2. Use the **Column Width** command to set the width of **column A** to **19** and **column B** to **14**.

3. Enter the data shown at right to the table.

4. Select **cell B6** and enter the function **=FV(B3/12,B4*12,-B5)**.

	A	B
1	Savings Account Analysis	
2		Acct. Details
3	Interest Rate	8.00%
4	Number of Years	18
5	Monthly Deposit	$200
6	Future Value	

   The result equals $96,017.23. Notice the minus (–) sign between the comma and B5. Without it, the FV function would return a negative number. Also notice that the interest rate in cell B3 is divided by 12 to produce a monthly rate. The number of years in cell B4 is multiplied by 12 to produce the total number of monthly payments.

Use Data Analysis Tools

5. Select **cell B5** and change the monthly deposit to **300**.

   Notice that this increases the future value of the investment to $144,025.84. In the next few steps, you will use Goal Seek to determine the interest rate necessary to achieve a future value of $200,000 with a monthly deposit of $300 for 18 years.

6. Select **cell B6** and choose **Data→Data Tools→What-If Analysis** 📖❓**→Goal Seek**.

7. Set the **To Value** option to **200000**.

8. Set the **By Changing Cell** option to **B3** (the interest rate cell).

9. Click **OK** and notice that a 10.91 percent interest rate is required.

10. Click **OK** in the Goal Seek Status dialog box to accept the change to the interest rate.

11. Use **Goal Seek** to determine the interest rate required to achieve a $275,000 future value with a $325 monthly deposit.

    Your worksheet should now display an interest rate of 12.92 percent. In spite of the increase in the monthly deposit, the significant increase in the Future Value necessitated a higher interest rate.

12. Save and close the workbook; exit **Excel**.

13. Submit your final file based on the guidelines provided by your instructor.

    To view examples of how your file or files should look at the end of this exercise, go to the student resource center.

REINFORCE YOUR SKILLS EX09-R03
Use Advanced Functions

In this exercise, you will use multiple functions and Goal Seek to evaluate a variety of investment options.

Create Formulas Using Criteria IF Functions

1. Start **Excel**. Open **EX09-R03-Investments** from the **EX2013 Lesson 09** folder and save it as **EX09-R03-Investments-[FirstInitialLastName]**.

    In the next steps, you will create a formula to count the number of funding pools within each investment.

2. Select **cell D12** and click **Insert Function** f_x.

3. Choose the **Statistical** category and double-click **COUNTIF** in the list.

    The Function Arguments dialog box displays.

4. Select **cells D5:D9** in the worksheet for **Range**; convert these to absolute references.

5. Type **=1** in the **Criteria** box; click **OK**.

    The result is 3. Excel added quotation (") marks around the criteria in the formula =COUNTIF($D$5:$D$9," =1").

6. Copy the formula in cell D12 to **cell D14**, and change "**=1**" to "**=2**" within the formula.

    The result is 2.

Use Logical Functions in Formulas

Kids for Change will not invest more than four funding pools in a single investment. To make the investment worthwhile, the company will only invest if more than one funding pool is committed.

7. Select **cell H7** and type **=IF(AND(D12>1,D12<5),"Yes","No")**.

    Because the number of pools being invested falls between 1 and 5, the word Yes displays.

8. Rewrite the same IF formula in **cell I7**, substituting **D14** for cell D12.

    Once again, the word Yes is displayed.

Use Functions to Format Text

You will now create a summary cell for each formula in which the name of the funding pool and the monthly investment will be displayed.

9. Select **cell C5** and type **=CONCATENATE(A5," - ",B5)**.

   The result displays as Pool #1 – 600. *This description can now be used to quickly refer to any of the funding pools.*

10. AutoFill this formula within the **range C6:C9**.

Create Financial Functions

11. Select **cell E5** and enter the function **=FV(H5/12,H6*12,-B5)**.

    The result equals $50,259. Notice that the interest rate in cell H5 is divided by 12 to produce a monthly rate, and the number of years in cell H6 is multiplied by 12 to produce the total number of monthly payments.

12. Create similar formulas to calculate the future value of the remaining four investments in the **range E6:E9**.

    Be certain to use the Investment #2 figures when calculating the Future Value of funding pools within Investment #2.

Use Data Analysis Tools

Because of Kids for Change's investment history, the company may be able to obtain a more favorable interest rate for Investment #1. They want to determine what interest rate would be necessary for Investment #1 in order to have at least $250,000 total from these investments.

13. Select **cell E10** and choose **Data→Data Tools→What-If Analysis 📑→Goal Seek**.

14. Set the **To Value** option to **250000**.

15. Set the **By Changing Cell** option to **H5** (the interest rate cell).

16. Click **OK** and notice that a 5.51 percent interest rate is required.

17. Click **OK** in the Goal Seek Status dialog box to accept the change to the interest rate.

18. Save and close the workbook; exit **Excel**.

19. Submit your final file based on the guidelines provided by your instructor.

Apply Your Skills

Create Multiple Advanced Functions

In this exercise, you will create a SUMIF function, NOT function, and CONCATENATE function.

Use Criteria IF Functions and Logical Functions

1. Start **Excel**. Open **EX09-A01-Payroll** from the **EX2013 Lesson 09** folder and save it as **EX09-A01-Payroll-[FirstInitialLastName]**.

2. In **cell E15**, create a **SUMIF** function that adds the gross pay of all employees who worked overtime hours.

3. In **cell E16**, create a **SUMIF** function that adds the gross pay of all employees who did not work overtime hours.

   These employees display a zero in the Overtime Hours Worked column. Use this worksheet element when creating your formula.

4. In **cell I4**, create a **NOT** function that indicates whether Millie Aberdeen has worked 40 regular hours this week. The result TRUE or FALSE should display in the cell.

	E	F	G	H	I
3	Reg Hours Worked	Overtime Hourly Rate	Overtime Hours Worked	Gross Pay	Did Not Work 40 hours
4	40	$18.00	4	$552.00	FALSE

5. Copy the formula in **cell I4** down **column I** for the other employees.

   A TRUE result indicates the employee did not work exactly 40 regular hours.

6. Apply conditional formatting to the **column I** formula cells to draw attention to the TRUE results.

Use Functions to Format Text

7. In **cell J4**, create a **CONCATENATE** function that combines the first employee's last name with the total number of overtime hours worked.

   The first employee's abbreviation displays as Aberdeen4.

8. Copy the formula from cell J4 to the **range J5:J13**.

9. Save and close the workbook; exit **Excel**.

10. Submit your final file based on the guidelines provided by your instructor.

    To view examples of how your file or files should look at the end of this exercise, go to the student resource center.

Use the FV Function and Solver

In this exercise, you will calculate the future value of a mutual fund investment. Then you will use Solver to determine the rate of return needed to achieve a specific future value.

The Solver add-in must be installed for this exercise.

Create Financial Functions

1. Start **Excel**. Start a new workbook named **EX09-A02-MutualFund-[FirstInitialLastName]** and saved to the **EX2013 Lesson 09** folder.

2. Create the worksheet shown. Copy the currency formatting in cell B5 to **cell B6**.

	A	B
1	Investment Projections	
2		Utilities Mutual Fund
3	Projected Annual Rate of Return	11.00%
4	Number of Years	20
5	Monthly Contribution	$300
6	Future Value	

3. Taking care to display the answer as a positive number, use the **FV** function to calculate the future value in **cell B6**.

Use Data Analysis Tools

4. Use **Solver** to determine the annual rate of return needed to achieve a future value of $300,000 with a monthly contribution of $400 or less. Accept Solver's suggested answer.

5. Save and close the workbook; exit **Excel**.

6. Submit your final file based on the guidelines provided by your instructor.

   To view examples of how your file or files should look at the end of this exercise, go to the student resource center.

Excel 2013

Pursue a Business Loan

In this exercise, you will determine which projects Universal Corporate Events will pursue and calculate the monthly payment for a business loan.

Use Criteria IF Functions and Logical Functions

1. Start **Excel**. Open **EX09-A03-BusinessLoan** from the **EX2013 Lesson 09** folder and save it as **EX09-A03-BusinessLoan-[FirstInitialLastName]**.

2. In **cell B5**, create a **SUMIF** function that adds the required funding for all projects with a priority level of 1.

3. Copy the formula in **cell B5** and paste values in the same cell to replace the SUMIF formula.

   To use Goal Seek later, cell B5 must contain a value instead of a formula.

   Universal Corporate Events would like to initially pursue those projects which represent more than one-third of the total loan amount.

4. Create a formula in **cell D9** to determine if each project should initially be pursued. Display a response of *Yes* or *No*.

   Remember that the AND function should be used within the IF function here, and that projects must have a priority level of 1 and represent more than one-third of the total loan amount to be pursued first.

5. Ensure that absolute formatting was correctly applied to the formula in **cell D9**. AutoFill the formula to the **range D10:D12**.

   The Auto Purchase is the only project that should initially be pursued.

Use Functions to Format Text

6. Select **cell E9** and type **Office Refurb. - 1**.

7. Select **cell E10** and use **Flash Fill** to complete the entries in the **range E10:E12**.

Create Financial Functions and Use Data Analysis Tools

8. Taking care to display the answer as a positive number, use the **PMT** function to calculate the monthly payment in **cell B6**.

9. Use **Goal Seek** to determine the loan amount if the monthly payment is $200. Accept Goal Seek's suggested answer.

10. Save and close the workbook; exit **Excel**.

11. Submit your final file based on the guidelines provided by your instructor.

Extend Your Skills

In the course of working through the Extend Your Skills exercises, you will think critically as you use the skills taught in the lesson to complete the assigned projects. To evaluate your mastery and completion of the exercises, your instructor may use a rubric, with which more points are allotted according to performance characteristics. (The more you do, the more you earn!) Ask your instructor how your work will be evaluated.

EX09-E01 That's the Way I See It

In this exercise, you will determine the monthly payment needed for a business loan. Open Excel and create a new worksheet. Save it as **EX09-E01-BusinessLoan-[FirstInitialLastName]** in the **EX2013 Lesson 09** folder.

Use the PMT formula to determine the monthly payment needed if the loan amount is $1,500,000, the annual interest rate is 7 percent, and number of years is 5. Then, create a formula to calculate the total cost of the loan. The generic formula is Total Loan Cost = Monthly Payment * Number of Payments. Next, use Goal Seek to determine the interest rate required to generate a monthly payment of $30,000. Lastly, use the UPPER function to convert all text headers within the worksheet to uppercase (use the formula in a blank row, then cut and paste the result in place of the original headers).

You will be evaluated based on the inclusion of all elements specified, your ability to follow directions, your ability to apply newly learned skills to a real-world situation, your creativity, and the relevance of your topic and/or data choice(s). Submit your final file based on the guidelines provided by your instructor.

EX09-E02 Be Your Own Boss

A national landscaping corporation is interested in purchasing your company, Blue Jean Landscaping. As you consider the offer, you examine multiple scenarios for projected expenses. To begin, open **EX09-E02-BudgetScen** from the **EX2013 Lesson 09** folder and save it as **EX09-E02-BudgetScen-[FirstInitialLastName]**.

Display the entries in the range B16:B17 as percentages with one decimal place, and paste their values in place of the existing formulas. Next, to facilitate the national landscaping corporation's computer analysis, create a new column in which the LEFT function is used to display the first three letters within the name of each expense item (rows 4–9 and 12–13). Using the existing sales and customer support figures as variables, create the first scenario. Then create two more scenarios, one where sales is $2,500,000 and customer support is $100,000, and a second where sales is $2,000,000 and customer support is $85,000. Display scenario 3 within the worksheet, and display a scenario summary report that includes salaries and wages total, staffing expenses total, sales staffing ratio, and customer support staffing ratio.

You will be evaluated based on the inclusion of all elements specified, your ability to follow directions, your ability to apply newly learned skills to a real-world situation, your creativity, and your demonstration of an entrepreneurial spirit. Submit your final file based on the guidelines provided by your instructor.

Transfer Your Skills

In the course of working through the Transfer Your Skills exercises, you will use critical-thinking and creativity skills to complete the assigned projects using skills taught in the lesson. To evaluate your mastery and completion of the exercises, your instructor may use a rubric, with which more points are allotted according to performance characteristics. (The more you do, the more you earn!) Ask your instructor how your work will be evaluated.

EX09-T01 Use the Web as a Learning Tool

Throughout this book, you will be provided with an opportunity to use the Internet as a learning tool by completing WebQuests. According to the original creators of WebQuests, as described on their website (WebQuest.org), a WebQuest is "an inquiry-oriented activity in which most or all of the information used by learners is drawn from the web." To complete the WebQuest projects in this book, navigate to the student resource center for this book and choose the WebQuest for the lesson on which you are currently working. The subject of each WebQuest will be relevant to the material found in the lesson.

WebQuest Subject: Using functions and Flash Fill to complete a worksheet

Submit your file(s) based on the guidelines provided by your instructor.

EX09-T02 Demonstrate Proficiency

Stormy BBQ has decided to open a new restaurant, but they must first secure the necessary capital. You have been asked to use the FV function to show the total investment if monthly contributions are $5,000 and the annual interest rate is 4 percent. The intention is to open the new restaurant in three years. Then, use Goal Seek to determine the monthly contributions needed to achieve a future value of $200,000, which is the current estimate of the required funding. Lastly, use the LEN function to calculate the text length of each title within the worksheet and ensure that these formulas are displayed in an appropriate location. Save your file as **EX09-T02-FutureVal-[FirstInitialLastName]** in the **EX2013 Lesson 09** folder.

Submit your final file based on the guidelines provided by your instructor.

EXCEL 2013

Creating Tables and Outlines

LESSON OUTLINE

LEARNING OBJECTIVES

After studying this lesson, you will be able to:

- Create and format tables from worksheet data
- Display totals and use functions to perform calculations
- Sort data using various specifications
- Display specific data records by filtering
- Outline and group to summarize data

In this lesson, you will enter data into a table, format in table style, and quickly create calculation formulas. Some formulas will include structured references that point to specific areas within a table. You will sort and filter the table contents, and use both the SUBTOTAL function and the Quick Analysis button. You will also hide detail data using the outline and grouping commands so you can view summary data only.

Organizing Related Sales Data

Your janitorial product supplier and cleaning service company, Green Clean, sells its products throughout the United States. You would like to analyze the performance of your sales staff, and you plan to organize related sales data using an Excel table. You will sort table data to view the "big picture" and filter employee data on specific criteria to display relevant data. You also want to count staff members, sum sales totals, and calculate an average for the entire group. You believe that Excel tools will help you identify positive and negative trends in less time so you can lead your staff effectively.

	A	B	C	D	E	F	G	H	I	J
1	Green Clean									
2	Sales Performance Table									
3										
4	Last Name	First Name	Years	Review Date	Position	Region	State	A-Sales	B-Sales	Total Sales
5	Alvizo	Alex	7	1-Mar	Senior Account Mgr	Western	CA	602,000	622,000	1,224,000
6	Clayton	Taneisha	2	1-Mar	Sales Rep	Central	IL	230,000	120,000	350,000
7	Cray	Karen	1	15-Apr	Sales Rep	Western	WA	123,000	130,000	253,000
8	Fernandez	Maria	1	15-Jun	Sales Account Mgr	Eastern	MA	228,000	216,000	444,000
9	Hasan	Taz	3	15-Jul	Sales Account Mgr	Western	CA	446,000	120,000	566,000
10	Hill	Patricia	1	1-Jun	Sales Rep	Central	IL	120,000	170,000	290,000
11	Huy	Lin	5	1-Aug	Senior Account Mgr	Central	IL	234,000	560,000	794,000
12	Knapp	Mai	2	15-Nov	Sales Rep	Eastern	FL	140,000	130,000	270,000
13	Martinez	Carlos	4	15-Sep	Senior Account Mgr	Eastern	FL	450,000	450,000	900,000
14	Mathis	Gerhardt	3	15-Sep	Sales Rep	Western	CA	156,000	160,000	316,000
15	McGee	Olivia	8	1-Jun	Senior Account Mgr	Eastern	MA	317,000	513,000	830,000
16	Sutton	David	6	1-Sep	Sales Account Mgr	Central	CO	162,000	151,000	313,000
17	Williams	LaShaun	3	1-Sep	Sales Account Mgr	Central	CO	210,000	340,000	550,000
18	Zain	Elizabeth	7	1-Feb	Sales Account Mgr	Western	CA	340,000	700,000	1,040,000
19	Total		4		14			3,758,000	4,382,000	8,140,000
20		Avg Years			Total Sales Staff			Total A-Sales	Total B-Sales	

A table with rows sorted by last name

Working with Tables

Video Library   http://labyrinthelab.com/videos   Video Number: EX13-V1001

You will often work with ordinary worksheet lists, but at times you will want to convert a list into a table. An Excel table manages related data, such as the sales performance data for each sales employee. The table data may be sorted, filtered, and calculated in various ways. Features specific to tables include:

- **Automatic expansion:** As you type more data rows at the bottom or columns to the right, the table expands to include them. Cell formatting and formulas are copied automatically to the new rows.
- **Calculated columns:** Entering a formula in one cell automatically copies the formula to all cells in the table column.
- **Table styles:** Selecting any of the formatting presets in the table style library applies consistent formatting to the entire table.
- **Filtering:** Displaying only rows that meet certain criteria is available immediately after you create a table, but you must turn on filtering in columns of a worksheet list.
- **Functions:** You may display a total row and create summary formulas instantly by choosing from a list of frequently used functions such as SUM and AVERAGE.

Table Rows

In Excel, each row in a table holds a collection of facts about a certain person, event, or other item. For example, the sales performance table will have one row for each sales employee.

Table Columns

Each column in a table contains one piece of information, such as last name or total sales achieved by the employee. For example, the sales performance table could have columns for each sales employee's last name, first name, position, and sales performance.

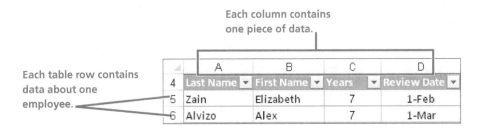

Each column contains one piece of data.

Each table row contains data about one employee.

Creating a Table

Video Library   http://labyrinthelab.com/videos   Video Number: EX13-V1002

You start a table by entering data in worksheet cells as you normally would. Don't use blank rows or columns to separate areas within lists because Excel does not automatically include areas after blanks in tables. You may apply formatting as desired. A worksheet may include multiple tables.

	A	B	C
4	**Last Name**	**First Name**	**Years**
5	Zain	Elizabeth	7
6	Alvizo	Alex	7
7	Clayton	Taneisha	2
8	Cray	Karen	1

Worksheet data prior to creation of a table.

Converting a Range to a Table

You may convert a worksheet list to a table by selecting any cell in the list and choosing the Format as Table command. Excel includes all adjacent cells in the table until a blank row and column are encountered. You may change the suggested table range if necessary. The table appears in place of the original cells. During the conversion process, you choose a table style, also known as a Quick Style. The Table Tools Design tab appears on the Ribbon after you create the table, allowing you to apply additional formatting.

FROM THE RIBBON

Home→Styles
→Format as Table

FROM THE KEYBOARD

Ctrl+T to create a table

If checked, the first row will be used as the header row.

The table range

	A	B	C
4	**Last Name** ▾	**First Name** ▾	**Years** ▾
5	Zain	Elizabeth	7
6	Alvizo	Alex	7
7	Clayton	Taneisha	2
8	Cray	Karen	1

The resulting table

Use Insert→Tables→Table 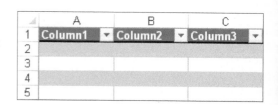 if you prefer to create a table using the default table style.

Creating a New Blank Table

As an alternative, you may start with blank cells in a table. After you select a range and choose the Format as Table command, the new table displays. Column headings and table data can then be entered.

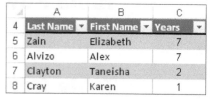

	A	B	C
1	**Column1** ▾	**Column2** ▾	**Column3** ▾
2			
3			
4			
5			

Renaming a Table

Excel names tables as Table1, Table2, and so on. Although you may use the generic names, renaming with a more descriptive title is a good practice because table names often are used in formulas. As with defined names for a cell or range, table names may not include spaces but may include underscores.

QUICK REFERENCE	CREATING AND RENAMING TABLES
Task	**Procedure**
Create a table from an existing range	▪ Select the desired range in the worksheet.
	▪ Choose Home→Styles→Format as Table 🗒 and choose a table style from the list; or, press Ctrl+T.
	▪ Change the suggested table range in the dialog box (if necessary) and click OK.
	▪ Edit column headings in the first table row as necessary and type data if not already entered.
Rename a table	▪ Choose Table Tools→Design→Properties.
	▪ Click in the Table Name box, type the new name, and tap Enter.

DEVELOP YOUR SKILLS EX10-D01

Create a Table

In this exercise, you will create a table for Green Clean's sales force. You will work with this table throughout the lesson.

1. Open **EX10-D01-SalesPerf** from the **EX2013 Lesson 10** folder and save it as **EX10-D01-SalesPerf-[FirstInitialLastName]**.

    Replace the bracketed text with your first initial and last name. For example, if your name is Bethany Smith, your filename would look like this: EX10-D01-SalesPerf-BSmith.

2. Select **cell A4** in the **Sales Performance Table** worksheet.

3. Follow these steps to create a table:

Ⓐ Choose **Home→Styles→Format as Table**. Ⓑ Choose **Table Style Light 9**.

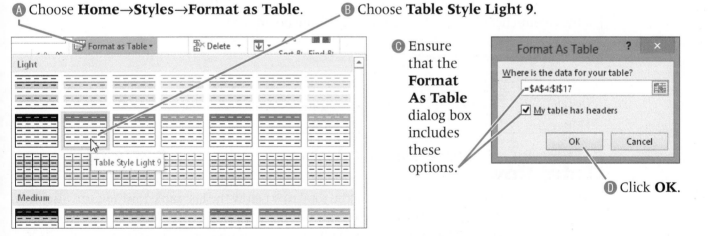

Ⓒ Ensure that the **Format As Table** dialog box includes these options.

Ⓓ Click **OK**.

Notice that although you selected only one cell in the range A4:I17, Excel based the table on the entire range.

Rename the Table

The Table Tools Design tab appears on the Ribbon when a table cell is selected.

4. Choose **Table Tools→Design→Properties** and click in the **Table Name** box to select the existing generic table name. Type **Sales_Performance** and tap Enter.

   You should rename a table to provide a clear description of any table names that may be used in formulas.

5. Deselect the highlighted table cells.

6. Save the file and leave it open; you will modify it throughout this lesson.

Header Row

Video Library   http://labyrinthelab.com/videos   Video Number: EX13-V1003

Always enter column headings in the first row of a table, which Excel treats as the header row. Excel uses the following rules for column headings:

- **One item per column:** Each column must contain one piece of information (such as last name or street address) to enable full sorting and filtering.
- **Unique headings:** Each heading should be different.
- **Special characters:** You may use spaces, multiple capital letters, and special characters (such as comma [,] or dollar sign [$]) in column headings. Avoid using the "at" symbol (@), the pound sign (#), brackets ([and]), and single quotes ('), as those have special meanings in formulas.

With any table cell selected, the header row labels operate like frozen titles. They display in place of the column headings (A, B, C, etc.) as you scroll down the table.

The header row is frozen as you scroll down.

	Last Name ↓↑	First Name ▼	Years ▼	Date ▼
10	Hill	Patricia	1	1-Jun
11	Huy	Lin	5	1-Aug

Total Row

After you create a table, you may display the total row below the last table row. You can also turn off its display. If the last table column contains numbers, a total is calculated automatically when the total row is displayed. If the last column contains text or dates, the populated cells in the column are counted.

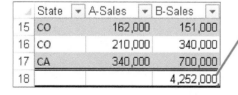

	State ▼	A-Sales ▼	B-Sales ▼
15	CO	162,000	151,000
16	CO	210,000	340,000
17	CA	340,000	700,000
18			4,252,000

The total row displays an automatic sum in the last column.

Creating Summary Formulas

A summary formula is a calculation displayed in the total row and based on the contents of its table column. You may create summary formulas by choosing from the total cell's list of commonly used functions.

Formatting a Table

The Table Tools Design tab activates when any table cell is selected. You may change the table style and toggle on or off a number of table options from the Design tab. Banded rows and columns contain a light fill and dark fill that alternate for each row or column in order to facilitate reading the table.

Other Excel functions can be accessed here.

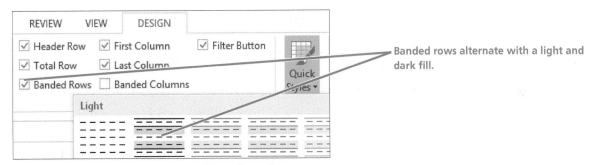

Banded rows alternate with a light and dark fill.

The table styles change to match the Table Style Options set within the Design tab.

Excel 2013

QUICK REFERENCE	CHOOSING TOTAL ROW FORMULAS AND TABLE STYLE
Task	**Procedure**
Display/hide the header row or total row	■ Select any table cell and choose Table Tools→Design→Table Style Options→Header Row or Total Row.
Create a formula in the total row	■ Select the desired cell in the total row and either type a formula, choose the formula name, or choose More Functions (then select the desired function and click OK).
Change or remove a table style	■ Select any table cell and choose Table Tools→Design→Table Styles→More ▼ menu. ■ Choose a different table style or None.
Emphasize data in a table	■ Choose Table Tools→Design→Table Style Options. ■ Turn on/off First Column, Last Column, Banded Rows, and Banded Columns as desired.

Create Totals and Format a Table

In this exercise, you will view the header row and total row. You will create totals for some of the table columns. You also will change the table style.

1. Save your file as **EX10-D02-SalesPerf-[FirstInitialLastName]**.

2. Select any cell in the table and review the column headings in **row 4**. (Choose **Table Tools→Design→Table Style Options→Header Row** if the header row is not displayed.)

3. Double-click the **Date** column heading and change *Date* to **Review Date**.

4. With any table cell selected, scroll down (don't change the active cell) until the table column headings replace the worksheet column headings—A, B, C, etc.

	Last Name	First Name	Years	Date
10	Hill	Patricia	1	1-Jun
11	Huy	Lin	5	1-Aug

The column headings freeze automatically as you scroll so they are always visible.

5. With any table cell still selected, scroll up until row 1 is visible. Choose **Table Tools→Design→Table Style Options→Total Row** if the total row is not displayed in row 18.

   Excel added a total in the last column automatically because the column contains numbers.

6. Select **cell C18**.

7. Follow these steps to create a formula:

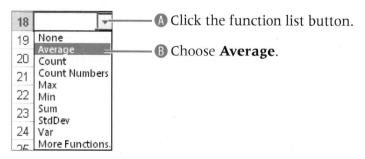

   Ⓐ Click the function list button.

   Ⓑ Choose **Average**.

   The average years employed displays as 4, while the Formula Bar displays =SUBTOTAL(101,[Years]). Notice that you did not have to type an equals (=) sign or select cells to create the formula.

8. Select **cell E18**, choose **Count** from the function list, and center-align the contents.

   The formula =SUBTOTAL(103,[Position]) appears in the Formula Bar; the formula result is 13.

9. Select **cell H18**, choose **Sum** from the function list, and type these labels in **row 19**.

18	Total		4		13			3,618,000	4,252,000
19			Avg Years		Total Sales Staff			Total A-Sales	Total B-Sales

These labels are optional and are not part of the table because they are below the total row.

10. Center-align the labels in **row 19** and AutoFit **columns H–I**.

Change the Table Style

11. Select any table cell and choose **Table Tools→Design→Table Styles→More ▼→Table Style Medium 16**.

    Excel formats the table in blue with white bands on alternating rows. Notice that the Banded Rows option is selected in the Table Style Options group.

12. Choose **Table Tools→Design→Table Style Options** and place checkmarks next to **First Column** and **Last Column**.

    The first and last columns are now highlighted with a blue fill color to draw attention to them.

13. Choose **Table Tools→Design→Table Styles→More ▼→Table Style Medium 7**.

14. Choose **Table Tools→Design→Table Style Options→Banded Rows** to turn off alternating banded rows. Verify that the settings match those shown to the right.

    The table is formatted in orange without shaded bands on alternating rows. The text in the first and last columns displays in bold.

☑ Header Row	☑ First Column
☑ Total Row	☑ Last Column
☐ Banded Rows	☐ Banded Columns

    Table Style Options

15. Save the file and leave it open; you will modify it throughout this lesson.

Adding and Deleting Rows and Columns

Video Library   http://labyrinthelab.com/videos   Video Number: EX13-V1004

You can easily add and delete records within a table.

Table Rows

You may insert a row by selecting a cell below the desired location and choosing the Insert command. The simplest way to add rows is to include them at the end of the table, which can be done by tapping Tab while the right-most cell in the last data row is active. You use the Delete command to remove rows after selecting a cell in the desired row(s).

Click Undo 🔄 if you accidentally tap Tab after the last cell in the row.

Table Columns

You may insert a column by selecting a cell to the right of the desired location and choosing the Insert command. You may simply type in the blank column to the right of the last column to add it to the table. The command for deleting a column varies based on the selected cell(s). The Delete command on the Ribbon may be used when entire columns are selected. If you select only one cell in a column, you must use the Ribbon command to delete the column.

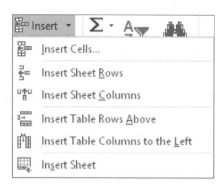
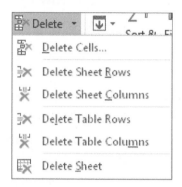

Automatic Extension

When new rows and/or columns are added to a table, calculations are updated and consistent formatting is applied automatically.

Selecting Table Rows and Columns

At times you may need to select all cells in a table row or column, such as when you want to change their text color. Selecting a table row or column is different from selecting a row or column within a worksheet in that you must click in the first cell of the table's row or column, instead of in the row or column header.

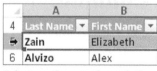

Selects entire row through the
end of the worksheet

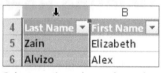

Selects entire column through
the end of the worksheet

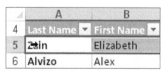

Selects entire row within
the table

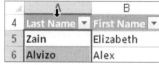

Selects entire column within
the table

Task	Procedure
Add records to a table	■ Select the last cell in the last data row and tap Tab. ■ Type a cell entry and tap Tab. Continue until all records are added.
Insert one or more rows in a table	■ Select one cell or multiple cells below the desired location. ■ Choose Home→Cells→Insert (one row), or Home→Cells→Insert menu ▼→ Insert Table Rows Above (multiple rows).
Delete one or more rows from a table	■ Select one cell in each row to be deleted. ■ Choose Home→Cells→Delete (one row), or Home→Cells→Delete menu ▼→ Delete Table Rows (multiple rows).
Insert one or more columns in a table	■ Type data or a formula in the column to the right of the last column. Or, select one cell or multiple cells to the right of the desired location and choose Home→Cells→Insert menu ▼→Insert Table Columns to the Left.
Delete one or more columns from a table	■ Select one cell in each column to be deleted (select adjacent cells if deleting multiple columns) and choose Home→Cells→Delete menu ▼→Delete Table Columns.
Select a table row	■ Place the mouse pointer over the first cell of the row to display the arrow pointer and click.
Select a table column	■ Place the mouse pointer at the top of the table column heading to display the arrow pointer and click.

DEVELOP YOUR SKILLS EX10-D03

Add and Delete Table Rows and Columns

In this exercise, you will add a record to the table and explore commands to insert and delete rows and columns.

1. Save your file as **EX10-D03-SalesPerf-[FirstInitialLastName]**.

2. Select **cell I17** and tap Tab.

   The insertion point wraps to a newly inserted row.

3. Enter the following record, tapping Tab after each cell except the last. Tap Enter to complete the last entry.

18	Knapp	Mai	2	15-Nov	Sales Rep	Eastern	FL	140,000	130,000

   The table expanded to include the new row. Formulas in the total row automatically recalculated to include the new numbers.

4. Select **cell E14** and choose **Home→Cells→Insert** 🔲.

   Excel inserts a blank table row above the selected cell.

13	Huy	Lin	5	1-Aug	Senior Account Mgr	Central
14						
15	Sutton	David	6	1-Sep	Sales Account Mgr	Central

5. Select **cell K9** and type `Revised`. Then type `Tuesday` in **cell K10**.

6. Select the **range E9:E10** and choose **Home→Cells→Insert menu ▼→Insert Table Rows Above**.

   Two rows are inserted above the data that was previously displayed in row 9. Notice that the text in cells K9 and K10 (outside the table) did not move.

7. Select **cell D7** and choose **Home→Cells→Insert menu ▼→Insert Table Columns to the Left**.

8. Select **cell D4** and replace the generic Column1 heading with **Phone**.

9. Right-click any cell in table **row 16** and choose **Delete→Table Rows**.

   Table row 16 (a blank row) is deleted.

10. Select the **range D9:D10**, right-click one of the two selected cells, and choose **Delete→Table Rows**.

    Table rows 9 and 10 (blank rows) are deleted.

11. With the **range D9:D10** still selected, right-click one of the two selected cells and choose **Delete→Table Columns**. Click another table cell to deselect the highlighted range.

    Now the table contains no blank rows or columns.

Select and Format Both Rows and Columns

12. Point inside **cell A9** near its left border until the mouse pointer displays as an arrow and then click.

9	Hill	Patricia

    Excel selects the range A9:I9 within the table.

13. Choose **Home→Styles→Cell Styles ▦→Data and Model→Warning Text** to apply formatting to the entire row.

14. In **cell D4**, point near the top of the Review Date column heading until the mouse pointer displays as an arrow. Then drag to select the **Review Date** and **Position** table columns.

    Notice that the cells below the table are not included in the selection.

15. Select any table cell to deselect the columns.

16. Save the file and leave it open.

Calculated Columns

Video Library http://labyrinthelab.com/videos Video Number: EX13-V1005

Any blank table column can become a calculated column, in which you create a formula in one cell and Excel copies the formula to all of the other cells in the column. If you do not want a calculated column, type text or a number in at least one cell within the column before creating any formulas.

Converting a Table to a Range

You may convert a table to a normal range in the worksheet. But be aware that some table formatting may be lost if you convert the list back into a table at a later time.

Printing a Table

The Print Selected Table option in the Print tab of Backstage view is used to print a table without including the other cells on the worksheet. The option is available only when you select a cell in the table before displaying the Print tab.

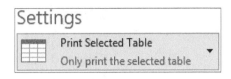

Deleting a Table

Delete tables when you no longer need them. You can delete a table by selecting all table cells, including the total row if visible, and tapping Delete or choosing Delete Table Rows.

QUICK REFERENCE	CREATING CALCULATED COLUMNS, PRINTING, AND DELETING TABLES
Task	**Procedure**
Create a calculated column	■ Create a formula in any cell of a blank table column. The formula copies to all other column cells automatically.
Convert a table to a normal range	■ Select any cell in the table. ■ Choose Table Tools→Design→Tools→Convert to Range and click Yes.
Print a table only	■ Select any cell in the table. ■ Choose File→Print, click the first option under Settings, choose Print Selected Table, and click Print.
Delete a table	■ Select all table cells, including the header row and total row, and tap Delete.

DEVELOP YOUR SKILLS EX10-D04
Create a Calculated Column

In this exercise, you will create a Total Sales column as a calculated column to sum the Product Line A sales and Product Line B sales for each employee.

1. Save your file as **EX10-D04-SalesPerf-[FirstInitialLastName]**.

2. Select **cell J10**, type an equals sign, and select **cell H10**.

f_x	=[@[A-Sales]]

   Excel uses a different type of reference for cell H10. This structured reference will be explained a bit later.

3. Tap + on the keyboard, select **cell I10**, and click **Enter** ✓.

   The table expands to include column J and the formula copied automatically for all other employees. This calculated column is now the last column in the table, so bold formatting transferred from column I to column J.

4. Select **cell J19** and choose **Sum** from the cell's function list.

5. Select the **range J5:J19** and format it as **Comma Style** with **no decimal places**.

6. Select **cell J4** and replace the generic column heading with **Total Sales**. AutoFit the column width.

7. Select any cell in the table and choose **File→Print**.

8. In the Settings area of Backstage view, click **Print Active Sheets** and choose **Print Selected Table** from the list.

   Only one page containing just the table will now print.

9. Exit **Backstage view**; delete the contents of **cells K9** and **K10**.

10. Save the file and leave it open.

Understanding Structured References

Video Library   http://labyrinthelab.com/videos   Video Number: EX13-V1006

Formulas in normal worksheet lists use cell references such as E7, but Excel uses structured references to refer to cells used in table formulas. Structured references allow formulas to adjust results automatically as rows and columns are added to, or deleted from, the table. They also adjust as you rename tables, edit column headings, and move or copy formulas. The generic syntax (language) of structured references allows you to create one formula in a calculated column so that the formula doesn't need to be copied to specific cells in the column, as would be necessary in a normal worksheet range.

Formulas with Structured References

To understand how structured references differ from cell references, compare the two formulas shown.

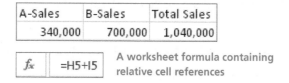

The syntax of the table formula converts the relative reference of cell H5 to a structured reference containing brackets ([ ]) and the "at" symbol (@).

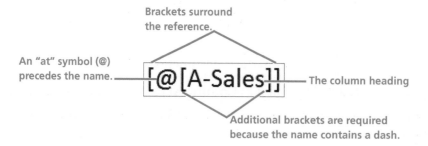

QUICK REFERENCE	CREATING STRUCTURED REFERENCES IN TABLE FORMULAS
Task	**Procedure**
Create a structured reference	Use point mode to select a cell or a cell range while you write the table formulas. Excel creates the necessary structured references for you.

Excel 2013

DEVELOP YOUR SKILLS EX10-D05
View Structured References

In this exercise, you will review formulas in the Total Sales column that you created as a calculated column. You will also view formulas in the table's total row.

1. Save your file as **EX10-D05-SalesPerf-[FirstInitialLastName]**.

2. Select **cell J5**. Review the addition formula containing two structured references for the values in the **A-Sales** and **B-Sales** columns.

3. Select **cell J6**.

   Notice that the same formula displays for every cell in the calculated column.

4. Review the formulas in **cells H19 and C19**.

   These SUBTOTAL functions use structured references.

5. Save the file and leave it open.

Using Enhanced Sorting and Filtering

Video Library   http://labyrinthelab.com/videos   Video Number: EX13-V1007

Excel's AutoFilter feature operates in the same manner for both lists and tables. A table automatically displays an AutoFilter button in each column heading, while these buttons can be turned on in a normal worksheet list. The AutoFilter feature allows you to sort by color and to filter with a wide variety of color, text, number, and date options. You can either use the search box to add items to the filter or select them from the list.

The Data→Sort & Filter→Filter ▼ command turns on/off the display of the column heading list buttons for the selected table or list.

Sorts

You can access the A to Z or Z to A commands via the column heading AutoFilter buttons to sort one column in a table. A column heading's AutoFilter button changes to indicate that the table or list is sorted based on that column. An up arrow indicates the sort is from lowest to highest, and a down arrow indicates highest to lowest.

You can sort table data on multiple columns through the Sort dialog box, which can be accessed from the custom sort option on the AutoFilter button menu. The Move Up and Move Down buttons within the Sort dialog box can be used to change the sort order.

4	Last Name	First Name	Years	
5	Alvizo	Alex	7	
6	Clayton	Taneisha	2	
7	Cray	Karen	1	

The up arrow indicates that the table is sorted by last name from A to Z.

DEVELOP YOUR SKILLS EX10-D06

Sort a Table

In this exercise, you will sort the table rows in alphabetic, numeric, and color order.

1. Save your file as **EX10-D06-SalesPerf-[FirstInitialLastName]**.

2. Follow these steps to sort the table by last name:

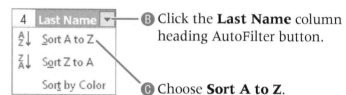

Ⓐ If necessary, click in the table and choose **Data→Sort & Filter→Filter**.

Ⓑ Click the **Last Name** column heading AutoFilter button.

Ⓒ Choose **Sort A to Z**.

The AutoFilter button image has now changed to a sort indicator, and the table rows are sorted in alphabetical order by last name.

3. Click the **Position** column heading **AutoFilter** ▼ button and choose **Sort by Color→red color box**.

The table rows are sorted by color with the single row of red text displayed first.

4. Click the **Total Sales** column heading **AutoFilter** ▼ button and choose **Sort Largest to Smallest**.

The table rows are sorted by total sales from highest to lowest.

5. Save the file and leave it open.

Filters

Video Library   http://labyrinthelab.com/videos   Video Number: EX13-V1008

Filtering allows you to display only rows that meet certain criteria. For example, you may display just the records for which the sales total is greater than $500,000 or only records for employees with three years' experience. The records not meeting your criteria are hidden until you clear the filter. You may filter by text color, cell fill color, or cell contents including text, numbers, or dates. You can filter for a color or icon applied by conditional formatting. The column heading AutoFilter button displays a filter icon to alert you that the table is filtered and does not currently display all rows. The current filter setting appears in a screen tip when you hover the mouse over the button. You may filter on multiple columns using the AutoFilter buttons.

The row numbers change color to indicate that some rows are hidden temporarily.

⊿	A	B	C
4	Last Name ▼	First Name ▼	Years 🔽
10	Hasan	Taz	3
11	Williams	LaShaun	3
14	Mathis	Gerhardt	3
19	Total		3
20			Avg Years

The AutoFilter button indicates that a filter based on this column is in effect.

Formulas in the total row recalculate for the filtered records.

Excel 2013

Filtering with Multiple Criteria and Searches

An AutoFilter list contains all unique items in the column. After removing the checkmark from Select All, you may choose one or more items to include in the filter. Alternatively, you can search for filters within the Search box.

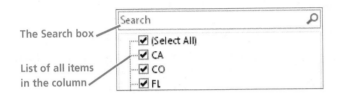

The Search box

List of all items in the column

Custom Filters

The Custom Filter command, accessed via the column heading AutoFilter list, displays a dialog box that may be used to filter by two criteria in the same column. For example, you may use the AND option to filter for records with a review date between April 15 and June 15. The Or option displays every record that meets either one of the two criteria—the record need not meet both criteria. The dialog box also displays after you choose any text filter option or some of the number and date filter options. You may choose one or both specifications in the dialog box as needed.

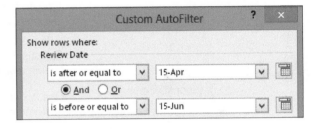

Task	Procedure
Sort a table/list using an AutoFilter button	■ If necessary, select a table cell or list range and choose Data→Sort & Filter→Filter. ■ Click the desired column heading AutoFilter ▾ button and then click: ◆ Sort A to Z, Smallest to Largest, or Newest to Oldest ⬇. ◆ Sort Z to A, Largest to Smallest, or Oldest to Newest ⬇. ◆ Sort by Color and the desired color or icon. ◆ Sort by Color→Custom Sort to sort multiple columns.
Filter by selection in a table/list	■ Right-click the desired item and choose Filter→Filter by Selected Cell's Value (or other characteristic).
Filter by a column's cell contents in a table/list	■ Click the column heading AutoFilter ▾ button. ■ Choose Text Filters, Number Filters, or Date Filters then choose the desired criterion.
Filter by multiple criteria in the same column	■ Click the column heading AutoFilter ▾ button and then: ◆ Uncheck the column entries to be excluded, or uncheck the Select All box, and then check the column entries to be included. ◆ Choose Text Filters, Number Filters, or Date Filters and choose an option. If the Custom AutoFilter dialog box is displayed, choose options for up to two criteria.
Filter using a search	■ Click the column heading AutoFilter ▾ button. ■ Type an entry in the Search box until the desired item appears, uncheck any unwanted items, and click OK. ■ If desired, search for another item, place a checkmark next to Add Current Selection to Filter (also uncheck Select All Search Results to *exclude* the current search results, if desired), and click OK.
Clear filter criteria	■ *One column:* Choose the column heading filter ⛛ button→Clear Filter From "[column name]" from the list. ■ *All columns:* Choose Data→Sort & Filter→Clear ⛛.

Filter a Table

In this exercise, you will perform single-column and multicolumn filters using text, numbers, and dates.

1. Save your file as **EX10-D07-SalesPerf-[FirstInitialLastName]**.

2. Right-click any **Eastern** cell in the **Region** column and choose **Filter→Filter by Selected Cell's Value**.

   Four records containing Eastern in the Region column display, and the calculations in the total row change to reflect those records.

3. Select any table cell and choose **Data→Sort & Filter→Clear** ⛛.

   The table redisplays all 14 records.

4. Follow these steps to filter for two job titles:

 Choose the **Position** column heading **AutoFilter** button.

Ⓑ Uncheck **Sales Rep**.

Ⓒ Click **OK** and view the filtered list.

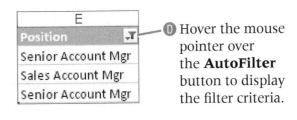

Ⓓ Hover the mouse pointer over the **AutoFilter** button to display the filter criteria.

You will now filter the previous results further to view only the records for Massachusetts.

5. Follow these steps to filter the previous results further:

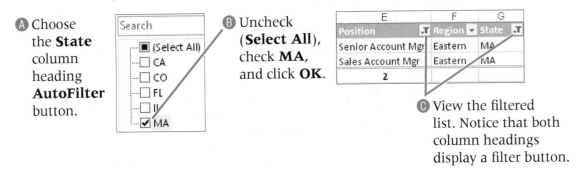

Ⓐ Choose the **State** column heading **AutoFilter** button.

Ⓑ Uncheck (**Select All**), check **MA**, and click **OK**.

Ⓒ View the filtered list. Notice that both column headings display a filter button.

6. Click the **Position** column heading **AutoFilter** button and choose **Clear Filter From "Position"**. Repeat the same process for the **State** column.

The list is restored to all 14 records.

7. Sort the table by **Last Name** in **A to Z order**.

8. Click the **Last Name** column heading **AutoFilter** ⊡ button and choose **Text Filters→Begins With**.

9. In the **Custom AutoFilter** dialog box, type **m** in the text box to the right of **Begins With**, and click **OK**.

Three records are displayed.

10. Click the **Last Name** column heading **AutoFilter** ⊡ button and choose **Clear Filter From "Last Name"**.

The text filter is now removed from the column.

11. Choose **B-Sales** column heading **AutoFilter** button→**Number Filters→Greater Than or Equal To**. In the Custom AutoFilter dialog box, choose **450,000** from the top list and click **OK**.

The filter displays five records.

Excel 2013

12. Filter the **State** column for **California (CA)**.

   Two employees in CA have B-Sales of $450,000 or greater.

13. In **cell A22**, type `California Employees with >$450,000 B-Sales`. Format this label in italics.

14. Select the **range A4:J20**, and copy and paste it to **cell A23**.

   Copying and pasting filtered rows allows you to save the results, so that you can further filter the list while maintaining the data.

15. Select any table cell and choose **Data→Sort & Filter→Clear** 📉.

Filter by Searching

16. Click the **Last Name** column heading **AutoFilter** ▾ button, click in the **Search** box and type `sutton`, and then tap `Enter`.

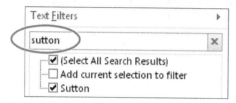

   The filter displays David Sutton's record.

17. Click the **Last Name** column heading **AutoFilter** 🔽 button.

18. Follow these steps to search for and add another name to the filter:

   Ⓐ Type `zain`.

   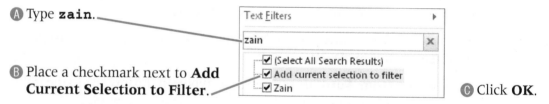

   Ⓑ Place a checkmark next to **Add Current Selection to Filter**.

   Ⓒ Click **OK**.

   Both David Sutton & Elizabeth Zain are now displayed on the worksheet.

19. Select any table cell and choose **Data→Sort & Filter→Clear** 📉 to display all 14 records sorted by last name.

20. Save the file and leave it open.

Using SUBTOTAL to Calculate Filtered Lists

Video Library   http://labyrinthelab.com/videos   Video Number: EX13-V1009

Formulas in the total row of a table use the SUBTOTAL function and automatically recalculate for the filtered records. When the records have not been converted to a table, you may use the SUBTOTAL function to calculate values in the filtered list.

SUBTOTAL Function Syntax

The structure of the SUBTOTAL function is SUBTOTAL(function number, range1, range2,...).

SUBTOTAL FUNCTION ARGUMENTS

Argument	Description
Function number	The arithmetic operation that will be performed
Range1	The range containing the values to be calculated
Range2, Range3, etc.	(Optional) Additional ranges, cell references, or specific values to be included in the calculation

The following table describes the basic functions you may use.

SUBTOTAL FUNCTION NUMBERS AND OPERATIONS

Function Number	Function	Operation Performed
1 or 101	AVERAGE	Averages the range
2 or 102	COUNT	Counts cells containing numbers in the range
3 or 103	COUNTA	Counts nonblank cells in the range
4 or 104	MAX	Returns the largest number in the range
5 or 105	MIN	Returns the smallest number in the range
6 or 106	PRODUCT	Multiples all values contained in the formula arguments
9 or 109	SUM	Adds the range

If a single-digit function number is used, hidden values are included in the calculation. If a three-digit function number is used, hidden values will be ignored.

How the SUBTOTAL Function Works

In the formula =SUBTOTAL(9,C5:C20), the argument 9 indicates that the SUM function will be used, while the range to be calculated is C5:C20. Regardless of whether the single-digit or three-digit function number is used, the SUBTOTAL function ignores any rows that are not displayed in the filter result.

Use the SUBTOTAL Function

In this exercise, you will use the SUBTOTAL function within a worksheet list and compare the results to subtotals within a table.

1. Save your file as **EX10-D08-SalesPerf-[FirstInitialLastName]**.

2. Reapply the filters greater than or equal to 450,000 to the **B-Sales** column and CA to the **State** column.

3. Follow these steps to create a SUBTOTAL function:

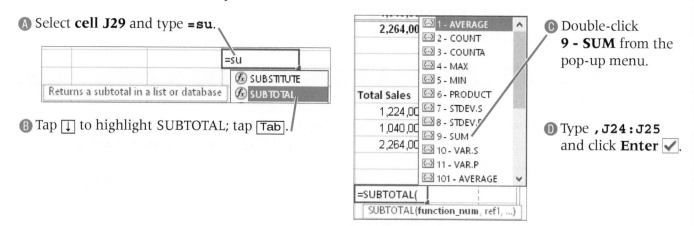

Ⓐ Select **cell J29** and type **=su**.

Ⓑ Tap ⬇ to highlight SUBTOTAL; tap Tab .

Ⓒ Double-click **9 - SUM** from the pop-up menu.

Ⓓ Type **,J24:J25** and click **Enter** ✓.

The formula =SUBTOTAL(9,J24:J25) appears in the Formula Bar. The result of the formula is 2264000, which is the same as the subtotal in cell J19.

4. Select **cell J19** and review the Formula Bar.

The formula =SUBTOTAL(109,[Total Sales]) appears in the formula bar. This structured reference within the table provides the same result as the cell reference you just created in cell J29.

5. Delete the contents of **cell J29**.

6. Save the file and leave it open.

Using Quick Analysis

Video Library   http://labyrinthelab.com/videos   Video Number: EX13-V1010

The Quick Analysis button allows you to more easily apply options, which are also available on the Ribbon, to data within both data tables and standard worksheet lists.

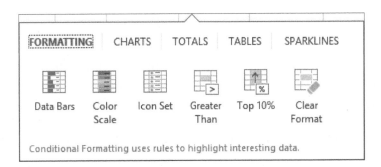

Available options include a variety of formatting, as well as the application of charts, column or row totals, and sparklines. In addition, the Quick Analysis button can be used to convert standard worksheet data into a table. You can also easily preview the impact of many of these options by holding the mouse pointer over the option.

DEVELOP YOUR SKILLS EX10-D09
Adjust Worksheet Data with Quick Analysis

In this exercise, you will create a data table and format worksheet data through Quick Analysis.

1. Save your file as **EX10-D09-SalesPerf-[FirstInitialLastName]**.

2. On the **Sales by Years** worksheet, highlight the **range A4:J18** and click the **Quick Analysis** button.

3. Select **Tables→Table**.

4. Choose **Table Tools→Design→Table Style Options→Total Row**.

   The total of the final column has been included within the table in cell J19.

5. Highlight the **range H5:J18**, click the **Quick Analysis** button, and choose **Formatting→Data Bars**.

   Note that formatting can be applied to a select portion of the table in this manner.

6. Click the **Undo** ↩ menu button and then click the first three items to revert the data table to worksheet data.

7. Save the file and leave it open.

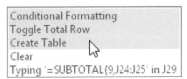

Using the Outline Feature

Video Library http://labyrinthelab.com/videos Video Number: EX13-V1011

Excel's Outline feature helps you to control the display of detail data in worksheets. You can see the big picture while still being able to view the details when necessary. Outlining works best in normal worksheet ranges, as opposed to tables.

How Outlines Work

When you create an outline for a worksheet list, Excel organizes the data into detail groups. This structure is displayed visually along the top border for columns and along the left border for rows. You may click the level number buttons to display various levels of detail, with 1 being the least detail and each higher number displaying more detail. The outline area also contains expand (+) and collapse (–) buttons you may click to display and hide individual groups of data.

Row level buttons collapse and expand groups of detail rows.

Column level buttons collapse and expand groups of detail columns.

This collapse button hides the detail columns H–I.

The expand buttons display detail row groups that are currently hidden.

	A	B	C	D	E	F	G	H	I	J
1	Green Clean									
2	Sales by Position									
3										
4	Last Name	First Name	Years	Review Date	Position	Region	State	ModSales	AppSales	Total Sales
5	Alvizo	Alex	7	1-Mar	Senior Account Mgr	Western	CA	602,000	622,000	1,224,000
6	Huy	Lin	5	1-Aug	Senior Account Mgr	Central	IL	234,000	560,000	794,000
7	Martinez	Carlos	4	15-Sep	Senior Account Mgr	Eastern	FL	450,000	450,000	900,000
8	McGee	Olivia	8	1-Jun	Senior Account Mgr	Eastern	MA	317,000	513,000	830,000
9					Senior Acct Mgr Total					3,748,000
10										
16					Sales Acct Mgr Total					2,913,000
17										
23					Sales Rep Total					1,479,000
24					Grand Total					8,140,000

This collapse button hides the detail rows 5–8.

Auto Outline

Excel can apply an outline to most worksheet lists automatically. The key to smooth automatic outlining is to arrange the detail and summary data consistently according to the following rules.

- **Detail columns:** Detail data in columns must appear all to the right or all to the left of the summary formulas.

- **Detail rows:** If you want the outline to group detail rows, sort the list by category and insert a subtotal formula after each change within the category.

Excel will try to outline all data related to summary formulas in the worksheet. If you are not satisfied with the results of the Auto Outline command, you may group rows and columns manually.

Outline a Worksheet Automatically

In this exercise, you will use the Auto Outline command to outline a worksheet that contains summary formulas. Then you will collapse and expand the outline.

1. Save your file as **EX10-D10-SalesPerf-[FirstInitialLastName]**.

2. Display the **Sales by Position** worksheet and note that it is grouped by position.

   Since a total row follows the detail rows for each position, Excel can group the worksheet data in an outline.

3. Choose **Data→Outline→Group ▦ menu button ▼→Auto Outline**.

   The rows are divided into three bracketed groups at Level 2 and one larger group at Level 1. Excel reviewed the formulas on the worksheet to create these groupings.

4. Select **cell A1** and scroll down until **row 4** displays just below the Excel column heading letters.

5. Follow these steps to collapse and expand the display of all detail data:

   Ⓐ Click the **Level 1** button for columns to collapse the individual sales columns.

   Ⓑ Click the **Level 1** button for rows to display only the grand total row.

   Ⓒ Click the **Level 2** button for rows to display the grand total and subtotal rows.

   Ⓓ Click the **Level 3** button for rows to display all detail rows.

6. Click the **Level 2** button for the row groups.

   Note that an outline level displaying a collapse button (-) shows detail data, while an outline level displaying an expand button (+) hides detail data.

7. Follow these steps to expand individual groups of row detail data:

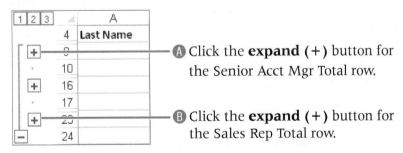

   Ⓐ Click the **expand (+)** button for the Senior Acct Mgr Total row.

   Ⓑ Click the **expand (+)** button for the Sales Rep Total row.

8. Click the **Level 3** button for the row groups to display all detail row groups.

9. Save the file and leave it open.

Excel 2013

Creating Groups Manually

Video Library   http://labyrinthelab.com/videos   Video Number: EX13-V1012

When the detail rows do not include summary formulas or Excel simply does not outline the worksheet as you expected, you may group rows and columns manually. Row groups must be separated by a blank row or Excel will combine all into one group.

QUICK REFERENCE	GROUPING AND UNGROUPING IN LISTS AND TABLES
Task	**Procedure**
Automatically outline rows and columns	■ Move columns of detail data all to the right or left of the summary formulas. ■ Sort the list by category and insert a subtotal formula after each change of category if you want the outline to group detail rows. ■ Choose Data→Outline→Group menu ▼→Auto Outline.
Manually group rows or columns	■ Insert a blank row between each section of rows to be grouped, if necessary. ■ Select the detail row(s)/column(s) to be grouped, choose Data→Outline→Group, and choose Rows or Columns.
Manually ungroup rows or columns	■ Select the detail row(s)/column(s) to be ungrouped, choose Data→Outline→Ungroup, and choose Rows or Columns.
Remove an entire outline	■ Select any single worksheet cell and choose Data→Outline→Ungroup menu ▼→Clear Outline.

DEVELOP YOUR SKILLS EX10-D11
Outline a Worksheet Manually

In this exercise, you will create groups manually in a table that has no summary formulas for the rows.

1. Save your file as **EX10-D11-SalesPerf-[FirstInitialLastName]**.

2. Display the **Sales by Years** worksheet.

3. Select any cell in the **Years** column and choose **Data→Sort & Filter→Sort Largest to Smallest**.

	A	B	C
4	Last Name	First Name	Years
5	McGee	Olivia	8
6	Alvizo	Alex	7
7	Zain	Elizabeth	7
8	Sutton	David	6

4. Choose **Data→Outline→Group 🖽 menu ▼ →Auto Outline**.

   Auto Outline grouped only columns H–I because Excel found total formulas in column J. The rows were not grouped because Excel found no summary formulas for them.

5. Follow these steps to insert a blank row at row 10:

9	Huy
➡	Martinez
11	Mathis

   Ⓐ Point at the **row 10** header until the pointer changes to an arrow.

   Ⓑ Right-click the **row 10** header and choose **Insert**.

   The blank row will now allow you to create a group for 1-4 years and a group for 5-8 years.

6. Select the **range C5:C9**, choose **Data→Outline→Group** 📲, choose **Rows** from the Group dialog box, and click **OK**.

7. Repeat the prior step for the **range C11:C19**.

Ungroup Rows

8. Select the **range E5:E9** and choose **Data→Outline→Ungroup** 📲. With **Rows** selected, click **OK**.

   Only the selected cells have been ungrouped.

9. Select **cell E5** and choose **Data→Outline→Ungroup** 📲 menu ▼→**Clear Outline**.

   When you select only one cell, all outline groups in the worksheet are cleared. You cannot undo after clearing the outline.

10. Regroup the rows, deselect the cells.

11. Save the file and leave it open.

Displaying Subtotals

Video Library   http://labyrinthelab.com/videos   Video Number: EX13-V1013

The Subtotal command creates subtotals and a grand total for numeric columns in a list (the command is not available in tables). You may specify the columns in which to display a subtotal. Excel automatically outlines rows of a list containing subtotals.

		F	G	H	I	J	
	4	Region	State	ModSales	AppSales	Total Sales	
	5	Central	CO	162,000	151,000	313,000	
	6	Central	CO	210,000	340,000	550,000	
	7		CO Total			863,000	
	8	Central	IL	230,000	120,000	350,000	
	9	Central	IL	120,000	170,000	290,000	
	10	Central	IL	234,000	560,000	794,000	
	11		IL Total			1,434,000	
	12	Eastern	FL	140,000	130,000	270,000	
	13	Eastern	FL	450,000	450,000	900,000	
	14		FL Total			1,170,000	Subtotals
	15	Eastern	MA	228,000	216,000	444,000	
	16	Eastern	MA	317,000	513,000	830,000	
	17		MA Total			1,274,000	
	18	Western	CA	602,000	622,000	1,224,000	
	19	Western	CA	446,000	120,000	566,000	
	20	Western	CA	156,000	160,000	316,000	
	21	Western	CA	340,000	700,000	1,040,000	
	22		CA Total			3,146,000	
	23	Western	WA	123,000	130,000	253,000	
	24		WA Total			253,000	
	25		Grand Total			8,140,000	Grand total

Excel automatically outlines the list based on the location of the subtotals.

Sorting the List

The first step in the subtotaling process is to sort the list on the column for which subtotals will be based. For example, sort on the State column if you want subtotals to appear each time the state changes. When you issue the Subtotal command, Excel groups all rows with the same state and calculates a subtotal for each group.

The Subtotal Dialog Box

The Subtotal command on the Ribbon displays the Subtotal dialog box. The options in the dialog box determine the column for which subtotals are calculated and the function used in the calculations.

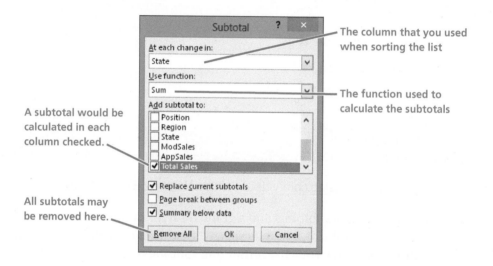

The column that you used when sorting the list

The function used to calculate the subtotals

A subtotal would be calculated in each column checked.

All subtotals may be removed here.

QUICK REFERENCE	DISPLAYING AND REMOVING SUBTOTALS FROM WORKSHEET LISTS
Task	**Procedure**
Display subtotals	■ Sort the list by the column on which you want subtotals to be based.
	■ Choose Data→Outline→Subtotal and set At Each Change In to the same column the sort is based on.
	■ Choose the desired function from the Use Function list, choose the numeric columns you want subtotaled in the Add Subtotal To list, and click OK.
Remove subtotals	■ Choose Data→Outline→Subtotal and click Remove All.

Display Subtotals

In this exercise, you will sort a worksheet list and display subtotals for each state. You also will use the Outline Bar to control the amount of detail displayed in the worksheet.

1. Save your file as **EX10-D12-SalesPerf-[FirstInitialLastName]**.

2. Display the **Sales by State** worksheet and select any cell in the list.

3. Choose **Data→Sort & Filter→Sort** 🔽, set options to sort first by region and then by state, and click **OK**.

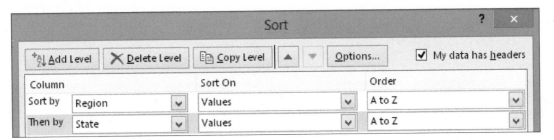

The states are now divided by region and listed in order. For subtotals to calculate correctly, the data for each state must be together. You could have sorted just by state without putting the states in region order.

4. Choose **Data→Outline→Subtotal** 🔢.

5. Follow these steps to set the subtotal options:

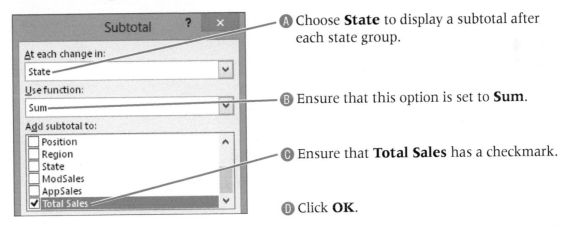

Ⓐ Choose **State** to display a subtotal after each state group.

Ⓑ Ensure that this option is set to **Sum**.

Ⓒ Ensure that **Total Sales** has a checkmark.

Ⓓ Click **OK**.

6. In **column J**, bold the six subtotal amounts and the grand total amount to make them stand out.

7. Follow these steps to experiment with the Outline Bar for rows on the left side of the worksheet:

Ⓐ Click the **Level 1** button to display the grand total row only.

Ⓑ Click the **Level 2** button to display the grand total and subtotal rows.

Ⓒ Click the **Level 3** button to display the grand total, subtotal, and detail rows.

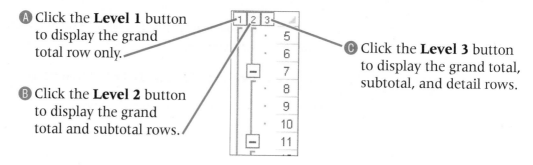

8. Save and close the file. Exit **Excel**.

Concepts Review

To check your knowledge of the key concepts introduced in this lesson, complete the Concepts Review quiz by choosing the appropriate access option below.

If you are...	Then access the quiz by...
Using the Labyrinth Video Library	Going to http://labyrinthelab.com/videos
Using eLab	Logging in, choosing Content, and navigating to the Concepts Review quiz for this lesson
Not using the Labyrinth Video Library or eLab	Going to the student resource center for this book

Reinforce Your Skills

Create, Sort, and Filter a Table

In this exercise, you will create a table to track supporters of a political candidate who is endorsed by Kids for Change. You will sort the records and filter the table by number and icons created by a conditional formatting rule.

Work with and Create a Table

1. Start **Excel**. Open **EX10-R01-Supporters** from the **EX2013 Lesson 10** folder and save it as **EX10-R01-Supporters-[FirstInitialLastName]**.

2. Select **cell A4**. Then, choose **Home→Styles→Format As Table** , choose **Table Style Light 12**, and click **OK**.

3. Choose **Table Tools→Design→Properties→Table Name** and change the existing name to **Contributions**.

4. Choose **Table Tools→Design→Table Style Options→Last Column**.
   The values in column G now appear bold.

5. Select the column headings in **row 4** and left-align the text.
   Left-aligning ensures that column headings are visible with their list buttons displayed.

6. AutoFit the table column widths so all text is visible in the table.
   Be careful not to AutoFit column A, as the entry in cell A1 would extend the column width too far.

7. Choose **Table Tools→Design→Table Style Options→Total Row** to display the total row in row 20.

8. Select **cell E20** and choose **Count** from the total cell's list.

9. Select **cell F20** and choose **Average** from the total cell's list.

10. Format the **range F20:G20** in **Accounting** number format with no decimal places.

Understand Structured References

11. Select **cell H4**, type **Difference** as the column heading, and AutoFit the column width.

12. Create a structured reference in **cell H5**, using point mode to select the cells, that adds cells E5 and F5 and then subtracts cell G5.

13. With **cell H5** selected, tap [F2] to display the formula in edit mode.

E	F	G	H	I	J
		Last Election			
Contribution 1 ▾	Contribution 2 ▾	Contribution ▾	Difference ▾		
1,000	230	-	=[@[Contribution 1]]+		
300	350	100	[@[Contribution 2]]-[@[Last Election		
1,000	1,250	2,000	Contribution]]		

Notice the three structured references in the formula. Excel copied this formula to all cells in the column except the total row.

14. Tap [Esc] to exit edit mode without making any changes.

15. Select **cell H19** and tap [Tab] to create a new blank row.

16. Enter the two records shown below in **rows 20–21**, tapping [Tab] after typing in each cell except the last. Don't replace the formula in the Difference column.

	A	B	C	D	E	F	G	H
19	Wilson	Flo	Union PAC	AFT	750	450	1,000	200
20	Takashima	Wendy	Private Individual	Homeowner	55	-	-	55
21	Lee	Young	Private Individual	Homeowner	40	50	50	40
22	Total				17	$ 359	$ 9,125	

Use Enhanced Sorting and Filtering in Lists and Tables

17. Click the **Difference** column heading **AutoFilter** ▼ button and choose **Sort Largest to Smallest**.

    The table rows are sorted from largest to smallest in value.

18. Click the **Contribution 1** column heading **AutoFilter** ▼ button and choose **Number Filters→Above Average**.

    The filter displays seven records higher than the average contribution amount.

19. Click the **Contribution 1** column heading **AutoFilter** ▼ button and choose **Number Filters→Top 10**. Click **OK**.

    The filter displays the 10 highest amounts sorted from largest to smallest.

20. Click the **Contribution 1** column heading **AutoFilter** ▼ button and choose **Clear Filter From "Contribution 1"**.

    The table view is restored to all 17 records.

21. Select the **range E5:E21**.

22. Choose **Home→Styles→Conditional Formatting** 📊 **→Icon Sets** and choose **3 Stars** under the Ratings category.

    The conditional formatting rule applies a star icon to each cell, with the yellow solid star representing the highest values in the column.

23. Click the **Contribution 1** column heading **AutoFilter** ▼ button and choose **Filter by Color**.

24. Choose the solid yellow star from the **Filter by Cell Icon** list.

    Two records containing the solid yellow star display. You can filter by any icon created by conditional formatting to locate trends in the data.

25. Sort the **Difference** column from largest to smallest.

26. Save and close the workbook; exit **Excel**.

27. Submit your final file based on the guidelines provided by your instructor.

    To view examples of how your file or files should look at the end of this exercise, go to the student resource center.

Create Subtotals and Use Outlining Tools

In this exercise, you will duplicate a worksheet and remove a filter. Then you will use Quick Analysis to apply formatting and create subtotals for the contribution amounts.

Use the SUBTOTAL Function to Calculate Filtered Lists

1. Start **Excel**. Open **EX10-R02-Contributions** from the **EX2013 Lesson 10** folder and save it as **EX10-R02-Contributions-[FirstInitialLastName]**.

2. Rename **Sheet1** as **List**.

3. Right-click the **List** sheet tab, choose **Move or Copy**, check the **Create a Copy** box, and click **OK**.

4. Rename the copied sheet as **Subtotals**.

5. Clear the filter from the **Last Election Contribution** column of the table.

   All 17 records should be displayed, and they remain sorted by last election contribution in largest to smallest order.

6. Sort by **Contact Type** in **A to Z** order.

7. Click the **Difference** column heading **AutoFilter** button and choose **Number Filters→Top 10**. Click **OK**.

   The filter displays the ten highest records.

8. Select **cell H22** and type **=SUBTOTAL (**.

9. Select **9-Sum** from the list, type a comma, highlight the **range H5:H20**, and tap Enter.

   The formula result is 5680, which is the sum of only those records presently displayed within the worksheet.

Use Quick Analysis

10. Highlight the **range H5:H20** and click the **Quick Analysis button** at the bottom-right of the selection.

11. Select **Formatting→Greater Than**, type **1000**, and click **OK**.

    Two donors whose contributions have increased by $1,000 or more are highlighted in red font with a red background.

Use the Outline Feature and Display Subtotals
You will now use the outline feature to create more extensive subtotals.

12. Delete the contents of **cell H22** and clear the filter from the **Difference** column.

13. Choose **Data→Outline→Subtotal**, set options as shown, and click **OK**.

    You will find the maximum contribution for each contact type in three columns of the worksheet list.

14. Click the **collapse (–)** button adjacent to Private Individual Max and Union PAC Max in the outline area.

1 2 3		A	B	C	
	4	Last Name ▼	First Name ▼	Contact Type ▼↑	Orga
	5	Lopez	Jesse	Business Owner	PC S
	6	Rogers	Thomasina	Business Owner	Stev
	7	Pretinger	Deneice	Business Owner	Cabl
	8	Watkins	Edward	Business Owner	Ron'
	9	Post	Wanda	Business Owner	Café
	10	Gardner	Aaron	Business Owner	Sym
−	11			Business Owner Max	
+	18			Private Individual Max	
+	24			Union PAC Max	
−	25			Grand Max	

The only detail rows that display are those related to Business Owners.

15. Click the **Level 3** button in the upper-left corner of the worksheet to expand all detail rows.

16. Click the **Level 2** button to display just the subtotals and grand maximum.

    Notice that no formula results display in the Difference column. You did not choose to calculate that column while setting up the outline options.

17. Save and close the workbook; exit **Excel**.

18. Submit your final file based on the guidelines provided by your instructor.

    To see examples of how your file or files should look at the end of this exercise, go to the student resource center.

REINFORCE YOUR SKILLS EX10-R03

Compare Table Data Using Multiple Methods

In this exercise, you will analyze community service data using multiple methods including data tables and Outlines.

Work with and Create a Table

1. Start **Excel**. Open **EX10-R03-TrackingLog** from the **EX2013 Lesson 10** folder and save it as **EX10-R03-TrackingLog-[FirstInitialLastName]**.

2. On the **Table** worksheet, select **cell A4**.

3. Choose **Home→Styles→Format As Table** 📊, choose **Table Style Light 11**, and click **OK**.

4. Reduce the column width for **columns D–F** to 17.

5. Select any table cell, choose **Table Tools→Design→Properties→Table Name**, and change the name to **Community_Service**.

6. Choose **Table Tools→Design→Table Style Options→Last Column**.

    The values in column F now appear bold.

7. Choose **Table Tools→Design→Table Style Options→Total Row** to display the total row in row 21.

8. Select **cell F21** and choose **Average** from the list.

9. In **cell A21**, replace *Total* with **Average**.

Understand Structured References

10. Select **cell G3**, type **Difference** as the column heading, and widen the column so the header is visible.

11. In **cell G4**, type **=**, select **cell D4**, type **+**, select **cell E4**, type **-**, select **cell F4**, and tap Enter.
    The bold formatting for the last column has been transferred to column G.

12. With **cell G4** selected, tap F2 to display the formula in edit mode.
    Notice the three structured references in the formula. Excel copied this formula to all cells in the column except the total row.

13. Tap Esc to exit edit mode without making any changes.

14. Select **cell G21** and choose **Average** from the total cell's list.

Use Enhanced Sorting and Filtering in Lists and Tables

15. Click the **Difference** column heading **AutoFilter** ⊡ button and choose **Sort Largest to Smallest**.
    The table rows are sorted from largest to smallest in value.

16. Click the **Days of Service: Prior Year** column heading **AutoFilter** ⊡ button and choose **Number Filters→Above Average**.
    The filter displays eight records higher than the average contribution amount.

17. Click the **Days of Service: Prior Year** column heading **AutoFilter** ⊡ button and choose **Number Filters→Top 10**. Click **OK**.
    The filter displays ten records.

18. Click the **Days of Service: Prior Year** column heading **AutoFilter** ⊡ button and choose **Clear Filter From "Days of Service: Prior Year"**.
    The table view is restored to display all 17 records.

19. Select the **range F4:F20**.

20. Choose **Home→Styles→Conditional Formatting** 🔢 **→Icon Sets** and choose **3 Flags** under the Indicators category.
    The conditional formatting rule applies a flag icon to each cell, with the green flags representing the highest values in the column.

21. Click the **Days of Service: Prior Year** column heading **AutoFilter** ⊡ button**→Filter by Color** and choose the red flag from the **Filter by Cell Icon** list.
    Four records containing the red flag display.

22. Sort the **Difference** column from largest to smallest if its column heading filter button does not display the sort icon.

Use the SUBTOTAL Function to Calculate Filtered Lists

23. In **cell G4** of the **Normal Range** worksheet, type **=D4+E4-F4** and confirm the formula.

24. Select **cell G3**, type **Difference**, and bold the text.

25. AutoFill the formula in **cell G4** through the end of **column G**.

26. Select any cell containing worksheet data and choose **Data→Sort & Filter→Filter**.

27. Widen the **Difference** column to fully display the header; sort by **Difference** in **largest to smallest** order.

28. Choose the **Difference** column heading **AutoFilter** button and choose **Number Filters→Top 10**. Click **OK**.

    The filter displays the ten highest records.

29. Select cell G21, and type **=SUBTOTAL (**.

30. Select **1-Average** from the list, type a comma, highlight the range **G4:G13**, and tap [Enter].

    The formula result is 9.2, which is the average of only those records presently displayed.

Use Quick Analysis

31. Highlight the **range G4:G13** and choose the **Quick Analysis button** 📋 at the bottom-right of the selection.

32. Choose **Formatting→Greater Than**, type **10**, choose **Green Fill with Dark Green Text** from the With box, and click **OK**.

    Five students, whose days of community service have increased by at least 10 days, have their differences displayed in green text with a green background.

Use the Outline Feature and Display Subtotals

You will now use the outline feature to create more extensive subtotals.

33. Delete the contents of **cell G21** and clear the filter from the **Difference** column.

34. Select the **range G4:G20** and choose **Home→Styles→Conditional Formatting→Clear Rules→Clear Rules from Selected Cells**.

35. Sort by **School** in **A to Z** ⬇ order.

36. Select a cell within the **range A3:G20** and choose **Data→Outline→Subtotal**.

37. Create subtotals so at each change in **School**, the **Average** function is used to add a subtotal to the **Difference** column.

38. Click the **collapse (−)** button adjacent to **High School West Average** and **High School East Average** in the outline area.

    Only the State University detail rows display.

39. Click the **Level 3** button to expand all detail rows.

40. Click the **Level 2** button to collapse the list to display just the subtotals and grand average.

41. Save and close the workbook; exit **Excel**.

42. Submit your final file based on the guidelines provided by your instructor.

Apply Your Skills

APPLY YOUR SKILLS EX10-A01

Convert to a Table and Create Formulas

In this exercise, you will convert a worksheet range to a table. You will change a formula in the total row, create a calculated column, and add a record. You will also sort the table.

Work with and Create a Table

1. Start **Excel**. Open **EX10-A01-Compensation** from the **EX2013 Lesson 10** folder and save it as **EX10-A01-Compensation-[FirstInitialLastName]**.

2. Convert the worksheet range to **Table Style Dark 3**.

3. Rename the table as **Retirement_Plan**.

4. Edit column heading names as necessary and adjust column widths.

5. Format the numbers in **columns D and E** with **Comma Style** and zero decimal places.

6. Create a calculated column that computes **Retirement Plan Contributions** divided by **Compensation**. Format the results with **Percent Style**.

7. Use **% of Compensation** as the column heading, apply wrap text to the heading, and widen the column to fully display *compensation*.

Use Structured References, and Enhanced Sorting and Filtering

8. Include a total row and delete the total in **column F**. Change the formula in the total row to one that averages the retirement plan contributions.

9. Change the label in **cell A18** to **Average**.

10. Review the formula in **cell E18** and note the structured references.

11. Sort by **% of Compensation** from largest to smallest.

12. Save and close the workbook; exit **Excel**.

13. Submit your final file based on the guidelines provided by your instructor.

    To view examples of how your file or files should look at the end of this exercise, go to the student resource center.

Outline a Worksheet and Use Subtotals

In this exercise, you will sort records in a list that tracks event costs. You will outline the worksheet and display subtotals that calculate averages.

Use SUBTOTAL to Calculate Filtered Lists and Quick Analysis

1. Start **Excel**. Open **EX10-A02-MarchExpenses** from the **EX2013 Lesson 10** folder and save it as **EX10-A02-MarchExpenses-[FirstInitialLastName]**.

2. Perform a multicolumn sort from A to Z by **Duration** and **Feedback**. Filter the worksheet to display those records with an **Extended** duration.

3. Use the **SUBTOTAL** function to calculate the Average Total Costs at the bottom of the Total Costs column. Format the result in **Accounting Number Format** and type a centered label of **Average** in the cell below.

   The result displays as $1,258.82.

4. Copy and paste the worksheet data, including the SUBTOTAL result and label, in **cell A29**.

5. Type an appropriate label above the pasted data; italicize the label.

6. Use **Quick Analysis** to highlight total costs within the pasted data that exceed $1,300.

Use the Outline Feature and Display Subtotals

7. Remove all filtering from the original worksheet list, delete the contents of the **range G24:G25**, and ensure that the list is still sorted by Duration and Feedback.

8. Include subtotals that average the total costs column and that are inserted at each change in feedback.

9. Bold the subtotal and grand total amounts.

10. Group **Variable Costs** and **Fixed Costs**, but do not group Total Costs.

11. Use outline buttons to hide details for the two **Extended** groups and to hide the Fixed **Costs** and **Variable Costs** columns.

12. Save and close the workbook; exit **Excel**.

13. Submit your final file based on the guidelines provided by your instructor.

    To view examples of how your final file or files should look at the end of this exercise, go to the student resource center.

Work with a Table, Subtotals, and Outline View

In this exercise, you will convert a worksheet range to a table. You will sort and filter the table, create a formula using the SUBTOTAL function, and use the outline feature.

Work with and Create a Table

1. Start **Excel**. Open **EX10-A03-Sales** from the **EX2013 Lesson 10** folder and save it as **EX10-A03-Sales-[FirstInitialLastName]**.

2. Convert the worksheet range to a data table with **Table Style Light 9**.

3. Rename the table as **Event_Sales**.

4. Align cell contents logically, and adjust column widths where necessary.

5. Format the numbers in **column F** with **Currency Style** and zero decimal places.

Use Structured References, and Enhanced Sorting and Filtering

6. Include a total row within the data table.

7. Create a formula in the total row for the Sales column that counts the number of sales reps. Create a **Count** label below the formula.

8. Review the formula and note the structured references.

9. Sort by **Sales** from smallest to largest. Filter by **New York** in the **Market** column.

Use SUBTOTAL to Calculate Filtered Lists and Quick Analysis

10. Use the **SUBTOTAL** function to calculate average sales below the Sales column. Format the result in **Accounting Format** with zero decimal places and type a centered label of **Average** in the cell below.

    The result displays as $41,497. Note in the Formula Bar that this formula does not contain a structured reference, due to the way in which it was created.

11. Use the **Quick Analysis** button to include a color scale within the Sales column.

    Karen Cray's total sales are now displayed in red.

Use the Outline Feature and Display Subtotals

12. Remove all filtering from the original worksheet list. Clear the conditional formatting (color scales), convert the data table back to a normal range, and delete the average information and Count label at the bottom of the Sales column.

13. Sort the data table based on the market.

14. Include subtotals that sum the sales column and that are inserted at each change in market.

15. AutoFit the market column; bold the subtotal and grand total amounts.

16. Group **First Name** and **Week**, and hide details for the group.

17. Use outline buttons to hide details for **Cincinnati**, **Las Vegas**, and **Phoenix**.

18. Save and close the workbook; exit **Excel**.

19. Submit your final file based on the guidelines provided by your instructor.

Extend Your Skills

In the course of working through the Extend Your Skills exercises, you will think critically as you use the skills taught in the lesson to complete the assigned projects. To evaluate your mastery and completion of the exercises, your instructor may use a rubric, with which more points are allotted according to performance characteristics. (The more you do, the more you earn!) Ask your instructor how your work will be evaluated.

EX10-E01 That's the Way I See It

You're shopping for a new car! To help you choose the best make and model, you will create an Excel table.

Open a new workbook and save it in the **EX2013 Lesson 10** folder as **EX10-E01-Automobiles-[FirstInitialLastName]**. Identify three automobile manufacturers whose models appeal to you, and then go online and research four car models for each manufacturer. In your worksheet, create a table listing each automobile's manufacturer, model name, classification (sedan, SUV, etc.), base price, general customer satisfaction (high, medium, or low, based on your research), and your personal rating (1–10, with 10 being the highest). Sort the table appropriately, and filter it to display the automobiles that earn your highest rating. Lastly, use the Quick Analysis button to apply a color scale to an appropriate set of data within the table.

You will be evaluated based on the inclusion of all elements specified, your ability to follow directions, your ability to apply newly learned skills to a real-world situation, your creativity, and the relevance of your topic and/or data choice(s). Submit your final file based on the guidelines provided by your instructor.

EX10-E02 Be Your Own Boss

As your company Blue Jean Landscaping continues to grow, you are finding the need to get more organized. Specifically, you want to track the different service packages that your largest clients are purchasing.

Open **EX10-E02-Customers** from the **EX2013 Lesson 10** folder and save it as **EX10-E02-Customers-[FirstInitialLastName]**. Convert the data to a table with the headings **Area**, **Customer**, **Package**, and **Sales**. Design the table in an appropriate, professional style. Create a total row and use it to calculate the number of packages sold. Sort the data by customer, and filter the data to display only packages costing more than $10,000. Finally, use the SUBTOTAL function to calculate the total cost of all packages displayed.

You will be evaluated based on the inclusion of all elements specified, your ability to follow directions, your ability to apply newly learned skills to a real-world situation, your creativity, and your demonstration of an entrepreneurial spirit. Submit your final file based on the guidelines provided by your instructor.

Transfer Your Skills

In the course of working through the Transfer Your Skills exercises, you will use critical-thinking and creativity skills to complete the assigned projects using skills taught in the lesson. To evaluate your mastery and completion of the exercises, your instructor may use a rubric, with which more points are allotted according to performance characteristics. (The more you do, the more you earn!) Ask your instructor how your work will be evaluated.

EX10-T01 Use the Web as a Learning Tool

Throughout this book, you will be provided with an opportunity to use the Internet as a learning tool by completing WebQuests. According to the original creators of WebQuests, as described on their website (WebQuest.org), a WebQuest is "an inquiry-oriented activity in which most or all of the information used by learners is drawn from the web." To complete the WebQuest projects in this book, navigate to the student resource center and choose the WebQuest for the lesson on which you are currently working. The subject of each WebQuest will be relevant to the material found in the lesson.

WebQuest Subject: Effectively using the Quick Analysis button

Submit your final file(s) based on the guidelines provided by your instructor.

EX10-T02 Demonstrate Proficiency

You have created a salesman training roster for Stormy BBQ in order to monitor the progress of the company's potential regional salespeople. You would like to more closely examine the results of a subset of individuals currently undergoing training.

Open **EX10-T02-Roster** from the **EX2013 Lesson 10** folder and save it as **EX10-T02-Roster-[FirstInitialLastName]**. Use the AutoFilter button to filter worksheet data for Level 1 trainees only. Below the data create formulas using the SUBTOTAL function to calculate the number of Level 1 trainees displayed and the maximum score achieved by these trainees. Use the Quick Analysis button to highlight those scores among the top 10 percent, and sort the data based on manager first, then trainee name. Apply appropriate formatting to the formula results.

Submit your final file based on the guidelines provided by your instructor.

EXCEL 2013

Utilizing Graphics and Templates

LEARNING OBJECTIVES

After studying this lesson, you will be able to:

- Insert and modify pictures and clip art on worksheets

- Draw, modify, and add text to shapes

- Customize SmartArt to convey ideas, processes, and data relationships

- Use existing workbooks and Office templates as the basis for new workbooks

- Create and modify custom templates

Enhancing workbooks with graphics may help you illustrate the worksheet theme and call attention to important details. In this lesson, you will locate and insert photos and clip art on worksheets. You will draw shapes using Excel's large gallery of drawing tools and move, size, rotate, and crop images. You will correct photos and apply special effects to images. You will use WordArt to further enhance your worksheets, and you will create text charts that visually demonstrate a process or relationship by using SmartArt. Lastly, you will use and customize templates to allow for more efficient worksheet development.

Enhancing Data Using Graphics and Templates

You will be attending a meeting of the corporate officers for Green Clean, your janitorial product supplier and cleaning service. At this meeting you will be reviewing two topics. First, you will examine the company's sales performance in comparison to the prior year. You think that adding some graphics will highlight and connect key points in your presentation. You will add graphics to several worksheets while applying principles of good design. Second, you will discuss Green Clean's charitable endeavors. You will create a template to record and share charity race results. The template will contain the text labels and formulas common to all events.

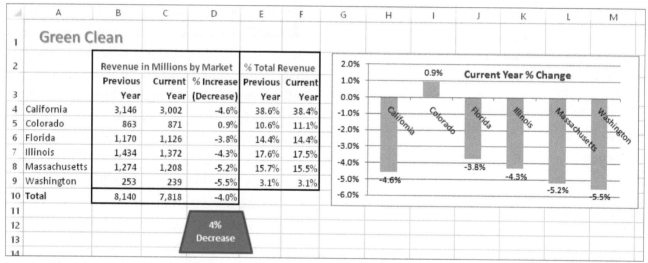

The chart is enhanced by a shape with text.

	A	B	C	D	E
1			Race Results		
2			[Type event name here]		
3			[Enter month and day here]		
4					
5	Place	Team	Team Captain	Points	
6	1				
7	2				
8	3				
9	4				
10	5				
11		Average		#DIV/0!	

[Type a message or select the graphic and press Delete.]

This template can be used repeatedly for each event.

Using Illustrations with Excel

Video Library http://labyrinthelab.com/videos Video Number: EX13-V1101

You can dress up your worksheets using the professionally designed clip art provided by Microsoft Office. You can also insert your own pictures, such as a company logo or a scanned picture.

Design Principles

Graphics are fun to create, but when adding art you should follow these generally accepted design rules.

- Each graphic should have a purpose, such as to call attention to an important number, summarize data, or contribute to the worksheet theme.
- Graphics should enhance, and not distract from or clutter, the worksheet.
- The image colors, size, alignment, and other formatting should be consistent with other worksheet objects.
- Copyright law prohibits the use of many images for commercial use without permission. However, there are websites featuring copyright-free art, and the clip art within Excel is free to use as long as it is not resold.

Inserting Pictures and Clip Art

The Picture command adds an image saved as a file, while the Clip Art command adds a drawing or photo from a gallery of images available in Microsoft Office. You may adjust several image characteristics, including sharpness, colors, and brightness. You may apply picture styles, such as a frame or blurred edges. Immediately after it is inserted, the picture or clip art image displays with sizing and rotation handles.

Inserting a Picture from a File

After you choose the Picture command, Excel displays the Insert Picture dialog box, similar to the Open dialog box for workbooks. Navigate to the folder containing the desired picture and select its file.

Insert a Picture

In this exercise, you will add a picture to a worksheet.

1. Open **EX11-D01-Comparison** from the **EX2013 Lesson 11** folder and save it as **EX11-D01-Comparison-[FirstInitialLastName]**.

    Replace the bracketed text with your first initial and last name. For example, if your name is Bethany Smith, your filename would look like this: EX11-D01-Comparison-BSmith.

2. **Maximize** ☐ the window and display the **By Market** worksheet.

3. Select **cell B12**, choose **Insert→Illustrations→Pictures** 🖼, and navigate to the **EX2013 Lesson 11** folder.

    None of the Excel workbook filenames are displayed because the Files of Type option is set to All Pictures.

4. Select the **EX11-D01-GreenClean** file and click **Insert**.

    The upper-left corner of the picture appears on cell B12, which you selected, but the picture is not attached to the cell.

5. Select the image and tap ⌗Delete⌗.

6. Save the file and leave it open; you will modify it throughout this lesson.

Inserting a Screenshot

Video Library   http://labyrinthelab.com/videos   Video Number: EX13-V1102

You can insert a screenshot of any non-Excel window, or a specific area of that window. For example, you can capture a certain area of a web page or a Word document.

Insert a Screenshot

In this exercise, you will take a screenshot of a specific area of a Word document and insert it on a worksheet.

1. Save your file as **EX11-D02-Comparison-[FirstInitialLastName]**.

2. Open **Word 2013**.

3. In Word, open **EX11-D02-ExpenseData** from the **EX2013 Lesson 11** folder.

    This document contains a note about numbers to be used in the Revenue Comparison workbook.

4. In Excel, display the **Analysis** worksheet and select **cell B15**.

5. Choose **Insert→Illustrations→Take a Screenshot** 📷.

    You could insert the entire Word window by selecting the thumbnail in the Available Windows area, but you will select only the text area for the screenshot.

6. Choose **Screen Clipping** from the menu.

   The Word window appears dimmed and the mouse pointer appears as a plus (+) sign.

7. Follow these steps to take a screenshot:

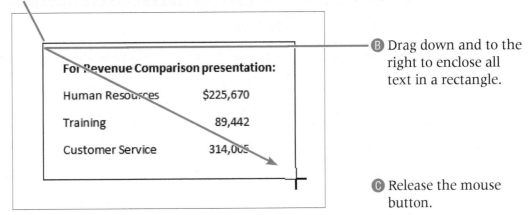

Ⓐ Place the mouse pointer above and to the left of the text.

Ⓑ Drag down and to the right to enclose all text in a rectangle.

Ⓒ Release the mouse button.

The Excel window appears, and your selection appears as a picture at cell B15.

8. Switch to the **Word** window in the Windows taskbar; exit **Word**.

9. Save the file and leave it open.

Inserting Clip Art

Video Library   http://labyrinthelab.com/videos   Video Number: EX13-V1103

The Online Pictures command on the Insert tab displays the Insert Pictures dialog box. This pane lets you search for clip art using keywords.

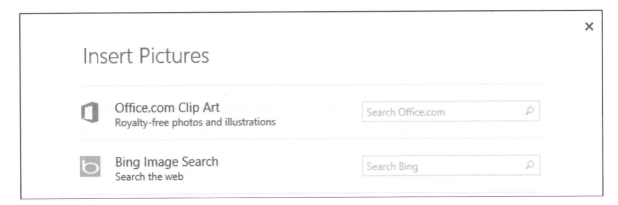

Two media types of clip art work with Excel: illustrations (drawings in a variety of designs and colors) and photographs (images from a camera).

Insert Clip Art

In this exercise, you will search for clip art images and add one to a worksheet.

1. Save your file as **EX11-D03-Comparison-[FirstInitialLastName]**.

2. If necessary, display the **Analysis** worksheet.

3. Select **cell C5** and choose **Insert→Illustrations→Online Pictures** .
   The Insert Pictures dialog box appears.

4. Follow these steps to conduct a search for clip art:

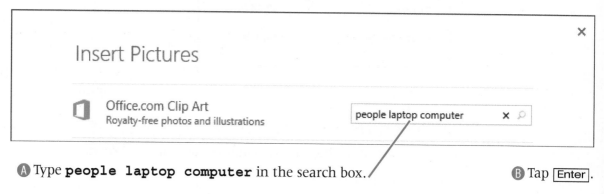

Ⓐ Type **people laptop computer** in the search box. Ⓑ Tap Enter .

You must be connected to the Internet in order to receive search results.

5. Scroll through the clips, click the one shown at right, and choose **Insert**.
   If this image is not available, choose a similar one. The image displays at cell C5.

6. Save the file and leave it open.

QUICK REFERENCE	INSERTING IMAGES
Task	**Procedure**
Insert a picture	▪ Select any cell and choose Insert→Illustrations→Pictures.
	▪ Navigate to and select the picture file, and choose Insert.
Insert clip art	▪ Select any cell and choose Insert→Illustrations→Online Pictures.
	▪ Type a keyword in the search box and tap Enter .
	▪ Select the desired clip art and choose Insert.
Insert a screenshot of a non-Excel window	▪ Click in the desired window to be captured.
	▪ Switch to Excel and do one of the following:
	◆ Choose Insert→Illustrations→Take a Screenshot and choose the desired window.
	◆ Choose Insert→Illustrations→Take a Screenshot →Screen Clipping and drag to select the desired window area.

Moving, Sizing, and Rotating Images

Video Library   http://labyrinthelab.com/videos   Video Number: EX13-V1104

When you select a picture or clip art image, sizing handles and a rotation handle appear. You can size, move, and rotate selected objects.

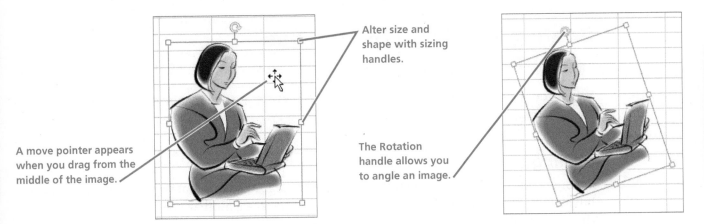

Alter size and shape with sizing handles.

The Rotation handle allows you to angle an image.

A move pointer appears when you drag from the middle of the image.

Excel 2013

Deleting a graphic that you no longer need is as simple as selecting it and tapping Delete .

DEVELOP YOUR SKILLS EX11-D04
Move, Rotate, and Size Images

In this exercise, you will modify the appearance of the clip art image you have previously inserted.

1. Save your file as **EX11-D04-Comparison-[FirstInitialLastName]**.

2. Follow these steps to move, rotate, and size an image:
   The positioning of your image may differ from these figures.

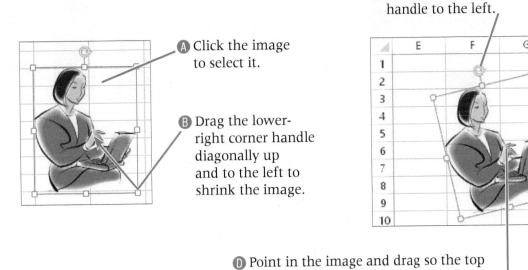

Ⓒ Drag the circle in the rotation handle to the left.

Ⓐ Click the image to select it.

Ⓑ Drag the lower-right corner handle diagonally up and to the left to shrink the image.

Ⓓ Point in the image and drag so the top of the image is near the top of **cell F3**.

3. Select the image and tap ⌈Delete⌉.
   The image is removed.

4. Click **Undo** ⌐↩⌐ to restore the image.

5. Save the file and leave it open.

Scaling and Cropping Images

Video Library   http://labyrinthelab.com/videos   Video Number: EX13-V1105

When you select an image, various Picture Tools become available on the Ribbon. To adjust most characteristics, you use the Format tab.

Scaling

Scaling a picture reduces its overall size to a percentage of its original size. The effect is equal to having dragged a corner handle on the object. You can scale more precisely, however, by typing the number of inches or using the spinner arrows.

Original size

Fifty percent of the original size

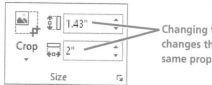

Changing the height or width also changes the other dimension in the same proportion.

Cropping

If you want to use part of a picture or clip art image, use the Crop command. The object remains the same size, and you drag the handles inward to cut off one or more edges of the image.

Drag a corner handle or side handle to **crop**.

The picture before cropping

The picture after cropping

The Format Picture Task Pane

The Format Picture task pane allows you to set a variety of picture options. It can be particularly useful when you need the same measurements for multiple objects.

Resetting an Image

If you want to start over, you may reset an image to its original characteristics by choosing a Reset command from either the Format tab or the Format Picture task pane.

The Reset Picture & Size command removes all changes to the image. If you're satisfied with the size and cropping, you may want to copy and paste a duplicate image (to preserve the characteristics) before experimenting with additional effects.

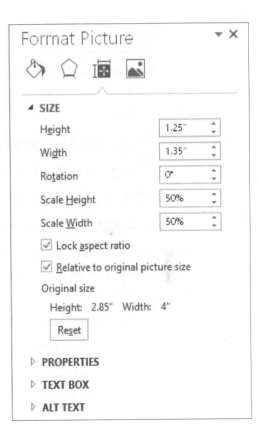

Format Picture

▲ SIZE

He**i**ght	1.25"
Wi**d**th	1.35"
Rotation	0°
Scale **H**eight	50%
Scale **W**idth	50%

☑ Lock a**s**pect ratio
☑ **R**elative to original picture size

Original size
    Height: 2.85"   Width: 4"
    Re**s**et

▷ PROPERTIES
▷ TEXT BOX
▷ ALT TEXT

QUICK REFERENCE	SCALING AND CROPPING IMAGES
Task	**Procedure**

Scale an image	■ Select the image and then:
	   ◆ Choose Picture Tools→Format→Size→Shape Height or Shape Width and edit the size; or
	   ◆ Launch the Format Picture task pane, choose Height or Width under Size, and change the percentage.

Rotate an image	■ Select the image and drag its rotation handle.
Crop an image	■ Select the image and choose Picture Tools→Format→Size→Crop . ■ Drag a cropping handle.
Reset size, rotation, and cropping	■ Select the image and choose Picture Tools→Format→Adjust→Reset Picture menu ▼→Reset Picture & Size.

Scale and Crop an Image

In this exercise, you will scale a clip art image to smaller than its original size. You will also crop the image.

1. Save your file as **EX11-D05-Comparison-[FirstInitialLastName]**.

2. Display the **Analysis** worksheet and select **cell B3.**

3. Choose **Insert→Illustrations→Online Pictures** .

4. Type **profit arrows** in the search box and tap Enter.

5. Scroll through the results, click this image, and select **Insert**.

   If this image is not available, choose a similar one. The clip art image is displayed at cell B3.

6. Select the image, and then choose **Picture Tools→Format→Size**.

7. Follow these steps to scale the image:

   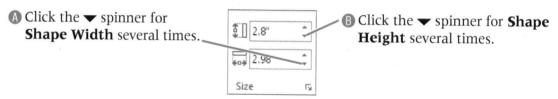

   Ⓐ Click the ▼ spinner for **Shape Width** several times.

   Ⓑ Click the ▼ spinner for **Shape Height** several times.

   Both commands scale the width and the height together. Your settings may be different from those shown.

Scale Using the Format Picture Task Pane

8. Choose **Picture Tools→Format→Size→dialog box launcher** to open the Format Picture task pane.

9. Follow these steps to scale the image:

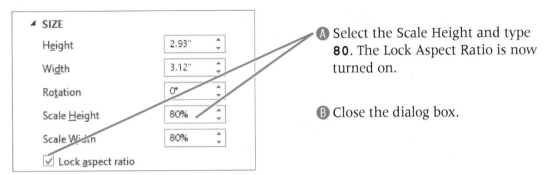

Ⓐ Select the Scale Height and type **80**. The Lock Aspect Ratio is now turned on.

Ⓑ Close the dialog box.

Excel 2013

The image displays at 80 percent of its original size.

10. Right-click the image and choose **Size and Properties**.

11. In the Format Picture task pane, edit the scale width to **50**, and then close the task pane.

If you are using a different image than the one shown, use an appropriate percentage.

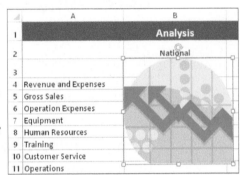

Use the Cropping Tool on the Ribbon

12. Select the image and choose **Picture Tools→Format→Size→Crop**.

13. Follow these steps to crop the image:

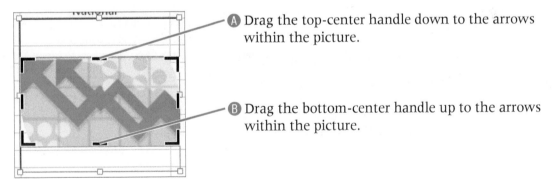

Ⓐ Drag the top-center handle down to the arrows within the picture.

Ⓑ Drag the bottom-center handle up to the arrows within the picture.

14. If needed, scale the image larger or smaller so it balances well with other objects on the worksheet. Click away from the image to deselect the cropping tool.

15. Select the image again and choose **Picture Tools→Format→Adjust→Reset Picture menu ▼→Reset Picture and Size**.

All changes are removed, and the original image is restored.

16. **Undo** the reset to restore the image.

17. Move the profit arrows image to **cell F11**.

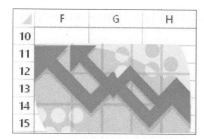

18. Click outside the image to deselect it.

19. Save the file and leave it open.

Correcting Images and Applying Special Effects

Video Library   http://labyrinthelab.com/videos   Video Number: EX13-V1106

The Picture Tools Format tab allows you to sharpen and soften photos and apply artistic effects to them. Additional options are available to adjust the brightness, contrast, and color of images. The Background Removal tool allows you to remove unwanted objects from a photo.

Picture Styles, Effects, and Borders

The Picture Styles group includes many options to frame an image or apply a reflection. With Picture Effects, you can give an image a 3-D appearance by choosing a preset, which includes multiple effects. You can also choose a single effect, such as a shadow or a bevel. With Picture Borders, you can apply and modify a wide variety of borders to any picture.

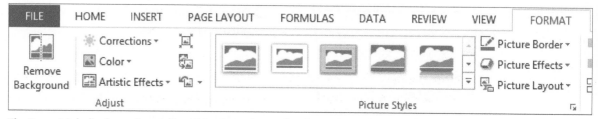

The Format tab displays when a clip art or picture image is selected.

Task	Procedure
Adjust image brightness and contrast	■ Select the image, choose Picture Tools→Format→Adjust→Corrections, and select a brightness and contrast preset option.
Adjust the image color	■ Select the image, choose Picture Tools→Format→Adjust→Color, and select a color saturation, color tone, or recolor preset option.
Set an option for an image precisely	■ Select the image, open the Format Picture Styles task pane, select the desired category, and enter the value for the desired option.
Sharpen or soften a photo	■ Select the photo, choose Picture Tools→Format→Adjust→Corrections, and select a sharpen or soften preset option.
Remove or restore background areas on a photo	■ Select the photo, choose Picture Tools→Format→Adjust→Remove Background, and drag handles on the masking rectangle to select the area to be adjusted.
	■ **Remove:** Choose Background Removal→Refine→Mark Areas to Remove, and click the pencil tool on an object or drag across an object.
	■ **Restore:** Choose Background Removal→Refine→Mark Areas to Keep, and click points on the object or drag across the object.
	When finished, choose Background Removal→Close→Close Background Removal and Keep Changes.
Apply an artistic effect to a photo	■ Select the photo, choose Picture Tools→Format→Adjust→Artistic Effects, and select a preset effect.
Apply a picture style to an image	■ Select the image, choose Picture Tools→Format→Picture Styles→More, and choose a style.
Apply a picture effect to an image	■ Select the image, choose Picture Tools→Format→Picture Styles→Picture Effects and choose a preset or other effect.
Apply a border to an image	■ Select the image, choose Picture Tools→Format→Picture Styles→Picture Border, and choose a border.

Excel 2013

DEVELOP YOUR SKILLS EX11-D06

Adjust Images and Apply Special Effects

In this exercise, you will change the brightness and contrast of an image, and then recolor it with a theme color. You will also apply a picture style and picture effects to images.

1. Save the file as **EX11-D06-Comparison-[FirstInitialLastName]**.

2. Display the **Analysis** worksheet and select the **profit arrows picture**.

3. Choose **Picture Tools→Format→Adjust→Corrections** 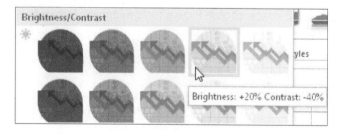 and point at the preset option in the center of the list.

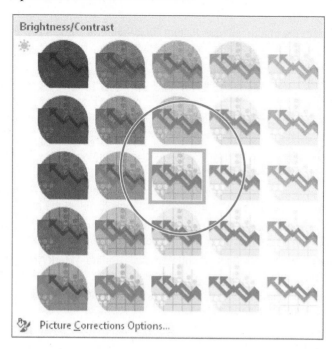

The frame around this preset option indicates that it is the current setting.

4. Point at a few other preset options to preview the effect on the image, and then choose **Brightness: +20% Contrast: –40%**.

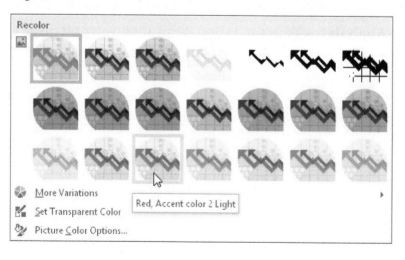

5. Choose **Picture Tools→Format→Adjust→Color** 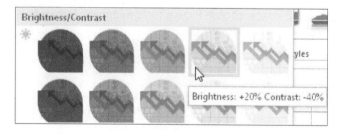 and choose **Red, Accent color 2 Light**.

Insert a Photo Image

6. Select **cell B3**, and then choose **Insert→Illustrations→Online Pictures** .

7. Type **business meeting women organizers** in the search box and tap ⎡Enter⎤.

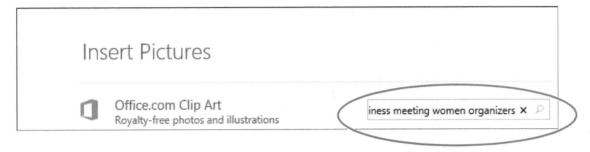

8. Choose this image (or a similar image if this one isn't available) and click **Insert**.

The image displays at cell B3 of the worksheet.

Remove Background Areas

9. Choose **Picture Tools→Format→Adjust→Remove Background** .

The Background Removal tab appears at the right of the File tab. A masking rectangle appears on the image. Areas outside the rectangle are masked in a single color. Masked areas will be removed from the image.

10. Drag the center handle of each side of the masking rectangle to surround the two women tightly.

11. Choose **Background Removal→Refine→Mark Areas to Keep** and place the pencil tool pointer near the top of the masked objects (likely the women's suit jackets and/or hair).

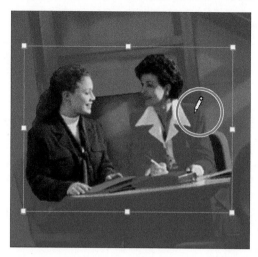

12. Drag down to the jacket sleeve (if a suit jacket is masked) to unmask part of the jacket. Continue pointing and dragging to unmask all areas on the women.

    You can use the Undo command if your selection is incorrect. You could also use the Mark Areas to Remove command to mask additional areas of the image.

13. When you are finished, choose **Background Removal→Close→Close Background Removal and Keep Changes**.

14. With the image still selected, choose **Picture Tools→Format→Size→Shape Height**, type **1.5**, and tap Enter.

    The image shrinks, the width remaining in proportion to the height. Ignore any changes to the masked areas that may occur from resizing the image.

15. Select the photo at **cell I3** and choose **Picture Tools→Format→Adjust→Artistic Effects→Paint Brush**.

16. Select the profit arrows image at **cell F11** and choose **Picture Tools→Format→Picture Styles→Drop Shadow Rectangle**.

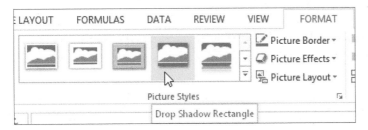

The image displays a drop shadow effect.

17. Select the laptop computer image at **cell F3** and scroll to the right so the image is fully visible, if necessary.

18. Choose **Picture Tools→Format→Picture Styles→Picture Effects** 🔲.

19. Follow these steps to choose a preset:

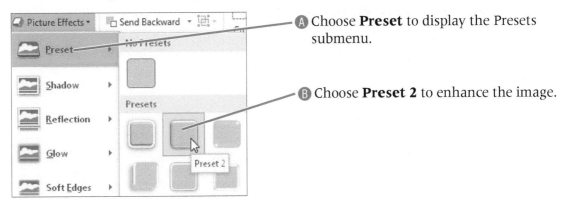

Ⓐ Choose **Preset** to display the Presets submenu.

Ⓑ Choose **Preset 2** to enhance the image.

20. Move the photo of the two women from **cell B3** to overlap the profit arrows image at **cell F11**.

21. Apply one or two effects (artistic effect, color adjustment, picture style, or picture effect).

22. Save the file and leave it open.

Getting Into Shapes

Video Library   http://labyrinthelab.com/videos   Video Number: EX13-V1107

With the Microsoft Office Shapes tools, you may draw lines, ovals, rectangles, arrows, and many other shapes. The Shapes command is used to add these objects. You can type text into most shapes, though certain lines cannot accept text.

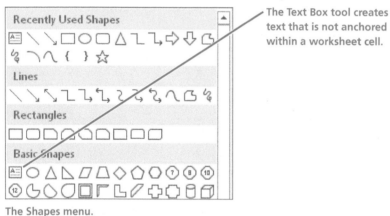

The Text Box tool creates text that is not anchored within a worksheet cell.

You may type text inside many shapes, including **callouts**.

The Shapes menu.

Inserting Shapes

To draw a shape, choose the desired tool from the Shapes menu and then either click or drag in the worksheet. Clicking creates a shape of a predefined size; dragging allows you to customize the width and height. After you create or select a shape, the Drawing Tools appear on the Ribbon. The Format tab contains options to change the size, fill, and outline; add an effect; and insert more shapes.

Constraining Objects

You hold down the Shift key to draw shapes that remain in equal proportion of width to height. You can also constrain lines to 90- or 45-degree angles.

Text Boxes

Text boxes are slightly different from rectangle shapes, which display centered text. As you type in a text box, text is left-aligned by default, and the text box lengthens automatically to display all the text. You may position a text box anywhere on a worksheet, even over worksheet entries, pictures, and other graphics. A text box may be layered over a cell, picture, clip art, or shape.

Applying Shape Styles and Effects

With a shape selected, you can apply options from the Shape Styles group on the Format tab. You may apply one of the Quick Styles that are predesigned with a workbook theme color, outline, fill, and bevel effect. As an alternative, you may create a custom outline or fill. The Shape Effects menu contains options to angle, bevel, shadow, or reflect the image for a 3-D appearance.

Revenue
Summary

QUICK REFERENCE	INSERTING AND EDITING SHAPES
Task	**Procedure**
Insert a shape	■ Choose Insert→Illustrations→Shapes ⬙ and choose a shape tool.
	■ Click in the worksheet to create the shape or drag to control the shape's size and hold down Shift while dragging to constrain the shape to a perfect square, circle, or 90- or 45-degree line.
Insert a text box	■ Choose Insert→Text→Text Box ▣, click in the worksheet, and type the text.
Apply an outline or fill to a shape	■ Select the image, choose Drawing Tools→Format→Shape Styles, and choose a predesigned style (or choose Shape Fill or Shape Outline for custom settings).
Apply a shape effect	■ Select the shape, choose Drawing Tools→Format→Shape Styles→Shape Effects, and choose a preset option or other effect.
Set an option for a shape precisely	■ Select the shape, choose Drawing Tools→Format→Shape Styles dialog box launcher, and enter the value for the desired option.

DEVELOP YOUR SKILLS EX11-D07
Insert and Edit Shapes

In this exercise, you will draw various shapes, including a callout and a text box. You will change the appearance of shapes, and you will apply a glow effect to one of the shapes.

1. Save the file as **EX11-D07-Comparison-[FirstInitialLastName]**.

2. In the **By Region** worksheet, choose **Insert→Illustrations→Shapes→Basic Shapes→Oval**.

3. Follow these steps to draw an oval on cell D5:

Ⓐ Position the mouse pointer above and to the left of **-2%** and drag down and right.

Ⓑ Release the mouse button.

The oval hides the number because the oval contains a fill.

4. Choose **Drawing Tools→Format→Shape Styles→Shape Fill** **→No Fill**.

   The number now appears through the oval.

5. Choose **Drawing Tools→Format→Shape Styles→Shape Outline** ✎, choose an orange shade, and move and resize the oval to center it over the number.

6. Choose **Insert→Illustrations→Shapes→Callouts→Line Callout 1** ⌐□.

7. Follow these steps to draw a callout on cell G9:

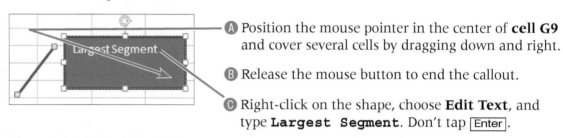

   Ⓐ Position the mouse pointer in the center of **cell G9** and cover several cells by dragging down and right.

   Ⓑ Release the mouse button to end the callout.

   Ⓒ Right-click on the shape, choose **Edit Text**, and type **Largest Segment**. Don't tap ⌗Enter⌗.

8. Drag the **bottom-right handle** to reduce the size of the box so no blank space appears around *Largest Segment*.

9. Choose **Drawing Tools→Format→Shape Styles→More** ▼ and select **Moderate Effect – Red, Accent 2**.

   Your callout should contain text, a graduated red fill, and a thin shadow.

10. Follow these steps to rotate and lengthen the callout line:

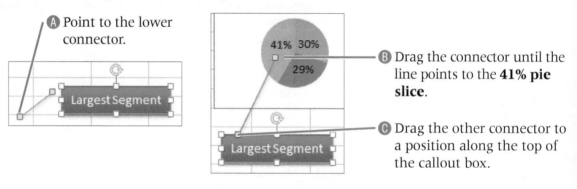

   Ⓐ Point to the lower connector.

   Ⓑ Drag the connector until the line points to the **41% pie slice**.

   Ⓒ Drag the other connector to a position along the top of the callout box.

11. Display the **Analysis** worksheet and choose **Insert→Text→Text Box** 🄰.

12. Follow these steps to draw a text box on the laptop computer image:

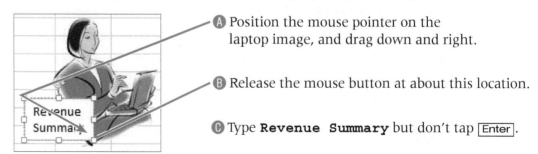

   Ⓐ Position the mouse pointer on the laptop image, and drag down and right.

   Ⓑ Release the mouse button at about this location.

   Ⓒ Type **Revenue Summary** but don't tap ⌗Enter⌗.

13. If necessary, point to the border to move and resize the shape.

14. Display the **By Market** worksheet and choose **Insert→Illustrations→Shapes→Basic Shapes→Trapezoid**.

15. Follow these steps to draw a trapezoid across several cells:

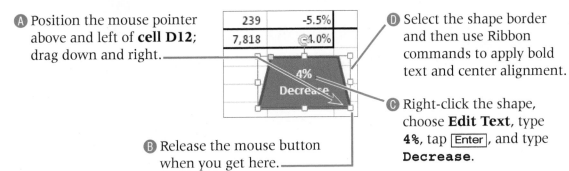

Ⓐ Position the mouse pointer above and left of **cell D12**; drag down and right.

Ⓑ Release the mouse button when you get here.

Ⓓ Select the shape border and then use Ribbon commands to apply bold text and center alignment.

Ⓒ Right-click the shape, choose **Edit Text**, type **4%**, tap ⎵Enter⎵, and type **Decrease**.

16. With the trapezoid selected, choose **Drawing Tools→Format→Shape Styles→More** and choose a red style.

17. With the trapezoid still selected, choose **Drawing Tools→Format→Shape Styles→Shape Effects→Bevel** and choose a bevel option.

    Because the shape has a bevel effect, the Soft Edges effects in the Shape Effects menu are not available. The shape will not preview a change when you point to those effects on the menu.

18. Copy and paste the trapezoid and move the duplicate to **row 26**. With the duplicate selected, choose **Drawing Tools→Format→Shape Styles→Shape Effects→Bevel→No Bevel**.

19. Save the file and leave it open.

Illustrating with SmartArt and WordArt

Video Library http://labyrinthelab.com/videos Video Number: EX13-V1108

With SmartArt, you can illustrate a procedure, process, or decision tree more easily than you can with simple shapes. SmartArt includes predefined charts to show relationships between ideas, illustrate an information cycle, and sequence project workflow steps. With WordArt you highlight important words/phrases through the use of predefined formatting within text boxes.

Using SmartArt

The Choose a SmartArt Graphic dialog box displays charts within categories. When you select a chart, its description displays to the right.

Chart categories.   Charts available within a category

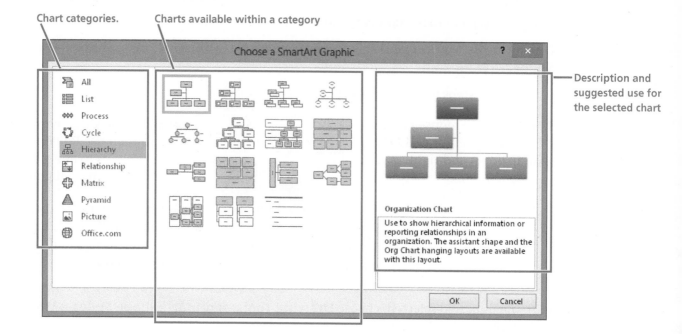

Description and suggested use for the selected chart

Choose a SmartArt Graphic

All
List
Process
Cycle
Hierarchy
Relationship
Matrix
Pyramid
Picture
Office.com

Organization Chart

Use to show hierarchical information or reporting relationships in an organization. The assistant shape and the Org Chart hanging layouts are available with this layout.

OK   Cancel

Adding Text to SmartArt

After a SmartArt chart is inserted, you can select one of its graphics and begin typing text into it. Depending on the chart type, you may prefer to display the Text pane and enter all text as an outline. You can add/delete levels and type as many items within a level as needed.

The expand button displays the Text pane.

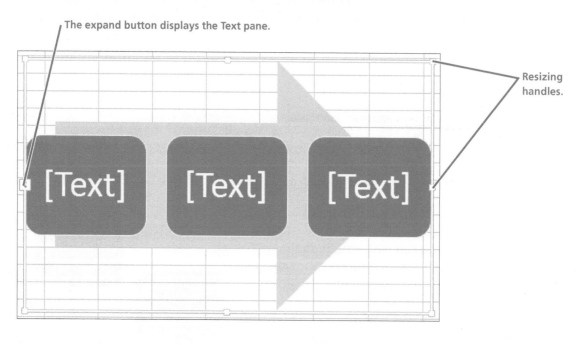

Resizing handles.

[Text]   [Text]   [Text]

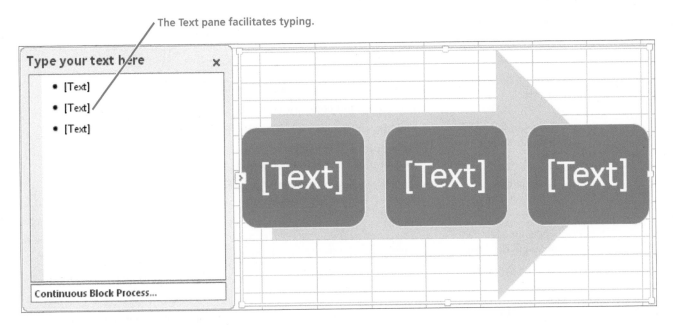

The Text pane facilitates typing.

Keep text brief in SmartArt. Use ⌷Tab⌷ to demote text to the next lower level and ⌷Shift⌷+⌷Tab⌷ to promote text to the next higher level.

Formatting SmartArt

The SmartArt Tools display when a SmartArt graphic is selected. You may change the chart's layout, colors, and number of shapes on the Design tab. There you also will find SmartArt Styles. These Quick Style designs combine shape fills, shadows, and 3-D effects that you can apply with the click of a button. You may use the Format tab to apply a shape style, outline, fill, or effect to one or multiple shapes in the SmartArt chart.

Using WordArt

WordArt allows you to insert a text box with formatted text, based on the predefined options. As with other objects, WordArt can then be further customized through the Drawing Tools Format tab. You may also convert existing text within a text box to WordArt.

WordArt can be used to emphasize text.

Task	Procedure
Insert a SmartArt chart	■ Choose Insert→Illustrations→SmartArt. ■ Choose a chart category, choose a chart type, and click OK.
Type text in a SmartArt chart	■ **One graphic:** Select a graphic and type the desired text. ■ **All graphics at once:** Click the expand button, delete all existing text, and type the new text for each component.
Change the SmartArt chart styles	■ Click in the SmartArt chart or on its frame, choose SmartArt Tools→Design→SmartArt Styles→More ▼, and select a style.
Apply an effect to a shape in SmartArt	■ Select the desired shape(s), choose SmartArt Tools→Format, and choose an option from the desired menu(s).
Insert a WordArt object	■ Choose Insert→Text→Insert WordArt, choose a WordArt type, and type the desired text.
Change text to WordArt	■ Select the border of the text box containing the desired text, choose Insert→Text→Insert WordArt, and choose a WordArt type.
Apply an effect to a WordArt object	■ Select the desired WordArt object, choose Drawing Tools→Format, and choose an option from the desired menu(s).

DEVELOP YOUR SKILLS EX11-D08

Insert SmartArt and WordArt

In this exercise, you will create a SmartArt graphic to convey a relationship. You will move, resize, and change colors on the graphic. You will also apply a style to the SmartArt and work with WordArt.

1. Save your file as **EX11-D08-Comparison-[FirstInitialLastName]**.

2. On the **Analysis** worksheet, select any cell and tap [Home] to ensure that **column A** is displayed.

3. Select **cells B2:C2** and tap [Delete] to remove the labels.

4. Choose **Insert→Illustrations→SmartArt**.

5. Follow these steps to insert an arrow ribbon chart:

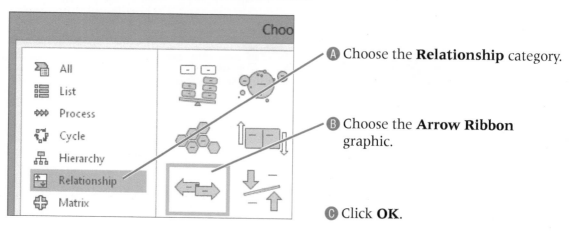

Ⓐ Choose the **Relationship** category.

Ⓑ Choose the **Arrow Ribbon** graphic.

Ⓒ Click **OK**.

6. With the graphic selected, choose **SmartArt Tools→Design→SmartArt Styles→Change Colors**.

7. Scroll down to **Accent 6** and select an appropriate shade.

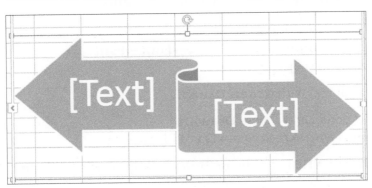

8. Select the text box on the left and type **National**, but do not tap ⌜Enter⌟. Select the text box on the right and type **Sector**, but do not tap ⌜Enter⌟.

9. Follow these steps to change the text to italic:

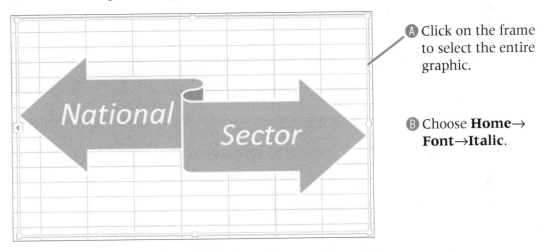

Ⓐ Click on the frame to select the entire graphic.

Ⓑ Choose **Home→ Font→Italic**.

10. Follow these steps to shrink the graphic and move it into position:

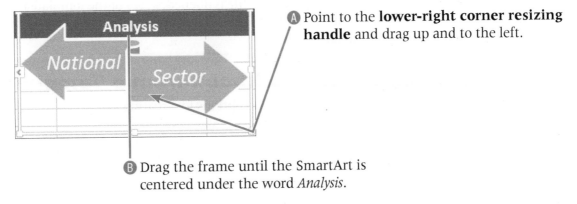

Ⓐ Point to the **lower-right corner resizing handle** and drag up and to the left.

Ⓑ Drag the frame until the SmartArt is centered under the word *Analysis*.

11. Choose **SmartArt Tools→Design→SmartArt Styles→More** and select any **Best Match for Document** options.

Insert WordArt

12. Display the **By Market** worksheet and select **cell A1**.

13. Choose **Insert→Text→Insert WordArt** and select **Fill – Black, Text 1, Shadow**.
    The WordArt object overlaps the existing data.

14. Select the **WordArt border**, choose **Home→Font→Font Size→18**, and drag the object to **cell A1**.

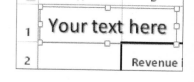

15. Replace the default text with `Green Clean`.

16. Select the object border and choose **Drawing Tools→Format→WordArt Styles→Text Fill→Green**.

17. Highlight the **range A1:B1** and choose **Home→Alignment→Merge & Center**.
    You have now created a WordArt title for the worksheet.

18. With the **range A1:B1** still selected, choose **Home→Clipboard→Copy**. Then, select **cell A1** of the **By Region** worksheet and choose **Home→Clipboard→Paste**.
    The title is copied to the By Region worksheet.

19. Save and close the file.

Using Templates

Video Library   http://labyrinthelab.com/videos   Video Number: EX13-V1109

You may use Excel's predesigned templates or create your own templates as the basis for new workbooks.

Template Features

Any Excel workbook may be saved as a template. Templates can include any type of cell entries, pictures, shapes, charts, and formatting available in Excel that you wish to reuse for a new workbook. A standard workbook filename includes the extension .xlsx, while a template contains the extension .xltx. When the file is opened, a *copy* of the template is displayed. The original template remains unchanged; a new file is created using the copy. You may, however, open the template to make revisions.

Creating a New Workbook from a Template

The New tab in Backstage view displays options for creating a new workbook. Here you may choose from different types of templates.

New

| Info |
| New |
| Open |
| Save |
| Save As |
| Print |
| Share |
| Export |
| Close |
| Account |

Search for online templates

Suggested searches: Budget   Invoice   Calendars   Expense   List   Loan   Schedule

Blank workbook   Welcome to Excel   My financial portfolio

Take a tour

Excel 2013

Templates display below the search options.

Office.com Templates

If connected to the Internet, you may choose from a variety of templates located on the Microsoft website, including calendars, budgets, calculators, and accounting worksheets. Selecting one of these displays a preview of the template worksheet in the New tab. The Create command transfers the template from the website to your computer.

Template Storage Locations

When an Office.com template is selected, a workbook copy is created. This copy can then be modified and saved as a workbook—or saved as a template to be used repeatedly in the future. Custom templates you create are saved by default to the Templates folder on your computer.

QUICK REFERENCE	CREATING AND USING TEMPLATES
Task	**Procedure**
Create a workbook based on an existing workbook	■ Open the existing workbook on which you will base the new workbook. ■ Choose File→Save As→Computer→Browse. ■ Navigate to the desired folder, change the filename, and click Save.
Create a workbook based on an Office.com template	■ Choose File→New. ■ Choose a category or search for a template, select a template, and click Create.
View the path to the Templates folder	■ Choose File→Save as→Computer→Browse. ■ Change the Save as Type option to Excel Template and click the folder button to display the path to the Templates folder. ■ Cancel the Save As command.

Create a New Workbook from an Excel Template

In this exercise, you will use an installed template to create a new workbook.

1. Choose **File→New** to display the New tab of Backstage view.

2. Follow these steps to select the template named Expense Report:

Ⓐ Search for **Expense Report**.

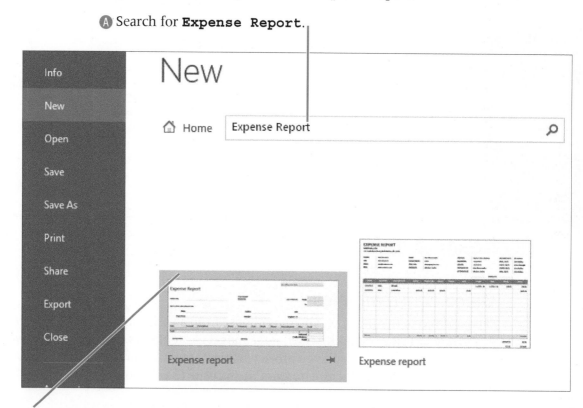

Ⓑ Select the first **Expense Report** template.   Ⓒ Choose **Create**.

If Expense Report is not available, choose another template. Notice that the Excel title bar for the new workbook displays Expense report1, indicating that you are working in a copy of the template. (Expense report1 is a temporary document name for display only.)

3. Save the file in your **EX2013 Lesson 11** folder as **EX11-D09-ExpenseReport-[FirstInitialLastName]**.

4. Scroll through the worksheet and click cells to view the included formulas. Notice the table within the template.

5. Fill in part of the form by typing text and numbers into some cells.

6. Save and close the file.

Customizing Templates

Video Library   http://labyrinthelab.com/videos   Video Number: EX13-V1110

If a predesigned template doesn't suit your needs, just create a workbook and save it as a template. You may revise your custom template, but note that workbooks based on the previous template version do not update when these revisions are made.

Creating Your Own Templates

To create a template, first create a workbook as usual with the cell entries, formatting, graphics, and other settings you want to reuse. When you save the file, use the template file format. To see the template within the New tab of Backstage view, it must be saved in the default personal templates location.

Excel 2013

QUICK REFERENCE	USING CUSTOM TEMPLATES
Task	**Procedure**
Create a custom template	■ Create the workbook as usual, and then choose File→Save As→Computer→Browse. ■ Type the filename, choose Excel Template from the Save as Type list, and click Save to store the file in the Templates folder. (If you don't have privileges to save in that folder, choose a different location.)
Create a new workbook based on a custom template in the Templates folder	■ If necessary, choose File→Options→Save. ■ Type the Templates folder path in the Default Personal Templates Location box and click OK. ■ Choose File→New, choose Personal, and select a template.
Create a new workbook based on a custom template outside the Templates folder	■ Choose File→Options→Save. ■ Type the alternate folder path in the Default Personal Templates Location box and click OK. ■ Choose File→New, choose Personal, and select a template.
Modify a custom template	■ Choose File→New, choose Personal, and select a template. ■ Make the desired changes in the template and choose File→Save or Save As→Computer→Browse. ■ Choose Excel Template in the Save as Type list, select the original filename, and click Save; click Yes to confirm.

DEVELOP YOUR SKILLS EX11-D10
Create a New Template

In this exercise, you will save your workbook as a template.

1. Open **EX11-D10-Results** file from the **EX2013 Lesson 11** folder and save it as **EX11-D10-Results-[FirstInitialLastName]**.

2. **Maximize** ☐ the window, select **cell B2**, and replace *Richmond 5K Run* with the generic heading **[Type event name here]**.

3. Select the text in the callout graphic and replace it with this text:
   [Type a message or select the graphic and press Delete.]

4. Delete the race results from the **range B5:D9**.

   The D10 formula cell displays an error message because you deleted the data. When the race results are entered, the formula will calculate correctly.

Save the Workbook as a Template

5. Select **cell B2**.

   It is a good practice to select a specific cell before saving. When you start a new workbook, the mouse pointer will be in that cell, ready for typing the event name.

6. Choose **File→Save As→Computer→Browse**.

7. Follow these steps to save the workbook as a template:

   Ⓐ Change the filename to **EX11-D10-ResultsTemplate-[FirstInitialLastName]**.

   Ⓑ Choose **Excel Template** as the file type.

   Remember: Replace the bracketed text with your actual first initial and last name.

8. Navigate to your **EX2013 Lesson 11** folder and click **Save**. (*Don't* save in the default Templates folder.)

   The Excel title bar now displays EX11-D10-ResultsTemplate-[FirstinitialLastName] as the filename. The original Results file remains unchanged.

9. **Close** ☒ the template workbook.

Base a New Workbook on the Template

Use the following steps to access templates stored in locations that prevent them from appearing on the New tab of Backstage view, such as a USB drive.

10. Choose **File→Options→Save**.

11. In the **Default Personal Templates Location** box, type the **EX2013 Lesson 11** folder path.

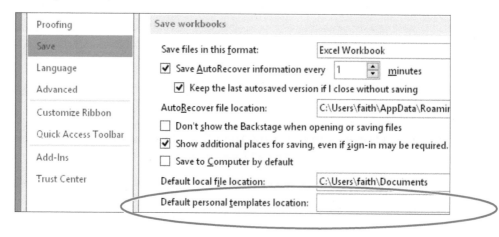

12. In the New tab of Backstage view, select **Personal** and choose your **EX11-D10-ResultsTemplate**.

   A new generic workbook based on the template appears, and the temporary document name EX11-D10-ResultsTemplate-[FirstInitialLastName]1 appears in the title bar.

13. Follow these steps to enter data for the Coastal Classic race:

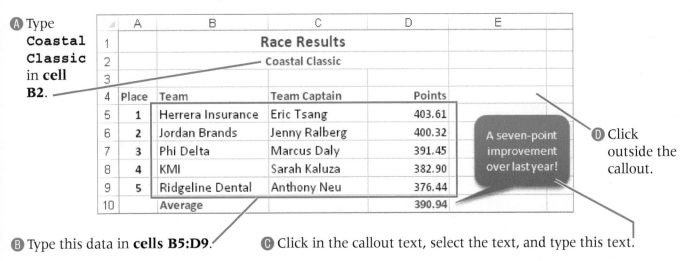

Ⓐ Type **Coastal Classic** in **cell B2**.

Ⓑ Type this data in **cells B5:D9**.

Ⓒ Click in the callout text, select the text, and type this text.

Ⓓ Click outside the callout.

A seven-point improvement over last year!

14. Click **Save** 💾 on the Quick Access toolbar and choose **Computer→Browse**.

   The Save as Type setting is set to Excel Workbook. Your changes will be saved in the new workbook, leaving the underlying template unchanged.

15. Type **EX11-D10-CoastalResults-[FirstInitialLastName]** as the filename, select your **EX2013 Lesson 11** folder, and click **Save**. Close the file.

Modifying Custom Templates

Video Library   http://labyrinthelab.com/videos   Video Number: EX13-V1111

You may modify a custom template after it has been created. To modify a template, you must open it from within Excel. If you double-click the template from a folder window, you will simply create a new workbook.

DEVELOP YOUR SKILLS EX11-D11
Modify the Template

In this exercise, you will open the custom template, make a change, and resave.

1. Open **EX11-D10-ResultsTemplate** from the **EX2013 Lesson 11** folder.

   The title bar now displays the name EX11-D10-ResultsTemplate-[FirstInitialLastName]. You are now working with the original template—not a workbook based on the template.

2. Insert a blank row at **row 3**.

3. Select **cells B3:D3** and choose **Home→Alignment→Merge & Center**.

4. Select **cell B3** and choose **Home→Cells→Format→Format Cells** ⊞.

⊿	B	C	D
1	Race Results		
2	[Type event name here]		
3	[Enter month and day here]		

The Format Cells dialog box opens.

5. Follow these steps to set a date format that displays the month and day in figures:

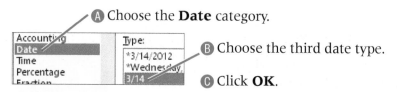

Ⓐ Choose the **Date** category.

Ⓑ Choose the third date type.

Ⓒ Click **OK**.

6. In **cell B3**, type **[Enter month and day here]**.

7. Select **cell B2** to position the mouse pointer for data entry when a new workbook is created.

8. Save and close the template.

Test the Modified Template

9. Choose **File→New→Personal** and select your **EX11-D10-ResultsTemplate**.
   A new workbook based on the modified template appears.

10. Select **cell B3** and enter **October 28**.
    The date formatted as 10/28 replaces the generic instruction.

11. **Close** ✕ the new workbook without saving it. Exit **Excel**.

Concepts Review

To check your knowledge of the key concepts introduced in this lesson, complete the Concepts Review quiz by choosing the appropriate access option below.

If you are...	Then access the quiz by...
Using the Labyrinth Video Library	Going to http://labyrinthelab.com/videos
Using eLab	Logging in, choosing Content, and navigating to the Concepts Review quiz for this lesson
Not using the Labyrinth Video Library or eLab	Going to the student resource center for this book

Reinforce Your Skills

Insert Clip Art and Shapes

In this exercise, you will search for and insert appropriate graphics to illustrate a worksheet. You will also create a text box and a shape. Then you will format the graphics to unify them with the workbook theme.

Use Illustrations, and Insert Pictures and Clip Art

1. Start **Excel**. Open **EX11-R01-Expenses** from the **EX2013 Lesson 11** folder and save it as **EX11-R01-Expenses-[FirstInitialLastName]**.

2. **Maximize** ☐ the window.

3. Select **cell A1** and choose **Insert→Illustrations→Online Pictures** 🖼️.

4. Type **children community service** in the search box, tap [Enter], select the third result (or a similar image, if this one is not available), and click **Insert**.

5. Resize the image to fit in the **range A1:A5** by dragging the lower-right corner sizing handle.
   The image's proportion of height to width is maintained when you use a corner handle.

6. Choose **Picture Tools→Format→Arrange→Rotate** 🔄**→Flip Horizontal**.
   The clip art image reverses from left to right.

7. Choose **Picture Tools→Format→Adjust→Color** 🖼️ and then choose **Lavender, Accent Color 5 Light** to better match the color of the data bars within the chart.

Get Into Shapes

8. Choose **Insert→Text→Text Box** 🔲 and click **cell B2**.

9. Type this text: **Marketing Theme: Help kids help our world!**

10. Resize the text box, if necessary, by dragging the corner handle. Then, center it below *Kids for Change* by dragging the border.

11. Choose **Insert→Illustrations→Shapes** . Under Block Arrows, choose **Right Arrow**.

12. Place the mouse pointer in **cell E15**, hold down ⟨Shift⟩, and drag to the right until the arrow tip reaches the right edge of **column G**. Release the mouse button, and then release ⟨Shift⟩. *The arrow's height is in proportion to its width because you held* ⟨Shift⟩.

13. With the arrow shape still selected, choose **Home→Font→Font Size→10** and type **Negative Balance**.

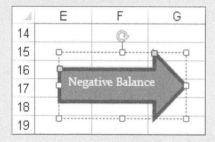

14. Point in the arrow shape and drag it to **cell A16**; resize and position it as shown.

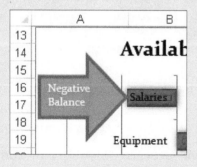

15. Choose **Drawing Tools→Format→Shape Styles→More ▼** and select **Moderate Effect - Olive Green, Accent 1**.

16. Select the text box on **row 3**.

17. Choose **Drawing Tools→Format→Shape Styles→Shape Fill** and then choose **Olive Green, Accent 1, Lighter 80%**.
    A light fill shade provides good contrast so the text is easy to read.

18. Choose **Drawing Tools→Format→Shape Styles→Shape Effects** .

19. Choose **Shadow** in the menu, and then choose **Offset Diagonal Bottom Right** from the Outer category.

20. Save and close the workbook; exit **Excel**.

21. Submit your final file based on the guidelines provided by your instructor.

    To see examples of how your final file or files should look at the end of this exercise, go to the student resource center.

REINFORCE YOUR SKILLS EX11-R02

Use a Workbook as a Template

In this exercise, you will use one workbook as the basis for a new workbook. Before that, though, you will insert a SmartArt object and create and customize a template that can be used for all sailing events.

Illustrate with SmartArt and WordArt

1. Start **Excel**. Open **EX11-R02-Race** from the **EX2013 Lesson 11** folder and save it as **EX11-R02-Race-[FirstInitialLastName]**.

2. Choose **Insert→Illustrations→SmartArt** .

3. Select the **Continuous Block Process** object from the Process category and click **OK**.

4. Click the expand button to display the Text pane, if necessary.

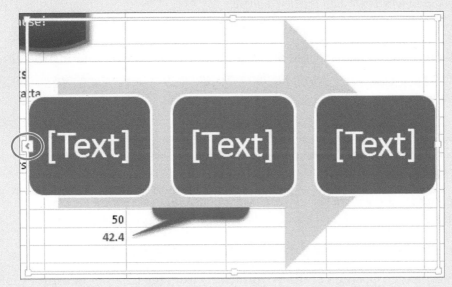

You could type text directly in the graphics, but you probably will find it easier to enter all the text in the outline pane.

5. Type the bulleted text as shown.

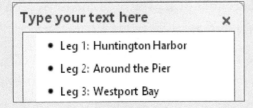

6. Click the expand button to minimize the text pane.

7. Click the outside border of the SmartArt object and choose **SmartArt Tools→Design→SmartArt Styles→More ▼**. Under 3-D, choose **Bird's Eye Scene**.

8. Drag the outside border of the SmartArt object so it begins in **column E** and is positioned as high as possible within the worksheet.

9. Hold down ⌈Shift⌉, drag the bottom-right resize handle, and reduce the size of the SmartArt object so it fits entirely within **columns E–G**.

Use Templates

10. Choose **File→Save As→Computer→Browse**.

11. Save the file to your **EX2013 Lesson 11** folder, naming it **EX11-R02-RaceTemplate-[FirstInitialLastName]** and using **Excel Template** as the file type.

    You have now created a template that can be modified for use with all races.

Customize Templates

12. Click in **cell B9** and type this text: **[enter race name here]**

13. Delete all race data within the **range B12:D16**.

14. Replace the text in the callout with this text: **[highlight race results here]**

    The average in cell D17 now displays an error. This is acceptable, as the formula in this cell will populate when race data is entered above.

15. Save and close the workbook; exit **Excel**.

16. Submit your final file based on the guidelines provided by your instructor.

    To see examples of how your final file or files should look at the end of this exercise, go to the student resource center.

REINFORCE YOUR SKILLS EX11-R03

Create a Profit Template

In this exercise, you will include clip art, a shape, and SmartArt within an existing worksheet. You will also create a template based on the worksheet, and you will customize the template contents.

Use Illustrations, and Insert Pictures and Clip Art

1. Start **Excel**. Open **EX11-R03-Donations** from the **EX2013 Lesson 11** folder and save it as **EX11-R03-Donations-[FirstInitialLastName]**.

2. Open **EX11-R03-PledgeForm** (a Word document) from the **EX2013 Lesson 11** folder.

3. In **Excel**, select **cell A1** of the **Donations** workbook.

4. Choose **Insert→Illustrations→Screenshot** 📷 and then choose **Screen Clipping**.

5. Enclose everything from the top of the pledge form to the Fax/Email line in a rectangle.

6. Resize the image to fit in the **range E1:G5** by dragging the lower-right corner sizing handle.

    The image's proportion of height to width is maintained when you use a corner handle.

Get Into Shapes

7. Choose **Insert→Illustrations→Shapes** ⬦. Under Callouts, choose **Line Callout 2**.

8. Place the mouse pointer at the right edge of **cell G17** and drag until the arrow tip reaches the center of **cell J13**.

9. With the callout selected, type this text: **Why are Milton donations lower? Send more mailers ASAP.**

10. Choose **Drawing Tools→Format→Shape Styles→Shape Effects** ⬛.

11. Choose **Glow** and then choose **Blue, 5 Pt Glow, Accent Color 5**.

Illustrate with SmartArt and WordArt

12. Delete the contents of **cell A1**.

13. Choose **Insert→Text→Insert WordArt** 🅰.

14. Choose **Fill – Black, Text 1, Outline – Background 1, Hard Shadow – Accent 1** and replace the default text with **Kids for Change**.

15. With the WordArt object selected, choose **Home→Font→Font Size→16**.

16. Click the border of the WordArt object and drag it to **cell A1**. Drag the bottom-right sizing handle so the object fits within the **range A1:B1**, if necessary.

17. Save the file and leave it open.

Use Templates

18. Delete the contents of the **range A5:D7**, the **range B4:D4**, and **cell A2**.
    The worksheet is now ready to be converted into a template.

19. Choose **File→Save As→Computer→Browse**.

20. Save the file to your **EX2013 Lesson 11** folder as **EX11-R03-DonationsTemplate-[FirstInitialLastName]** and use the **Excel Template** file type.
    You have now created a template that can be modified for use with all quarters and counties.

Customize Templates

21. Click in **cell A2** and type this text: **[enter fiscal quarter here]**

22. Replace the text in the callout with this text: **[modify callout to highlight data]**
    The formulas in the range B8:D8 will populate when donation amounts are entered above.

23. Save and close the workbook; exit **Excel**.

24. Submit your final file based on the guidelines provided by your instructor.

Apply Your Skills

Format Clip Art and a Shape

In this exercise, you will insert a clip art image and draw a star shape that contains text. You will crop, resize, and move objects. You will also apply shape style to an object.

Use Illustrations, and Insert Pictures and Clip Art

1. Start **Excel**. Open **EX11-A01-RevenueStar** from the **EX2013 Lesson 11** folder and save it as **EX11-A01-RevenueStar-[FirstInitialLastName]**.

2. Maximize the window, insert two blank rows above **row 1**, and move the titles in the **range A3:A4** to the **range C2:C3**.

3. Search for clip art of an event. Insert an appropriate image for the company.

4. Crop away some of the edges around the image.

5. Scale the image smaller and move it into position in the **range A1:B4**. Crop again, if necessary.

6. Use the **Corrections** options to adjust the sharpness, brightness, or contrast of the image.

Get Into Shapes

7. Choose the **16-point star shape** and use Shift to draw a perfect circle about 1-inch wide.

8. Type **Sale** in the shape and center-align the text.

9. Apply a shape style that complements the chart colors.

10. Move the star shape onto the chart as shown.

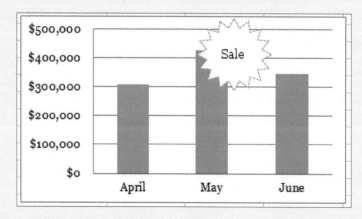

11. If necessary, resize the star and change the text size, while maintaining a perfect circle.

12. Save and close the workbook; exit **Excel**.

13. Submit your final file based on the guidelines provided by your instructor.

    To see examples of how your file or files should look at the end of this exercise, go to the student resource center.

Create and Use a Template

In this exercise, you will create a template for Universal Corporate Events that displays the budget for each company event. You will insert a SmartArt object within the template, and you will create a new workbook.

Illustrate with SmartArt and WordArt

1. Start **Excel**. Open **EX11-A02-Budget** from the **EX2013 Lesson 11** folder and save it as **EX11-A02-Budget-[FirstInitialLastName]**.

2. Add a **Horizontal Bullet List** SmartArt graphic. Add two categories to the existing three, each with two sub-bullets.

3. Type the five budget category names at the top of each category box within the SmartArt graphic.

4. Move the SmartArt graphic to an appropriate location within the worksheet.

Use and Customize Templates

5. Delete the sample data in the **range B4:B8**, then deselect the range and select an appropriate cell to be ready for data entry.

6. Display a print preview to verify that the workbook and chart will print on one page. *Notice that a footer displays the filename in the center section.*

7. Close the preview without printing.

8. Save the file as a template named **EX11-A02-BudgetTemplate-[First Initial Last Name]**. Make sure to save it in the **EX2013 Lesson 11** folder (not the Templates folder).

9. Issue the **Save As** command, naming the file **EX11-A02-BarrettBudget-[FirstInitialLastName]**. Be sure to save the file as an **Excel Workbook**.

   You are now creating a workbook based on the template and, therefore, are saving the file as an Excel workbook in your lesson folder.

10. Rename the **Sheet1** tab as **Barrett**, and enter the data shown into the **range B4:B8**. The chart in your new workbook should display the new percentages.

    Details regarding each budget item could now be entered within the SmartArt object.

	A	B
1	Universal Corporate Events	
2		
3	Item	Budget
4	Facilities	$2,000,000
5	Employee Costs	$1,500,000
6	Transportation	$200,000
7	Equipment	$1,500,000
8	Misc.	$700,000

11. Adjust the position of any chart data labels, if necessary.

12. Save and close the workbook; exit **Excel**.

13. Submit your final file based on the guidelines provided by your instructor.

    To see examples of how your file or files should look at the end of this exercise, go to the student resource center.

Excel 2013

Create an Income Projection Template

In this exercise, you will use clip art, shapes, and SmartArt to create a template that can be used by each event planning unit within Universal Corporate Events.

Use Illustrations, and Insert Pictures and Clip Art

1. Start **Excel**. Open **EX11-A03-Accounting** from the **EX2013 Lesson 11** folder and save it as **EX11-A03-Accounting-[FirstInitialLastName]**.

2. Search for the accounting clip art object shown (or a similar object, if this one is not available) and insert it on the worksheet.

3. Scale the image smaller and move it into position in the **range D3:F8**.

4. Use the **Corrections** options to adjust the image's sharpness, brightness, and/or contrast.

Get Into Shapes, and Illustrate with SmartArt and WordArt

5. Choose the oval; insert the shape so it completely surrounds the contents of **cell C6**.

6. Remove the shape fill so the figure in **cell C6** is legible and apply a red outline color.

7. Insert a **Fill – Blue, Accent 1, Shadow** WordArt object that displays **Universal Corporate Events**.

8. Move the WordArt so it begins in **cell A1**. Modify the font size and resize the object within the **range A1:C2**.

Use and Customize Templates

9. Delete the data in the **range B4:C5** and in **cell D2**, and select an appropriate cell to be ready for data entry.

10. Save as a template named **EX11-A03-AccountingTemplate-[First Initial Last Name]**. Make sure to save your template in the **EX2013 Lesson 11** folder (not the Templates folder).

11. Issue the **Save As** command, naming the file **EX11-A03-AccountingUnitA1-[FirstInitialLastName]**. Be sure to save the file as an **Excel Workbook**.

    You are now creating a workbook based on the template and therefore are saving the file as an Excel workbook in the EX2013 Lesson 11 folder.

12. Rename the **Sheet1** tab as **Unit A1**, enter the data shown into the **range B4:C5**, and **cell D2**.

13. Save and close the workbook; exit **Excel**.

14. Submit your final file based on the guidelines provided by your instructor.

	B	C	D
2			Unit A1
3	Current Year	Next Year	
4	38.5	42.6	
5	24.3	30.1	

Extend Your Skills

In the course of working through the Extend Your Skills exercises, you will think critically as you use the skills taught in the lesson to complete the assigned projects. To evaluate your mastery and completion of the exercises, your instructor may use a rubric, with which more points are allotted according to performance characteristics. (The more you do, the more you earn!) Ask your instructor how your work will be evaluated.

EX11-E01 That's the Way I See It

In this exercise, you will create a scoring template that can be used to track a fantasy sports league. You will remove all league-specific data from a previously used template, and you will modify the format to facilitate its use for all leagues.

Open **EX11-E01-League** from the **EX2013 Lesson 11** folder and save it as **EX11-E01-League-[FirstInitialLastName]**. Delete all data within the scoring template that is specific to the league displayed. Use a Count function to determine the number of players registering scores each week, and insert a shape containing generic text that can be modified to display the league name. Lastly, insert a sports-related clip art image to make the template more visually appealing.

You will be evaluated based on the inclusion of all elements specified, your ability to follow directions, your ability to apply newly learned skills to a real-world situation, your creativity, and the relevance of your topic and/or data choice(s). Submit your final file based on the guidelines provided by your instructor.

EX11-E02 Be Your Own Boss

In this exercise, you will insert WordArt into a document for your company, Blue Jean Landscaping. The WordArt object will identify the company and enhance the overall presentation.

Open **EX11-E02-Sales** from the **EX2013 Lesson 11** folder and save it as **EX11-E02-Sales-FirstInitialLastName**. Sort the data by Customer and subtotal by Sales. In cell A1, insert a WordArt object identifying the company, and size the object appropriately for the worksheet. Then insert two versions of a landscaping-related clip art image for comparison, so that the more visually appealing version can be selected. One version will be uncropped, while the second will be cropped both vertically and horizontally. Lastly, insert a text box beside the clip art images, in which you describe which clip art image you prefer, and why.

You will be evaluated based on the inclusion of all elements specified, your ability to follow directions, your ability to apply newly learned skills to a real-world situation, your creativity, and your demonstration of an entrepreneurial spirit. Submit your final file based on the guidelines provided by your instructor.

Transfer Your Skills

In the course of working through the Transfer Your Skills exercises, you will use critical-thinking and creativity skills to complete the assigned projects using skills taught in the lesson. To evaluate your mastery and completion of the exercises, your instructor may use a rubric, with which more points are allotted according to performance characteristics. (The more you do, the more you earn!) Ask your instructor how your work will be evaluated.

EX11-T01 Use the Web as a Learning Tool

Throughout this book, you will be provided with an opportunity to use the Internet as a learning tool by completing WebQuests. According to the original creators of WebQuests, as described on their website (WebQuest.org), a WebQuest is "an inquiry-oriented activity in which most or all of the information used by learners is drawn from the web." To complete the WebQuest projects in this book, navigate to the Student Resource Center for this book and choose the WebQuest for the lesson on which you are currently working. The subject of each WebQuest will be relevant to the material found in the lesson.

WebQuest Subject: Applying an appropriate SmartArt object

Submit your files based on the guidelines provided by your instructor.

EX11-T02 Demonstrate Proficiency

You would like to create a Purchase Order template that can be used for all purchase orders for Stormy BBQ. Creating this template will ensure consistency for all orders, and will therefore simplify the record-keeping process. You will modify an Office.com template so it will be specifically applicable to Stormy BBQ.

Open a new Excel file, locate the Office.com templates, search for **purchase order templates**, open the Purchase Order (Simple Blue Design) template, and save the template as **EX11-T02-POTemplate-[FirstInitialLastName]** in the **EX2013 Lesson 11** folder. Customize the template by inserting WordArt for Stormy BBQ in cell A1. Delete the company name and company slogan in the range A3:A4. Insert a cropped image that is appropriate for a BBQ restaurant, and a SmartArt image that displays the basic steps in the purchase order process (you can identify these via an Internet search). Lastly, insert a text box in which you instruct the user where purchase order information should be placed within the template.

Submit your file based on the guidelines provided by your instructor.

Index

Notes

Notes

Notes

Notes

Notes

Notes

Notes

Notes

Notes

Notes

Notes

Notes

Notes

Notes

Notes

Notes

Notes

Notes